The Global Debt Crisis

The Global Debt Crisis
Haunting U.S. and European Federalism

Paul E. Peterson
Daniel J. Nadler
editors

BROOKINGS INSTITUTION PRESS
Washington, D.C.

ABOUT BROOKINGS

The Brookings Institution is a private nonprofit organization devoted to research, education, and publication on important issues of domestic and foreign policy. Its principal purpose is to bring the highest quality independent research and analysis to bear on current and emerging policy problems. Interpretations or conclusions in Brookings publications should be understood to be solely those of the authors.

Copyright © 2014
THE BROOKINGS INSTITUTION
1775 Massachusetts Avenue, N.W., Washington, DC 20036
www.brookings.edu

Library of Congress Cataloging-in-Publication data

The global debt crisis : haunting U.S. and European federalism / Paul E. Peterson and Daniel J. Nadler, editors.
      pages   cm
  Includes bibliographical references and index.
  ISBN 978-0-8157-0487-4 (pbk. : alk. paper)
  1. Debts, Public—United States. 2. Debts, Public—Europe. 3. United States—Economic policy. 4. Europe—Economic policy. 5. Financial crises—Government policy. 6. Federal government—United States. 7. Federal government—Europe. I. Peterson, Paul E.
  HJ8119.G56 2013
  336.30973—dc23   2013034900

9 8 7 6 5 4 3 2 1

Printed on acid-free paper

Typeset in Minion

Composition by Cynthia Stock
Silver Spring, Maryland

Printed by R. R. Donnelley
Harrisonburg, Virginia

Contents

Preface   vii

PART I
FEDERALISM AND THE PENSION CRISIS IN THE UNITED STATES

1   Federalism's Emerging Fiscal Crisis   3
Paul E. Peterson and Daniel J. Nadler

2   Competitive Federalism under Pressure   15
Paul E. Peterson and Daniel J. Nadler

3   Can Market Discipline Survive in the
U.S. Federation?   40
Jonathan Rodden

4   Putting a Price on Teacher Pensions   62
Andrew G. Biggs and Jason Richwine

5   Structural Flaws in the Design of Public
Pension Plans   80
Cory Koedel, Shawn Ni, Michael Podgursky

6   Past and Present High-Risk Investments
by States and Localities   94
Daniel Shoag

PART II
THE FEDERALISM CRISIS WORLDWIDE

7 Between Centralization and Federalism in
    the European Union   113
    Daniel Ziblatt

8 German Federalism at the Crossroads   134
    Henrik Enderlein and Camillo von Müller

9 Spanish Federalism in Crisis   159
    César Colino and Eloísa del Pino

10 Regional Identity and Fiscal Constraints in
    Spanish Federalism   179
    Carlos Xabel Lastra-Anadón

11 The Resilience of Canadian Federalism   201
    Richard Simeon, James Pearce, and Amy Nugent

    Contributors   223

    Index   225

Preface

As this volume was going to press, Detroit, unable to pay creditors as much as $20 billion in outstanding debt, announced in July 2013 that it was filing for bankruptcy protection in federal court, thereby declaring the largest municipal bankruptcy in U. S. history. It remains uncertain whether it will be the wealth of creditors, pensioners, or taxpayers that will be grabbed by the dysfunctional municipal government of what was once a large, proud, prosperous American city. But however the costs of the bankruptcy are distributed, the event explains why Michelangelo Merisi da Caravaggio's *The Fortune Teller* was chosen to adorn the cover of this volume. The painting shows wealth being stolen while the victim is deluded by a sweet forecast of future bliss. The handsome young man's smug self-assurance of his own good fortune, displayed at the very moment of his exploitation, illustrates the dangers of complacency and serves as a reminder of the multiple, interactive ways in which theft takes place between the privileged and the exploited. Similar warnings against smugness and complacency are to be found throughout the pages that follow.

Many have assisted in the production of this volume, although we alone bear responsibility for errors of fact and interpretation, which should not be attributed to any other party or to the institutions with which we are affiliated. We are particularly appreciative of both the encouragement and the support of the Lynde and Harry Bradley Foundation, without which this undertaking would never have been brought to fruition. With the foundation's support, we were able to bring together an international team of scholars to address the federal dimension of the global debt crisis at a conference held at Harvard University in August 2012 under the auspices of the Harvard Program on Education Policy and Governance. The chapters in this volume are revised versions of the papers submitted for discussion at the conference.

We are indebted to Ashley Inman for table and figure construction and to Maura Roche, Alexandra Mandzak, and Antonio M. Wendland for administrative assistance and technical support. Finally, Paul E. Peterson wishes to thank his wife, Carol, for her unswerving support of his scholarly endeavors, and Daniel Nadler expresses his thanks to Nitzan, Harry, Doris, and Gabriel for the support and encouragement that they provided throughout the trajectory of this publication.

It is with heavy hearts that we note the passing of Richard Simeon at the time that this volume was in production. A leading figure in the study of federalism and the lead author of the volume's concluding chapter, on Canadian federalism, Richard was the first to suggest to us that we organize an international inquiry into the impact of the global debt crisis on federal systems.

The Global Debt Crisis

*Federalism and the Pension Crisis
in the United States*

PAUL E. PETERSON *and* DANIEL J. NADLER

1

Federalism's Emerging Fiscal Crisis

No pecuniary consideration is more urgent, than the regular redemption and discharge of the public debt: on none can delay be more injurious, or an economy of time more valuable.

—GEORGE WASHINGTON,
message to the House of Representatives, December 3, 1793

It is well understood that defaults, bankruptcies, and fluctuations in interest rates are shaped by business cycles, banking management, and financial engineering. However, credit risk among the lower tiers of government within a federal system also has political determinants and political consequences. Without downplaying the importance of economic conditions and technical considerations, this volume focuses on the political realities that affect the capacity of subnational governments to survive global financial crises. The material explored here serves as a reminder that the founding social science was called *political* economy and that visionaries from Adam Smith and David Ricardo to John Keynes, Milton Friedman, and Friedrich Hayek all considered themselves as much students of the subject identified by the first part of the term as students of that identified by the second.

Such students of political economy have never been as necessary as they are today. As the title of this book suggests, we are in the midst of a global debt crisis. Economists at the International Monetary Fund (IMF) suggest that the public debt of the ten leading developed nations will rise from 78 percent of GDP in 2007 to 114 percent by 2014. These governments, including those in the United States and in many European nations, will by then owe around $50,000 for every one of their citizens. That translates into more than $10 trillion of extra debt accumulated in less than ten years. The governments of rich nations have never borrowed so much in peacetime, and their massive debts will likely shape the world economy for decades to come. If current trends continue unchecked, demographic pressures combined with political paralysis will send the combined public debt of the largest developed economies toward 200 percent of their GDP by 2030. As if the 2008 recession did not do enough to overturn national and subnational balance sheets, a far longer-term and less cyclical fiscal crunch is currently in the making: the pension and health-care costs of a rapidly graying population. By 2050 a third of the developed world's population will be over 60 years of age, and economists estimate that this "demographic bill" is likely to be ten times larger than the recession's fiscal costs. Politicians in most industrialized nations have failed to confront these fiscal and demographic forces. The debt that they are accumulating portends an even greater financial catastrophe than the one that the international community is still struggling to survive. And so it is that leading economists are now beginning to acknowledge the resurgence of the venerable, if old-fashioned, field of political economy. In an era that until recently was defined by quantitative economics—derivatives, default swaps, and other exotic forms of financial engineering—the quaint field of political economy is seeing a rebirth among leading economists as the lens through which the present global crisis must be viewed to be understood. In 2013, a U.S. Federal Reserve Bank president, Eric Rosengren, criticized a widely circulated and fairly conventional economic model of sovereign credit risk for its oversimplification of the subject and its "parsimoniousness," especially the extent to which it "omitted" what Rosengren called the "*political* determinants of risk premiums." In a sign of just how far the pendulum has recently swung back to the political origins of the field of economics, Rosengren—a leading monetary specialist who, like most of his central bank colleagues, usually exhibits the putatively clinical nonpartisanship of his profession—openly observed, "One frequently sees that credit default rates spike around elections, and that countries that are politically destabilized have difficulty generating the political will to address problems."[1]

The notion that "political will" is as important as economic capacity in dealing with a crisis, though intuitive to students of political economy, is an important warning coming from a top U.S. central banker and one that may presage the reunification of the fields of politics and economics. Even more strikingly, Rosengren specifies a promising first candidate for close inspection in the realliance of political science and economics, one that also happens to be the overarching subject of this volume—fiscal federalism:

Another political variable that might be relevant [to credit risk] is a variable that captures whether there is stable fiscal federalism in a country.

For example in Spain, debt and banking problems have been exacerbated by the reality of regions that were autonomous but not necessarily fiscally responsible. A variable that might capture this impact is state and local government debt to GDP.[2]

Echoing those comments, Federal Reserve governor Jerome H. Powell observed, on the same day:

Many advanced economies are in an extended period of slow growth and high deficits, and face long-term fiscal pressures from aging populations. Terribly difficult fiscal adjustments lie ahead. Although there is still time to make them, delay will sharply increase the pain of adjustment. The time to act is now. *In my view, the problem is not principally one of economics or fiscal policy; it is one of governance. The real threat to the fiscal standing of the United States is that of inaction caused by a long period of political polarization and dysfunction.* That would be a self-inflicted wound. *And that is a problem that can't be derived from the traditional fiscal metrics* [emphasis added].[3]

This volume takes Powell's remarks as its point of departure.

Tales from Three Cities

While by now virtually everyone has come to understand that Greece, Ireland, Portugal, and Spain have, in some form or another, defaulted on their sovereign debts, the U.S. cities of Stockton, Vallejo, and Central Falls initially attracted far less attention. For decades, municipal bankruptcies were rare occurrences in the massive $3.7 trillion U.S. municipal bond market. Mostly limited to utilities and over-budget public projects, they were handled in isolation, rarely touched whole cities—let alone states—and posed few deeper questions regarding the political-economic structure of the nation as a whole. Quite apart from the events in Detroit, seven U.S. cities, towns, and counties have filed for bankruptcy since 2010. Prior to that year, no large municipality had failed to fully repay its principal debt since the Great Depression, when about 4,000 municipalities defaulted—including about forty that never fully repaid their debt.[4] But the modern trend of ultimate municipal creditworthiness might be changing, with several cities and counties having recently attempted to pass on losses to either bondholders or higher tiers of government. Alternatively, they may need to alter their contractual commitments to their employees. While each of the U.S. cities, towns, and counties that have filed for bankruptcy since 2010 has approached insolvency in different ways, the overall options available and the choices that each has made in dealing with the specter of bankruptcy provide a window into some of the broader national and international themes addressed by this volume.

Stockton, California

Stockton's 2012 bankruptcy made it the largest U.S. city in history to declare bankruptcy. At its bankruptcy hearing, the municipal government faced a $26 million annual deficit and had incurred a debt of as much as $1 billion— substantial for a city of 290,000. Stockton's choices were emblematic: either public sector employees or bondholders must take the brunt of the cuts. As the authors in this volume argue, which group Stockton chooses will have implications beyond the city itself; the consequences of its choice will reverberate across America's federalist structure as a whole.

In the summer of 2012, Stockton indicated that it might try to impose substantial losses on lenders as well as public employees in order to spread losses across both types of creditors. Since at least 1981 and possibly as far back as the 1930s, no U.S. municipality has used bankruptcy to force bondholders to take less than the full principal due, according to Bloomberg.[5] But as Stockton city manager Bob Deis told city council members at a June 26, 2012, hearing, "We're trying to spread the pain, unfortunately, to others besides employees." Punishing bondholders has generally been unsuccessful at the municipal level: of the forty-three municipal bankruptcies filed since 1981, thirty-three were either dismissed by a judge or failed to win a court ruling discharging their debt. Court records for the remaining ten do not list the disposition. According to Bloomberg, those cases ended with a cut in the principal owed to lenders.[6] Some cities have avoided trying to force investors to take a loss in court or outside of it since most market analysts have thought that the bond market would punish any future borrowing with higher interest rates or possibly by locking a defaulting municipality out of credit markets entirely. But the fear of credit market discipline is changing. For example, in 2013 Detroit asked both bondholders and pensioners to accept less than the amount originally contracted.

Central Falls, Rhode Island

Central Falls may be the municipality that has been most successful in extracting itself from its debt crisis—and it did so without burning its bridges to the bond market. In September 2012, it won court permission to exit bankruptcy status by repaying bondholders in full (including even their legal costs) while cutting municipal workers' pensions (by as much as 55 percent, including an additional requirement that pensioners pay 20 percent of their health-care costs until they turn 65 years of age). The court ruling ended a storm of controversy following the passage of a state law, signed by Governor Lincoln Chafee in 2012, that gave investors a lien on the city's tax and general revenue. Following the court's ruling that Central Falls can protect bondholders while forcing its employees to take cuts, the president of one of the Central Falls public sector unions said: "We've been pilfered and beaten down . . . we didn't have the power, the money, to fight it."[7]

Detroit, Michigan

Stockton and Central Falls can be ignored as exceptional instances, but the fiscal collapse in Detroit in the summer of 2013 is vastly more portentous. The nearly $20 billion bankruptcy suit that the city filed in federal court was the inevitable consequence of economic, social, and political trends only slightly more immediate and advanced than those undermining the fiscal well-being of Philadelphia, Chicago, Cleveland, Milwaukee, and many other U.S. central cities. Business and industry are moving to U.S. suburbs, ex-urbs, and rural areas and to countries across the globe. The quality of public services is deteriorating even as per capita costs are rising. Public officials are promising public sector employees health and pension benefits without putting aside the necessary resources to cover the costs. Taxes have been raised to levels that scare entrepreneurs into choosing more promising locations. Detroit's bankruptcy case can be expected to twist and turn as law, politics, and the fiscal reality on the ground are taken into account over the course of the litigation. All that can be said with certainty is that the competing demands of creditors and pensioners will take years to sort out.

The Fiscal Crisis of the U.S. States

The charged emotions surrounding Detroit's municipal bankruptcy and the city's and the unions' radically departing views on which party should bear the brunt of the cuts—the workers or the bondholders—are emblematic of every current sovereign and subsovereign fiscal solvency crisis, from the streets of Central Falls to the streets of central Athens, from the protests in Vallejo, California, to the protests in Valencia, Spain. The same difficult choices that Stockton and Vallejo, Jefferson County, and Central Falls have faced are confronting governments at the state and even national levels, with major consequences for the intergovernmental structure of the two largest and most important federations in the world: the European Union and the United States.

For the first time since the Great Depression, multiple U.S. states might find themselves unable to pay their employees or their bondholders, effectively going bankrupt (for our extended discussion, see chapter 2). As early as March 2010, the *Wall Street Journal* asked, "Who Will Default First: Greece or California?" (the answer was Greece), and in testimony before the Congressional Financial Crisis Inquiry Commission, investor Warren Buffett—who then owned more than $4 billion of state and local debt—stated that the federal government may ultimately be compelled to bail out states.[8]

If the failure of commercial banks posed a "systemic risk" in 2008, it will be difficult to argue that the U.S. states are not "too big to fail" in 2013: state and local governments represent more than 12 percent of the nation's GDP and more than 15 percent of its employment.[9] Millions of public employees stand to lose their jobs if the federal government does not step in.[10] The municipal bond market is more than $3 trillion in size, and state and local governments use it to finance their schools, highways, and other projects. More than two-thirds of outstanding state and local debt is held by small investors and public institutions.[11] Should states require a bailout by the federal government in 2013, it would likely rival the 2008 bailout of the U.S. banking system. Every day the pressure builds: in the summer of 2011, $160 billion in federal stimulus money—given to states and local governments during the financial crisis to keep them afloat—ran out.[12] The average U.S. state budget faced a roughly 20 percent deficit in 2011, with states like New Jersey and Illinois projecting 40 percent and 50 percent shortfalls, respectively.[13]

Arguments are already being made against such bailouts, ranging from the problem of moral hazard to the fact that it would likely change forever the face of American federalism—which historically considered the fiscal autonomy and independence of states as a defining feature of the federal system. Unprecedented alternatives are being sought: the *New York Times* reported in January 2011 that lawmakers were looking for ways to circumvent existing constitutional jurisprudence in order to allow states to declare bankruptcy.[14] (They currently cannot.)[15]

That sovereign entities may be at risk of default in the coming decades is well understood. It is not just Greece, Ireland, Portugal, Spain, and Italy whose debt situations have become a matter of urgent concern. According to Fred Bergstrom, even the United States has allowed itself to be placed at undue risk, as the net foreign debt of the U. S. central government, in the absence of corrective measures, is projected to rise within the next twenty years from about $14 trillion dollars in 2012 (more than 65 percent of GDP) to $50 trillion, or more than 140 percent of GDP—a level "far above any conceivably sustainable position."[16] As dramatic as those numbers are, they understate the looming crisis, for they do not include the sovereign debts of the fifty states of the union, which currently amount to more than $1 trillion, or about 7 percent of GDP. Nor do they take into account the value of the unfunded liabilities faced by public sector pension plans: although they are officially estimated at $438 billion by the states themselves, they could in fact be as high as $3 trillion, or about 20 percent of GDP.[17]

Bankruptcy protection for state governments has been proposed by University of Pennsylvania law professor David A. Skeel Jr., a specialist in corporate and bankruptcy law. In his view, the country needs a federal bankruptcy law designed specifically for sovereign debts. Such a law, which would "enable a state to restructure [its] obligations," would be constitutional if state sovereignty were protected by giving states the option to invoke bankruptcy procedures rather than requiring them to enter bankruptcy court if they would otherwise default. Voluntary participation in bankruptcy procedures would give states the opportunity to restructure their obligations to employees, pensioners, and bondholders, much as bankrupt corporations may continue to operate while under the protection of federal bankruptcy law. Bankruptcy protection would not only give states the opportunity "to restructure obligations that are [otherwise] extremely difficult to restructure" but also ensure that "most or all of a state's constituencies make sacrifices, not just one or two."[18] Jeb Bush and Newt Gingrich have proposed a similar plan that would give states the opportunity to seek bankruptcy protection in the event of a deficit crisis.[19]

On the other hand, Nicole Gelinas of the Manhattan Institute argues that a "state bankruptcy would create more problems than it would solve." States do not owe their debt through a single entity, making it difficult for any single bankruptcy court to handle the extraordinary complexities involved. Pension obligations are typically borne by local governments as well as by the state, adding to the number of participants in any bankruptcy procedure.[20]

In chapter 3, Jonathan Rodden advances the intriguing recommendation that the federal government clarify procedures for orderly default by sovereign states. Noting that states have defaulted in the past, he suggests that even in the midst of the 2008 financial crisis it was the markets, not the federal government, that imposed discipline on the states. He argues that in the United States the moment might be opportune to clarify once and for all that states can and will default if they do not achieve fiscal sustainability and to clarify for market actors the rules under which default would take place. Proceeding from the premise that for all parties an orderly default is preferable to a disorderly default, Rodden shows that by reducing fear of the latter, the federal government can reinforce its "no bailout" commitment.

Seeing a silver lining in the crisis, Rodden observes that while the U.S. system of federalism is under stress (especially from the problem of unfunded subnational obligations to retirees, which he argues is one of the largest policy challenges facing the United States today) and reform is needed at both the federal and the state level, any future reforms can (and should) *strengthen* rather than undermine the system of market discipline that has characterized U.S. federalism throughout the last century. Rodden contends that reformers should take the large state deficits of 2012 as opportunities to bolster definitively the foundations of market-based fiscal discipline in the states while bearing in mind that the most likely path to improved state fiscal discipline lies within the states themselves. For Rodden, bolstering discipline requires the federal government to have the courage and the steadfastness to treat states as mature, sovereign-like actors that must ultimately stand or fall on their own.

In chapter 4, beginning a three-part exploration of the problem of unfunded subnational obligations to retirees that Rodden cites as a significant threat to the future of American federalism, Andrew Biggs and Jason Richwine put a price on unfunded pension liabilities. Alarmingly, the authors reveal how public employee pension funds across the nation have come to suffer from unfunded liabilities that a growing number of economists, government agencies, and bond raters suspect are significantly understated. They estimate that if pensions are valued under a fair market approach, state and local pension obligations will increase significantly, moving unfunded liabilities from less than $1 trillion into the $2 trillion to $4 trillion range. These figures swamp reported state debt of $2.8 trillion as of 2010; furthermore, $4 trillion in pension debt is equal to about 27 percent of total U.S. GDP. If pension debt measured at market value as of 2010 is combined with explicit state, local, and federal government debt, U.S. obligations would register at 140 percent of GDP. In chapter 5, Cory Koedel, Shawn Ni, and Michael Podgursky tell us that retiree benefits in the public sector are usually designed as defined benefit plans, which place the full financial risk on the employer. In contrast, most employers within the private sector have switched to defined contribution plans, in which the employee bears the financial risk. Between 1973 and 2005, defined benefit plans declined from 88 to 33 percent of all pension programs while public sector policy remained essentially unchanged. Further, Koedel and Podgursky show that public sector plans tend to be "enhanced" when short-term returns from investments are larger than can be expected over the long run. The authors show how legislative pension "enhancements" that were enacted in the early 2000s—toward the end of an extended bull market in stocks that left many funds with substantial actuarial surpluses—led many states to transform a transitory increase in asset values into a permanent increase in liabilities, placing pension programs at grave risk in the aftermath of the 2008 financial crisis. The authors argue that pension enhancement legislation exposes the extent to which many U.S. state pension plans are open to rent capture by politically powerful entities and the ways in which senior public administrators are not at arm's length with respect to pension legislation—a highly problematic finding given the potentially potent fiscal impact that pensions and other legacy costs can have on the public enterprises that these administrators are charged with managing.

In chapter 6, Daniel Shoag completes the three-part exploration of the political economy of public pensions. He first identifies precedents for the contemporary public pension financing crisis by exploring the U.S. state defaults that occurred in the nineteenth century when states overinvested in transportation systems. He sees a strong resemblance between the risks taken by states during that period and the risks being taken by states now, with startling implications, given the disasters that befell many states then. According to Shoag, the risks posed by state and local pensions to fiscal federalism in the United States "are difficult to overstate" because states today, as in the mid-nineteenth century, rely heavily on risky investments to finance themselves, a reliance that in some cases led to state bankruptcy in the past. This does, of course, have deep implications for federalism and the country as a whole. Shoag also points out that many members of state and local pension systems are not currently covered by Social Security. Very likely, retirees who lost state pensions to state defaults would both demand Social Security benefits and pressure the federal government to bail out the defaulting states. Even more worryingly, the interconnectedness of financial markets opens the door for contagion: default by one state could lead to a run on the municipal debt market, making it impossible for other states to finance their obligations and forcing them into default as well. Shoag's work raises the possibility that the large size of public trust funds—which currently hold roughly 7.5 percent of all U.S. corporate equities—could mean that a rapid sell-off could force down asset prices, which would depress returns and hamper other states as well. In short, the viability of competitive federalism as it is known in the United States might depend largely on the viability of subnational financing and the management of system-wide pension risk.

Federalism in Crisis Abroad

The second half of this volume, which opens with chapter 7, looks at the political economy of federalist systems outside the United States. In chapter 7, Daniel Ziblatt examines the prospects for the continued functioning of fiscal federalism within the European Union (EU). Ziblatt examines whether a robust multi-tiered political system—in which the center and lower-tiered units have constitutionally protected separate spheres of influence and taxing and spending autonomy and in which subunits have representation in a second chamber— can be created and sustained through the institution of the European Union. At stake beyond even the fate of Europe is whether balanced systems of federalism can survive a financial crisis. Noting that all federations form atop local identities, Ziblatt argues that the tendency to view "strong national loyalties" as the major stumbling block to fiscal federalism in the EU is misplaced because federalism represents an effective and normatively attractive method of coping with precisely that sort of loyalty. In examining other less discussed causes of the major problems facing the European Union, Ziblatt draws on past instances of attempts to form larger political unions out of formerly sovereign states— in particular the nineteenth-century cases of German and Italian state formation—to argue that a potentially bigger problem over the long run comes from the temptation to over-centralize. There is today, just as in nineteenth-century Italy, a tendency to over-centralize in the face of uneven capacity at the lower tiers of a federalist system. EU policymakers repeatedly "rescue" weak states in "one-off" agreements that provide financial aid on the condition that centrally imposed austerity measures are adopted, thereby usurping lower-tier budget autonomy. As the European Union intrepidly pursues fiscal centralization without federalism, it runs the risk of centralization without political accountability, which could induce a crisis of a much higher order.

Turning to the largest federation within the European Union, in chapter 8 Henrik Enderlein and Camillo von Müller show the extent to which the German bond market's assessment of the risk of German *Länder* (state) bonds during the economic crisis has depended on the political climate within each state. Like many of the other federations covered by this volume, Germany is facing pressure to undergo fiscal centralization in response to the debt crisis, and it seeks at the very minimum to adopt mechanisms that would fiscally constrain the *Länder,* a move that places the already precarious German system of federalism in further jeopardy.

An even more rapid centralizing process is occurring in Spain, which César Colino and Eloísa del Pino explore in chapter 9 and Carlos Xabel Lastra-Anadón examines in chapter 10. Together, these chapters show the way in which the particular constitutional design of a federal system established as part of the democratizing processes of the 1970s encouraged lower-tier governments to run debts that now place them at risk of default. The crisis has been aggravated by the misplaced policies of national political leaders who were dependent on the support of regionally focused political parties. The authors suggest a need for a form of competitive federalism, with greater devolution of both taxation authority and fiscal responsibility to the Spanish regions. That would likely require a new constitutional arrangement that reflects both changing regional identities in several parts of Spain and continuing loyalty to the Spanish regime as a whole. Lastra-Anadón concludes that a form of competitive federalism similar to what was once enjoyed by the United States—with adequate oversight from the European Union—may be the best, if an imperfect, way forward for Spain.

Chapter 11 ends the volume with a surprisingly optimistic account of how a developed system of federalism might operate in a time of fiscal crisis. Richard Simeon, James Pearce, and Amy Nugent challenge the idea that high levels of fiscal decentralization necessarily lead to fiscal irresponsibility or incapacity. In their discussion of the impact of the global crisis on Canadian federalism, the authors offer what might be called the "Canadian paradox," a functional response to global financial crises by one of the most decentralized federations in the world. Canada grants its provinces sweeping fiscal autonomy, extraordinary freedom to tax and spend with minimal federal monitoring or regulation, and unlimited capacity to borrow in global credit markets. Furthermore, the country has serious linguistic divisions and highly uneven regional growth of the sort that has paralyzed other federal systems. Yet neither the country's robust decentralized federalist structure nor its economic growth rate was seriously disturbed by the massive tremors that have shaken the world economy since 2008. Why? While Canada's resource-based economy was admittedly well positioned to minimize the effects of the crisis, the authors show that political and institutional factors also played an important role: Canada's long experience in managing intergovernmental relationships and its surprisingly homogeneous ideological views on the role of government were critical in forming the national consensus on a coordinated federal-provincial response to the crisis that has eluded its neighbor to the south. The authors conclude that the strong tradition of fiscal coordination between federal and provincial treasuries in Canada—cooperation that arises not from federal coercion but from shared values—helped Canada stand apart during the global crisis and emerge with both its finances, and storied federalist structure, largely unscathed.

The Canadian experience shows that despite the overall warning sounded by this volume, there may still be cause for hope and time for change. Some of the countries that historically had been most associated with bloated public sectors and fiscal profligacy—think both Canada and the Nordic countries in the 1990s—are now serving as models to other developed nations with regard to how to rein in deficits, bring down debt, and cultivate efficient and responsive governance. Politicians around the world can therefore take some solace in the fact that no matter how bleak the global debt crisis seems at the moment, real solutions that bring down debt and increase government's fairness, efficiency, and responsiveness are possible—and that systems of competitive federalism may have a longer life than currently seems likely given the experiences in Spain, Germany, and the United States. But finding those solutions requires the political will to face up to the reality of financial problems and make them the responsibility of the current generation instead of future ones.

Notes

1. Eric S. Rosengren, "Comments on the Paper 'Crunch Time: Fiscal Crises and the Role of Monetary Policy,'" February 22, 2013 (www.bos.frb.org/news/speeches/rosengren/2013/022213/index.htm).

2. Ibid., pp. 4–5.

3. Jerome H. Powell, "Discussion of 'Crunch Time: Fiscal Crises and the Role of Monetary Policy,'" February 22, 2013 (www.federalreserve.gov/newsevents/speech/powell20130221a.htm).

4. Even New York City in the 1970s eventually fully repaid its debt, albeit with the help of New York State.

5. Steven Church, "Stockton Threatens to Be First City to Stiff Bondholders," June 30, 2013 (www.bloomberg.com/apps/news?pid=munievents&sid=amojnfWiMwU4).

6. Ibid.

7. "Bankruptcy Saves Tiny Rhode Island City, but Leaves Scars," Reuters, September 3, 2012 (www.reuters.com/article/2012/09/04/us-usa-rhodeisland-centralfalls-bankrupt-idUSBRE88300220120904).

8. "Buffett: U.S. Can Bail Out States, Insurers Pained," Reuters, May 1, 2010 (www.reuters.com/article/2010/05/01/berkshire-buffett-ratings-idUSN0118355720100501).

9. "State Budgets: The Day of Reckoning," CBS News, December 19, 2010 (www.cbsnews.com/stories/2010/12/19/60minutes/main7166220.shtml).

10. Ibid.

11. Ibid.

12. Ibid.

13. Ibid.

14. Mary Williams Walsh, "A Path Is Sought for States to Escape Their Debt Burdens," January 20, 2011 (www.nytimes.com/2011/01/21/business/economy/21bankruptcy.html).

15. Strictly speaking, states cannot declare "bankruptcy" (Chapter 9 of the U.S. Bankruptcy Code).

16. C. Fred Bergsten, "The Current Account Deficit and the U.S. Economy," testimony before the Budget Committee of the United States Senate, February 1, 2007 (www.iie.com/publications/papers/print.cfm?doc=pub&ResearchID=705). See also C. Fred Bergsten, "The Long-Term International Economic Position of the United States," Special Report 20 (Washington: Peterson Institute for International Economics, April 2009) (http://bookstore.piie.com/book-store/4327.html).

17. Andrew G. Biggs, "The Market Value of Public-Sector Pension Deficits," Outlook Series (Washington: American Enterprise Institute, April 2010).

18. David A. Skeel Jr., "Testimony," *State and Municipal Debt: The Coming Crisis? Hearing before the Oversight Subcommittee on TARP, Financial Services, and Bailouts of Public and Private Programs, U.S. House of Representatives,* February 9, 2011 (http://oversight.house.gov/hearing/state-and-municipal-debt-the-coming-crisis/).

19. Jeb Bush and Newt Gingrich, "Better Off Bankrupt: States Should Have the Option of Bankruptcy Protection to Deal with Their Budget Crises," *Los Angeles Times,* January 27, 2011.

20. Nicole Gelinas, "Testimony," *State and Municipal Debt: The Coming Crisis?*

PAUL E. PETERSON *and* DANIEL J. NADLER

2

Competitive Federalism under Pressure

One can hardly imagine how much [the] division of sovereignty contributes to the well-being of each of the States which compose the Union. In these small communities . . . all public authority . . . [is] turned towards internal improvements. . . . [T]he ambition of power yields to the less refined and less dangerous desire for well-being.

—ALEXIS DE TOCQUEVILLE[1]

It is one of the happy incidents of the federal system that a single courageous state may, if its citizens choose, serve as a laboratory; and try novel social and economic experiments without risk to the rest of the country.

—JUSTICE LOUIS BRANDEIS[2]

It is, of course, no longer politically correct to characterize anything American as exceptional. In days gone by, however, descendants of the Pilgrim faithful spoke easily of their country as a "city upon a hill," a "New Jerusalem"[3] whose hallowed light shone as a beacon for all nations to see. It was not difficult for nineteenth-century Americans to imagine that the nation was destined to spread from "sea to shining sea." Even in the mid-twentieth century, school children learned to sing of a "sweet land of liberty" made beautiful by its

This chapter is based on a paper prepared for "Understanding Education in the United States: Its Legal and Social Implications," a symposium held at the University of Chicago Law School on June 17 and 18, 2011. The authors would like to thank Romain Zamour, Yale Law School, JD Class of 2013, for his research assistance.

"purple mountain majesties," "spacious skies," and "amber waves of grain." Most felt that the United States had been called to end—or at least contain—tyrannies of unimaginable villainy in Nazi Germany, the Soviet Union, and Maoist China.[4] When Americans looked at their nation, they saw an exceptional land upon which God had shed his grace.

In the aftermath of World War II, university scholars joined in writing a secularized version of the hymn.[5] They marveled at a pluralist America that was able to hold its political leadership accountable while avoiding mass uprisings that could translate into totalitarian tyranny.[6] Such talk now seems antiquated, even self-indulgent. For many today, the United States is better understood as just another society at the advanced stage of capitalism.[7] American and European problems and politics are converging. If any country is exceptional, it is China, or one of the four Asian Tigers, or perhaps India or Brazil. To state the situation in the most undeniable terms: Every country is exceptional. Each has its own distinct geographical location, origin, history, social composition, and political institutions. The United States is no more exceptional than Canada, or Mexico, or what have you.

The Exceptional American Federalist System

Regardless of the new egalitarianism, the U.S. federal system, with its unique division of authority between the national and the state governments, is worth treating as exceptional. According to a recent count, only 25 of the world's 193 countries have federal systems,[8] and most of those 25 countries circumscribe the authority exercised by lower tiers of government in important ways. In some, the heads of lower levels of government hold office at the pleasure of the central government.[9] In others, the lower tiers are heavily dependent on the central government for revenue.[10] In all federal systems among the industrialized countries of the world, except Canada and Switzerland, state debts are implicitly or explicitly guaranteed by the central government.[11]

The design of the U.S. federal system owes as much or more to historical circumstances as to explicit theories of governmental organization. When writing the Constitution, those gathered in Philadelphia necessarily allowed for autonomous action by state governments for the very practical reason that no other form of government could have won ratification by the supermajority of states required before the founding document could take effect. Unless the national government's powers were limited and states continued to exercise considerable power of their own, the citizenry, fonder of their former colonial governments than of the new national entity, would not have agreed to the important limits that the Constitution did impose on the states, such as restrictions on their ability to declare war, coin money, and regulate interstate commerce. The cultural differences between the slaveholding South and an increasingly anti-slavery North could be contained only if each region was allowed to organize its own domestic affairs. But if the U.S. federal system was initiated to solve a very practical problem, it gradually became an institutional form so appropriate and effective that it has persisted into the twenty-first century, long after the Civil War was fought, slaves were freed, and a much more powerful federal government had been established.

This exceptional federal system, best characterized as competitive federalism, can be sustained only if the lower tiers of government are held accountable to the marketplace—most specifically, to the market for government bonds. Unless lower tiers are subject to independent movements in the interest rates on their bonds and unless lower tiers remain at risk of default—or something tantamount to default—the central government cannot afford to grant wide discretion to state or local governments. For more than two centuries, the U.S. federal system has survived multiple economic and political crises, but never has the autonomy of the lower tiers of government been circumscribed to such an extent that state and municipal bonds have not had their own independent standing in the marketplace. Yet a striking new political development—the granting of collective bargaining rights to those who work for state and local governments—has posed a dramatically new challenge to the viability of the American federal system as we have known it. Just how that occurred—and its potential consequences for the country's political institutions—is the topic of this chapter.

Competitive Federalism

Historically, competitive federalism helped to generate the extraordinary growth of the United States, the world's largest economic power.[12] Over the decades, states and localities developed and maintained canals, railroads, highways, sewage systems, schools, parks, and public safety agencies. As Lord James Bryce wrote nearly a century ago,

> [I]t is the business of a local authority to mend the roads, to clean out the village well or provide a new pump, to see that there is a place where straying beasts may be kept till the owner reclaims them, to fix the number of cattle each villager may turn out on the common pasture, to give each his share of timber cut in the common woodland.[13]

State and local governments are more sensitive than the federal government to political market forces, making them better equipped to design and administer such types of program. Unless local governments provide public services to meet the needs of local businesses and residents, citizens may "vote with their feet" and migrate to a locality that is better attuned to their needs. Since 12 percent or more of the U.S. population changes its residence each year,[14] the effects of policy choices on property values can be quickly felt.

Business and residential choices are influenced by factors other than the quality of local public services, of course. Businesses want to be close to both their sources of supply and the markets for their products. Individual and family residential choices are influenced by family ties, employment opportunities, and the quality of both the natural and the built environments. But the quality of publicly provided infrastructure also affects, on the margins, the choices that businesses and households make.[15]

Since small changes in supply or demand can have a significant effect on price, residents of a community, eager to protect their property values, can be expected to pressure government officials to employ public resources efficiently in order to meet local expectations and facilitate economic development. Poor policy decisions can have rapid and lasting effects on a municipality's property values and corresponding tax income.[16] Therefore, it is reasonable to expect most state and local governments to be relatively competent at designing and implementing development policies. Admittedly, lower-tier officials in a system of competitive federalism may exhibit "narrowness of mind and the spirit of parsimony," as Lord Bryce was the first to admit, but if it were otherwise, "there would be less of that shrewdness which the practice of local government forms."[17]

State and local governments can also facilitate the gathering of information regarding the most efficient way to organize public services. Each state or city is a laboratory wherein experiments can be tried. If the experiment is successful, other governments will copy it; if the experiment fails, the idea is soon abandoned. In addition, "states and localities pay close attention to the wages and salaries paid to employees in adjacent communities" and feel pressure to bring them into line with those of their neighbors.[18] So valuable is the role played by lower tiers of government within the U.S. federal system that despite the growth in the role of the federal government, more than 40 percent of all government spending for domestic purposes was, as late as 2008, paid for from revenues raised by state and local governments from their own sources (see figure 2-1). The lower tiers are also the predominant public sector employer: no less than 87 percent of all nonmilitary public sector employees work for either the state or local government (see figure 2-2).

In a system of competitive federalism, state and local governments resist taking responsibility for large-scale redistributive programs.[19] If states and localities

Figure 2-1. *Domestic Expenditures of Federal, State, and Local Governments in the United States, 2010*[a]

Percent of GDP

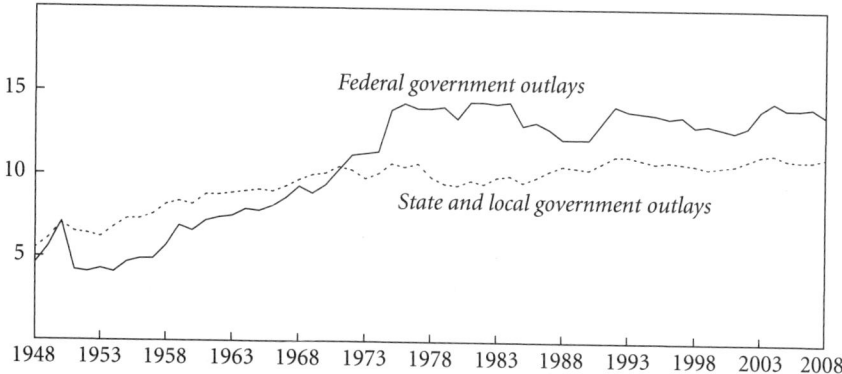

Source: Office of Management and Budget, *Historical Tables: Budget of the U.S. Government* (GPO, 2010), pp. 330–31, table 15.5.

a. Domestic expenditures minus defense and interest payments.

Figure 2-2. *Employment by Federal, State, and Local Governments in the United States, 1946–2008*

Employees, millions

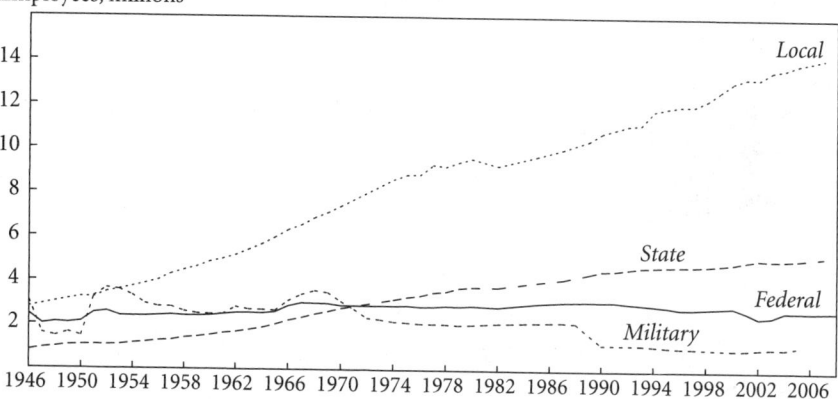

Sources: U.S. Census Bureau, *Historical Statistics of the United States: Colonial Times to 1970* (GPO, 1975), pp. 1100, 1141; U.S. Census Bureau, *Statistical Abstract of the United States*, 101st ed. (GPO, 1980), p. 318, table 519, p. 519, table 611; *Statistical Abstract of the United States*, 110th ed. (GPO, 1990), p. 339, table 552; *Statistical Abstract of the United States*, 119th ed. (GPO, 1999), p. 338, table 534, p. 367, table 587; *Statistical Abstract of the United States*, 127th ed. (GPO, 2008), p. 296, table 447, p. 322, table 482, p. 330, table 493; *Statistical Abstract of the United States 2010*, 130th ed. (GPO, 2010), tables 449, 484. This is a modification of a graph presented in Morris P. Fiorina and others, *The New American Democracy*, 7th ed. (Pearson, 2011), p. 397, figure 14.1.

attempt in a serious way to tax the rich and give to the poor, the rich will depart while the poor will be attracted. If the rich leave and the poor migrate into the state, tax revenues will plummet while expenditures escalate. Any debt acquired by state and local governments must be borrowed from investors; if a state borrows too much money, its bond rating falls and unless the fiscal situation of the state is corrected, the state will default on its debts.

Supreme Court Jurisprudence

If a state defaults, it may not be sued without its consent. That state sovereignty implies immunity from private lawsuits compelling payment of debt was established in the early years of the republic. When the Supreme Court, in *Chisholm v. Georgia*,[20] ruled that the state of Georgia had to pay a citizen of South Carolina a debt that it had incurred,[21] Congress passed the Eleventh Amendment to the Constitution, reversing that decision and subsequently "ma[king] it very difficult for creditors to force states to repay debts."[22] Early jurisprudence also established that a state's own citizens could not file a suit in federal court to secure repayment of a state debt[23] and that a foreign nation could not compel a state to pay its debt.[24]

A state is not immune to a suit filed by a sister state or by the federal government, but neither entity is likely to be a state bondholder.[25] Citizens within a state can file suit in the state's own courts, but historically state courts have not had much success in compelling other branches of state government to honor their debts; as a result, citizens have been "unable to collect on the bonds."[26]

One might think that decisions dating back to the earliest days of the republic are no longer pertinent. However, despite the array of civil rights litigation against states in recent decades, the original conception of the United States as a federal union in which sovereignty is enjoyed by both the federal and state governments has remained altogether relevant for contemporary jurisprudence. In *U.S. Term Limits, Inc.* v. *Thornton* (1995), Justice Anthony Kennedy, in a concurring opinion, characterized American federalism in words little different from those that James Madison might have used:[27]

> Federalism was our Nation's own discovery. The Framers split the atom of sovereignty. It was the genius of their idea that our citizens would have two political capacities, one state and one federal, each protected from incursion by the other. The resulting Constitution created a legal system unprecedented in form and design, establishing two orders of government, each with its own direct relationship, its own privity, its own set of mutual rights and obligations to the people who sustain it and are governed by it.[28]

Nor can the federal government order a state to compensate its creditors. The Rehnquist Court invalidated federal laws that were said to violate state autonomy by "commandeering" the states. In *New York* v. *United States* (1992),[29] the majority held that Congress may not simply "'commandeer' state governments into the service of federal regulatory purposes."[30] *Printz* v. *United States* (1997)[31] applied that reasoning to executive officers as well, holding invalid provisions of the Brady Handgun Violence Prevention Act[32] that required state and local law enforcement officers to conduct background checks on prospective handgun purchasers.[33] Writing for the majority, Justice Antonin Scalia concluded: "By forcing state governments to absorb the financial burden of implementing a federal regulatory program, Members of Congress can take credit for 'solving' problems without having to ask their constituents to pay for the solutions with higher federal taxes."[34]

With the passage of the Fourteenth Amendment and the application of its due process and equal protection clauses to the states, state sovereignty was eroded in a wide variety of civil rights lawsuits that were effectively prosecuted in both state and federal courts.[35] But Fourteenth Amendment suits generally have been viewed as constituting exceptions to state sovereign immunity. In *Alden* v. *Maine* (1999),[36] the Court reaffirmed the states' immunity to lawsuits filed in state courts.[37] Justice Kennedy rooted the decision in "the Constitution's structure, and its history," saying that "sovereign immunity derives not from the Eleventh Amendment but from the structure of the original Constitution itself."[38] However, Kennedy also said that state sovereign immunity does not extend to suits brought by the federal government itself and those pursuant to enforcement of the equal protection or due process clauses of the Fourteenth Amendment.[39]

Future attempts to limit state sovereignty can be expected to exploit Fourteenth Amendment exemptions from the doctrine of state sovereignty. Those who seek to compel states to honor state pension and health care policies and collective bargaining agreements can be expected to invoke equal protection and due process arguments. Bondholders will argue that defaults deny them property without due process of law. But it is doubtful that such suits could be successfully pursued in the absence of federal legislation requiring states to honor contracts with bondholders, pensioners, or public employees. In other words, the jurisprudence that allows states to claim sovereign status within the federal system seems as vibrant today as it has ever been. While the individual constitutions of many states may be interpreted as granting permission for lawsuits by bondholders, pensioners, or those protected by collective bargaining agreements,[40] states—as sovereign entities—appear to enjoy today the same legal prerogatives vis-à-vis bondholders and other creditors as states that have defaulted in the past, if they choose to exercise them.

Collective Bargaining in the Public Sector

Since the beginning of the republic, states have managed their fiscal affairs so well that in only a few instances have they defaulted on their debts. But in the twenty-first century, the risk of default by large and economically significant states has increased dramatically. Among the most important contributors to that change has been the rise of collective bargaining within the public sector. In this regard, events within the field of education are especially instructive, as school personnel are the largest segment of the state and local workforce and education costs constitute approximately one-third of all state and local expenditures paid for from locally generated revenues.[41]

Public sector collective bargaining was largely unknown prior to the 1960s. Even Franklin D. Roosevelt, the most significant presidential ally that the labor movement has ever enjoyed, rejected public sector bargaining within the federal government: "All Government employees should realize that the process of collective bargaining, as usually understood, cannot be transplanted into the public service. . . . The employer is the whole people, who speak by means of laws enacted by their representatives in Congress."[42] George Meany, the head of the American Federation of Labor, did not disagree. As late as the 1950s, he plainly stated, "It is impossible to bargain collectively with the Government."[43] Other organizations that represented government employees took the position that collective bargaining "was demeaning for civil service professionals."[44] The National Education Association (NEA), by far the largest of all teacher organizations, was firmly opposed to the idea.[45]

Collective bargaining was introduced into the public sector in part because the policy fit the political needs of the Democratic Party, which had been closely affiliated with the labor movement since the 1930s.[46] Since the 1950s, private sector unionization has been on the decline, slipping from roughly one-third to less than 10 percent of the nongovernment workforce.[47] Mobilizing new recruits to the Democratic Party became critical, and nothing was more appealing than reaching out to the growing segment of the workforce employed by the federal, state, and local governments. Previously, public sector workers had not shown any particular partisan loyalty, other than to the machine that hired them.[48] The many white-collar professionals working for government were, if anything, more inclined to the Republican side of the aisle.[49] But far-sighted union leaders and key Democratic members of Congress, perceiving an opportunity, began to campaign for collective bargaining rights for public sector workers.[50] Dwight Eisenhower, a Republican, stoutly resisted all congressional efforts to pass such legislation into federal law, but his Democratic successor, John Kennedy, promised that if elected president, he would take action.[51] Since the close balance of power on Capitol Hill precluded passage of collective bargaining legislation,

President Kennedy signed an executive order giving federal employees the right to bargain collectively.[52]

That executive order, in conjunction with the success of New York City teacher unions in obtaining collective bargaining rights, initiated a decisive transformation of the American public sector. In just three years, between 1964 and 1967, the number of teacher strikes increased from 9 to 107.[53] Faced with the prospect of school shutdowns and masses of teachers picketing outside once uneventful classrooms, school boards gave in to public pressure to settle strikes quickly and return children to school. Affiliates of the American Federation of Teachers (AFT) won recognition rights in many large cities, including Boston, Chicago, Cleveland, and Philadelphia.[54] "For the first time . . . since 1918, the AFT threatened to surpass the NEA," one historian noted.[55] That changed when the NEA, seeing its members rapidly defect to the AFT, dropped its principled opposition to collective bargaining. Eventually both organizations prospered, with "NEA membership climbing from 700,000 in 1960 to 3.2 million in 2007, while the smaller AFT grew from under 60,000 to 1.3 million over the same period."[56] Scarcely known in education before 1960, collective bargaining achieved predominance in most states outside the South.[57]

Today, collective bargaining within the public sector is so pervasive that few remember Franklin Roosevelt's objection to the practice. There remain a few critics who argue that collective bargaining subverts the democratic relationship between government and citizens by favoring a particular set of interests—those of government employees. Notably, such critics draw a distinction between collective bargaining in the public and in the private sector. In the private sector, collective bargaining is often appropriate, critics argue, because workers may need to bargain collectively in order to prevent a profit-maximizing management from abusing its superior bargaining position vis-à-vis individual employees. When resolute unions bargain with a management that is indifferent to all but its bottom line, each protects its own vital interests in the collective bargaining process. But within the public sector, such countervailing power cannot be assumed. The "management" in the public sector is made up of elected officials, such as school board members, to whom unions contribute heavily during the election process. Also, school employees participate more frequently than others in "school elections, which are often low-visibility, non-partisan affairs that engage the attention of only the most interested parties."[58] Campaign contributions and coordinated voting blocs give employees special influence over the very school board with which they negotiate. Though not quite self-dealing, teacher unions are certainly not bargaining with a hostile management whose interests are in opposition to those of teachers and other school employees.[59]

The political power of public sector unions has been expanded by collective bargaining agreements in other ways as well. Contracts in many districts require an amount equivalent to union dues to be deducted from an employee's pay-check, and the employee's union is given discretion in the use of the revenues thereby collected. The deductions include fees that may be used for political purposes unless a member specifically objects.[60] With such resources, teacher unions have become among the most influential groups in state politics. In 1985 "teachers' organizations" were identified as the most influential interest group in state politics; in 2002 they were found to be second only to business groups. In both surveys, they outranked such powerful groups as utility companies, insurance companies, hospitals, trial lawyers, manufacturers, and those repre-senting local governments more generally.[61]

Assessing the consequences of collective bargaining within the public sector is a controversial matter. But we do know that since the mid-1960s, per-pupil expenditures on elementary and secondary education have tripled in real-dollar terms—from less than $4,000 per pupil (in 2006 dollars) to nearly $12,000 in 2008.[62] Much of the increase is explained by the growth in the number of public school employees, both because the number of pupils per teacher fell by one-third (from twenty-five to sixteen pupils) and because many more nonteach-ing professionals were hired to provide ancillary services and to help manage an increasingly complex system.[63] In 1960, school districts employed 6 profes-sionals for every 100 students; by 2005 they were employing more than 12 for the same number. Nonprofessional hiring rose at a similar rate—from less than 2 per 100 students in 1960 to nearly 4 per 100 in 2005.[64] Most of the rising cost of education was borne by state and local governments, as the federal contribu-tion did not rise much above 10 percent of the total.[65]

During that period, teacher salaries kept pace with overall wage and salary increases nationwide.[66] In addition, teachers and other public sector employees have been guaranteed steep increases in pensions, health care, and other non-salary benefits as elected officials choose to reach collective bargaining settle-ments by rewarding workers with promises of future benefits rather than imme-diate increases in their salaries.[67] In most cases, the cost of those benefits was postponed into a future well beyond the current election cycle.[68] For years, the growing imbalance between rising costs and increasing liabilities, on one hand, and fiscal resources, on the other, was ignored, except by the Cassandras of the policy world.[69] But with the financial crisis of 2008, the possibility of state and municipal defaults shifted from the theoretical to the plausible.[70]

State Fiscal Crises

The lower tiers of the American federal system of government are facing a con-temporary fiscal crisis unprecedented since the days of the Great Depression. While some resource-rich, less populous states—Alaska, Montana, and North

Figure 2-3. *Yield Spread between Five-Year Bonds of Selected U.S. States and Five-Year U.S. Treasury Bonds*[a]

Spread, in basis points

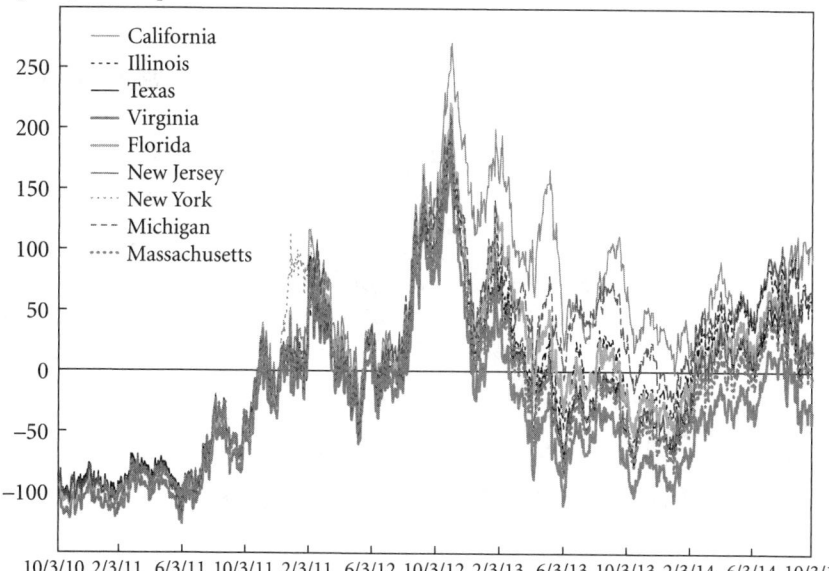

Source: Daniel J. Nadler and Sounman Hong, "Political and Institutional Determinants of Tax-Exempt Bond Yields," Harvard Kennedy School Report 11-04, p. 22 (www.hks.harvard.edu/pepg/PDF/Papers/PEPG_11-04_Nadler_Hong.pdf).

a. Solid vertical lines designate the date of pre-crisis and post-crisis measurement (June 30, 2008, and June 30, 2009, respectively) in the Harvard study. Figure constructed from Bloomberg Terminal data.

Dakota, for example—continue to have balanced budgets,[71] most states are confronting large deficits. New York's deficit for fiscal year 2012 was estimated in early 2011 to be 18 percent of the previous year's budget, California's to be 29 percent, Texas's to be 32 percent, and New Jersey's to be no less than 38 percent.[72] The gap in official state budgets was estimated to be $121 billion, or 19 percent of the budget in the forty-six states running deficits.[73] The projected deficits may have attenuated as state economies have begun to recover, but they would be considerably larger if they included the revenues necessary to fully fund state pension and health care obligations.[74]

With the onset of the financial crisis, the bond market immediately took note of the increased risk of sovereign state defaults. In late 2008 investors demanded a higher premium for state and local bonds than for safer U.S. Treasury securities, despite the exemption from federal taxation of interest received on most state and local bonds. Although all states were affected by the crisis, the perceived risk of default varied considerably by state (see figure 2-3). "Between

September and December of 2008, the premium that investors demanded to hold California debt over U.S. treasuries jumped from 24 basis points to 271 basis points, a ten-fold increase."[75] (100 basis points equals 1 percent.) Before the crisis, the difference between the premium paid in California and that in Texas was only 15 basis points, but by 2011 the gap between the two states had increased to 84 basis points.[76] Similar jumps in the cost of borrowing occurred in a number of other states as well. Clearly, investors had become increasingly sensitive to the variation in the risk of default among the sovereign states.

Impact of Collective Bargaining on Default Risk

State and municipal defaults are not unknown to American federalism.[77] Eight states defaulted on or repudiated their debt between 1841 and 1843, when a severe economic depression restricted their ability to pay interest on debt that they had assumed primarily for the purpose of constructing canals and railroads.[78] The federal government refused to assume responsibility, despite the efforts of both defaulting states and foreign banks to persuade the federal government to intervene.[79] While four states eventually repaid all of their debt, three made only a partial repayment, and one, Mississippi, never did.[80]

The boom-and-bust economy of the 1870s and 1880s provoked another ten defaults, and Arkansas was unable to cover its debts during the Great Depression.[81] Bondholders were not the only creditors that states ignored during hard times. During the Depression, Chicago teachers were on several occasions paid in scrip because the city did not have the cash on hand to compensate them.[82] Years later the scrip was made good, but few teachers themselves ever received payment in full, as they had used their highly discounted scrip to pay monthly bills.[83]

In none of those crises was there much hope that the federal government would come to the rescue of states at risk of default. During the 1840s, some political leaders invoked the precedent established when Congress, prompted by Alexander Hamilton, assumed the Revolutionary War debts incurred by some of the states.[84] But others argued that the precedent did not hold because states' Revolutionary War debts had been incurred on behalf of a common cause while the state debts prior to the 1840s were incurred in order to set up banking and transportation systems designed mainly for the benefit of the states themselves. Neither of the national political parties saw any advantage in coming to the rescue of a few states at the expense of the rest.[85]

Nor has the U.S. government guaranteed state debts in any subsequent crisis. As a result, each state is held accountable by the bond market in ways that lower-tier governments in most other countries are not. Consider, for example, the differing response of the bond market to the state bonds issued in the United

Figure 2-4. *Average Yield Spreads between U.S. and German State and Federal Bonds, June–December 2008*

Spread, in basis points

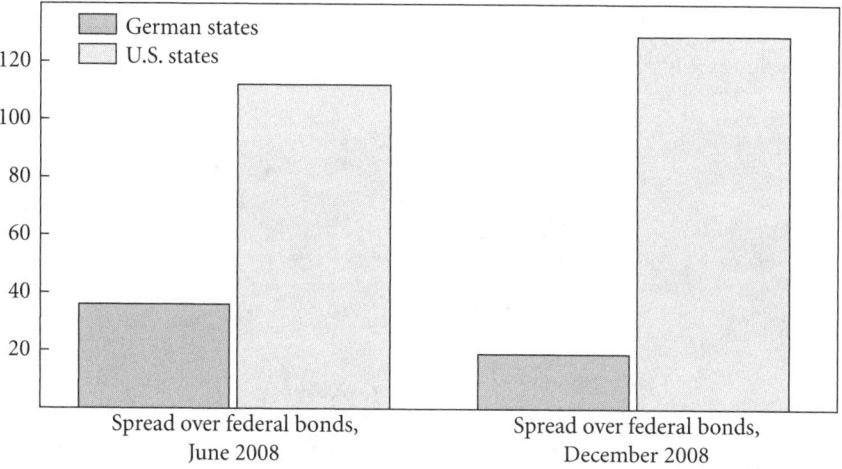

Source: Figure constructed from Bloomberg Terminal data, June–December 2008.

States and in the German Federal Republic. Even though the constitution of the German Federal Republic, adopted in the aftermath of World War II, was explicitly modeled on that of the United States and assigned major responsibilities to state governments, the German federal government has asserted control over state finances and guarantees state debts.[86] For that reason, the spread between German federal and state securities is less than the spread between such securities in the United States. As is shown in figure 2-4, the 2008 financial crisis had an impact on the perceived risk of default of the average German state relative to that of the German Federal Republic. The average yield spread between the two types of securities increased from 36 basis points to 112 basis points between June 2008, the eve of the financial crisis, and December 2008, when the crisis was at its peak. But during the same period, the average yield spread between U.S. state and federal securities increased from 19 basis points to 129 basis points. Clearly, the bond market believed that the risk of default by a state in Germany was attenuated by the guarantee supplied by the German Federal Republic.

In the United States, investors were willing to accept lower interest rates on state debt securities than on U.S. treasuries due to the federal tax-exempt status of state securities. After the financial crisis, however, as any tax advantages were overwhelmed by perceived increased risk, the yield on state bonds rose above that for comparable federal securities.[87] Moreover, the yield spread between

Figure 2-5. *Simple Relationship between Union Share of Public Sector Workforce and Yield Spread between State Bonds and Federal Securities*[a]

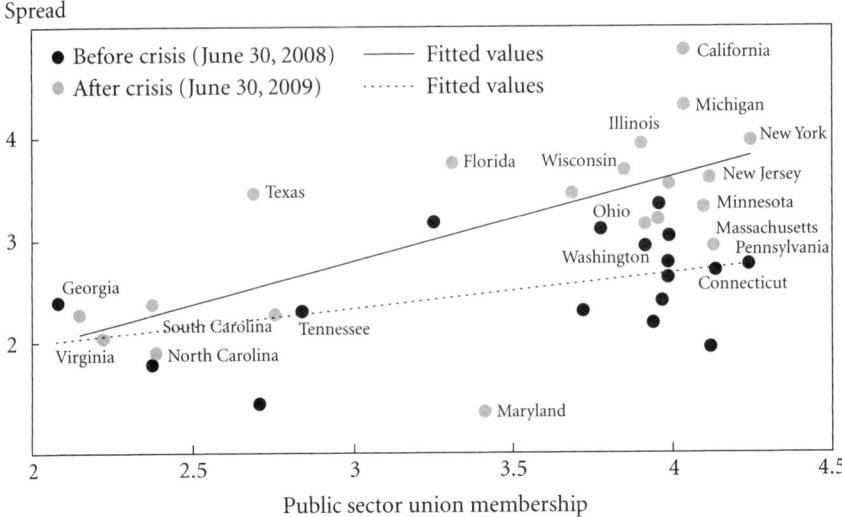

Source: Daniel J. Nadler and Sounman Hong, "Political and Institutional Determinants of Tax-Exempt Bond Yields," Harvard Kennedy School Report 11-04, p. 23 (www.hks.harvard.edu/pepg/PDF/Papers/PEPG_11-04_Nadler_Hong.pdf).

a. Variables are log transformed to make units of analysis visually comparable. June 2008 spread data are all shifted upward by 30 basis points to make the data visually comparable with June 2009 data.

state and federal bonds varied significantly from state to state, indicating that the market perceived greater default risk in certain states.[88]

Of note is the fact that investors' perceptions of the risk of default were correlated with the unionization rate of the public sector workforce.[89] As shown in figure 2-5, the relationship between union membership and default risk was noticeably weaker in June 2008, prior to the financial crisis, than it was over the following six months. The vertical axis shows the spread for federal securities and state bonds that mature in one year, while the horizontal axis shows the unionization rate for the state's public sector. "The relationship between the two variables, modest in June 2008, becomes pronounced by June 2009, as bondholders became highly sensitive to a state's perceived political capacity to take actions needed to bring budget deficits under control."[90] The differences in the steepness of the slopes of the regression lines in figure 2-5 describe the strengthening of the simple relationship between the union share of the public sector workforce and default risk.[91]

This relationship persists when other factors are controlled, as has been shown in a study by Daniel Nadler and Sounman Hong.[92] In their study, unbiased estimates of the impact of political variables on state default risk are estimated with models that solve for the endogenous relationship between credit and yield and that also take into account the economic factors that James Poterba and Kim Rueben have shown to be associated with state default risk: change in a state's unemployment rate, Gross Domestic Product (GDP), and deficit-to-GDP ratio.[93] Nadler and Hong present estimates of the impact of a range of state-level political variables—such as the union share of the public sector workforce and partisan representation in the legislature—on state municipal bond yield spreads in the context of the unexpected deficit shocks seen following the 2008 financial crisis. In particular, they evaluate the impact of the union share of the public sector workforce and partisan representation in the legislature using "separate models, because unionism and partisan balance are highly correlated with one another, making it difficult, with the small number of observations available, to identify the independent impact of each within a single model."[94]

Their results are reproduced here in table 2-1. According to Nadler and Hong, unexpected deficit shocks of the size that occurred in 2008 especially affect state yield spreads when certain political conditions are present. As can be seen in table 2-1, a difference of 1 percent in union membership in a state was associated with an additional 2.02 basis-point change in state borrowing cost, if the state had experienced a billion-dollar change in its unexpected deficit shock. In other words, a 20 percentage-point difference in the share of the public sector work-force that was unionized (1 standard deviation) was associated with an additional increase in the level of state bond spreads of 40.4 basis points for every billion-dollar change in unexpected deficit shock that a state experienced.[95]

Similarly, Nadler and Hong found that a 1 percentage-point increase in the Democratic Party's share of a state legislature was associated with an additional 3.02 basis-point increase in state borrowing costs for every billion-dollar change in a state's unexpected deficit shock. That suggests that an increase in the Democratic legislative representation of 20 percentage points was associated with a 60.4 basis-point increase in the state-to-federal bond yield spread in the context of a billion-dollar deficit shock. "The cost to the state taxpayer of a standard deviation shift in either variable is, roughly speaking, about one half of one percent on a five-year security note."[96] As Nadler and Hong argue, "That amount is non-trivial. In Illinois, an increase in the yield spread of that magnitude on its debt of $145.5 billion amounts to $727 million dollars in additional interest costs annually."[97]

However, one should not reify these two indicators of a state's political situation. Union share of the public sector workforce and partisan representation in the legislature are actually indicators of a broader set of factors affecting a state's risk of default.[98] As Nadler and Hong's work makes clear, the unionization rate of the public sector workforce is correlated with factors such as whether a state

Table 2-1. *The Effect of Unexpected Deficit Shocks, Partisan Representation, and Union Membership on State Bond Yields*[a]

Variable	Model 1	Model 2
Δ Defshock	24.17	−11.02
	(14.25)	(11.51)
Δ Defshock × Union membership	2.02***	
	(0.61)	
Δ Defshock × Democratic share in state legislature		3.02***
		(0.96)
Δ Unemployment rate	37.41	57.65*
	(23.11)	(27.48)
Δ Real GDP	131.5	−128.3
	(177.0)	(139.2)
Δ Deficit to GDP	8.598**	13.23***
	(3.335)	(4.267)
Constant	−100.3***	−131.9***
	(31.96)	
N	20	20
R^2	0.702	0.723

Source: Daniel J. Nadler and Sounman Hong, "Political and Institutional Determinants of Tax-Exempt Bond Yields," Harvard Kennedy School Report 11-04, p. 16 (www.hks.harvard.edu/pepg/PDF/Papers/PEPG_11-04_Nadler_Hong.pdf).

a. Data are for 2007–08 for twenty states. The independent variables are changes from 2007 (before crisis) to 2008 (after crisis) for twenty states, which include the fifteen largest states. The dependent variable has a six-month lag and thus is a change from June 2008 to June 2009. A six-month lag was used to allow for the fact that there might be some delays in market response. However, the results are highly robust and do not depend on whether they use lagged dependent variables. The twenty states are California, Connecticut, Florida, Georgia, Illinois, Maryland, Massachusetts, Michigan, Minnesota, New Jersey, New York, North Carolina, Ohio, Pennsylvania, South Carolina, Tennessee, Texas, Virginia, Washington, and Wisconsin. Standard errors are in parentheses. *p < 0.10, **p < 0.05, ***p < 0.01.

has a right-to-work law and whether the legislature has permitted public sector collective bargaining, both of which are correlated with the magnitude of bond yield spreads.[99]

The two interval variables emphasized by Nadler and Hong—public sector unionization and political orientation of the legislature—should be understood as useful proxies for a broader set of collective bargaining and partisan factors that affect bond yields. Economic factors—growth, change in the deficit-to-GDP ratio, and change in the unemployment rate—are also strongly associated with the substantial interstate variation in yield spreads that occurred in the wake of the financial crisis. But in addition to the impact of those economic factors, political realities are clearly also taken into account by bondholders: Nadler and Hong found that when both are entered into the same equation, the political variables seem to be at least as important as core economic indicators such as state-level growth in GDP and changes in state unemployment rates in explaining post-crisis interstate variation in yield spreads.[100]

Default Risks and Competitive Federalism

A system of competitive federalism has long been extolled as a permanent feature of American government.[101] Both early and modern Supreme Court jurisprudence have recognized states as sovereign entities that exercise autonomous power—and incur concomitant risks—within the sphere allocated to them by the Constitution.[102] States and localities play a major role in raising revenue, delivering public services, and servicing public debt. Nothing is as quintessentially American as the dual sovereignty granted to the states and the federal government.

Yet in a recent study of federal systems, Jonathan Rodden argues that attempts to sustain a system of competitive federalism usually fail, attributing to Alexander Hamilton a similar appreciation of competitive federalism's fragility.[103] When sovereignty is divided, lower-tier governments are tempted to run debts that place them at grave risk of default in times of financial crisis.[104] And central governments, both to safeguard their international credit rating and to respond to internal political pressures, cannot resist providing the assistance necessary to safeguard bondholders and other creditors from loss.[105] Central governments do not offer a helping hand without at the same time asserting their authority, however. When they rescue states and localities, they feel more than entitled to take preventive measures to preclude future defaults.[106] Irresponsibility at the state and local level thus undermines the dual sovereignty essential for the survival of competitive federalism. Celebrated in theory as an efficient system of government of Herculean proportions, competitive federalism is but a ten-pound weakling in practice.

It has long been argued by Rodden and others that the United States is an exceptional case. Because competitive federalism has been woven so deeply into the fabric of American society that it cannot be torn asunder—so the argument goes—even the pressures of a financial crisis were historically little match for the federalist cornerstone of American political culture: in the 1840s, the national government stood aside when multiple states defaulted, and it has never intervened to help them out in the decades since.[107]

Yet within little more than five years of the publication of Rodden's insightful study, competitive federalism in the United States seems more fragile than it has ever been. Many of the stabilizing factors are gradually being whittled away. In recent years, the size of federal, state, and local government has grown from less than 30 percent to more than 35 percent of GDP, the federal share of overall domestic expenditures has been on the increase,[108] intergovernmental grants are making up a greater share of total lower-tier expenditures, and state and national debt are escalating at an astounding rate. In the spring of 2009, Congress, as part of the stimulus package, transferred hundreds of billions of dollars to states and localities, and it appropriated tens of billions in additional aid the following year.[109] Although the package was presented as a means to protect public sector jobs,[110] the monies were most valued by governors and mayors as a mechanism for reducing fiscal deficits.[111] Though not a federal guarantee against default, the stimulus package nonetheless provided a dramatic example of the way that federal aid can ameliorate state and local distress when states find themselves at risk of default.

Within the United States, the sovereign state default crisis is for some states—Illinois, California, and New Jersey, for example—serious enough that Washington policymakers are currently debating the policy and constitutional implications of three alternatives: federal loans that would bail out states at risk of default;[112] bankruptcy procedures;[113] and simple defaults of the kind that occurred during the 1840s.[114] Representative Patrick McHenry (R-N.C.), chairman of a subcommittee of the Committee on Oversight and Government Reform, noted that "already state and municipal governments are coming to Washington, hat-in-hand, expecting a federal bailout."[115] Christopher Edley, dean of the law school at the University of California, Berkeley, has proposed that the federal government bail out states by lending them federal money at low interest in the expectation that it will be repaid in due course.[116] The Obama administration's proposal to loan monies to states to help them cover deficiencies in their state unemployment insurance accounts sets a precedent for larger and more consequential federal actions in the future.

If the state fiscal crisis became increasingly severe, as could happen if projected deficits in pension and health care accounts materialized, then multiple state and municipal defaults would likely provoke a nationwide political crisis that could affect the credit of the U.S. government, especially if its debt-to-GDP ratio continued to rise. Passage of bankruptcy legislation could allow for a more managed imposition of costs on the full range of creditors, including bondholders, pensioners, and beneficiaries of collective bargaining agreements; however, bankruptcy could also affect U.S. credit in world markets and would create a legal nightmare, given the complexity of state contractual arrangements with creditors. By comparison, federal loans to troubled states would provide a tempting option to those elected officials aligned with public sector unions, a constituency at risk in any bankruptcy proceeding. Even though power in Washington is divided between the two political parties, the fear of international consequences could induce compromises that require substantial federal contributions to states along the lines of the stimulus package passed in 2009.

Warren Buffett, a prominent investor with a large stake in the state and municipal bond market, expressed the hope that such federal action would be forthcoming, conceding that "[t]he bond insurers . . . have extraordinary liabilities" but doubting that "the federal government [would] turn away a state that is having extreme financial difficulties when in effect it honored" the debts of corporate entities, including General Motors.[117] Later, in an interview with the congressional Financial Crisis Inquiry Commission, he qualified that assessment, saying, "I don't know how I would rate [state bond default risks] myself. . . . It's a bet on how the federal government will act over time."[118]

Making a bet on the federal response to a state sovereign debt crisis is beyond the scope of this chapter. We claim only that the introduction of collective bargaining has magnified the risk of state sovereign defaults, complicated the resolution of deficit problems that provoke such crises, heightened the likelihood of a federal intervention if such crises materialize, and set the conditions for a transformation of the country's federal system. The costs of such actions are greater than just the explicit dollar amounts on the bargaining table. Within the past decade a system of competitive federalism that once enjoyed an exalted, even Olympian, standing in American political culture has now been placed at risk.

Notes

1. Alexis de Tocqueville, *Democracy in America,* ed. Francis Bowen, trans. Henry Reeve (Barnes and Noble, 2003), p. 141.

2. *New State Ice Co* v. *Liebmann,* 285 US 262, 311 (1932), Brandeis dissenting.

3. See Cecelia Tichi, "The Puritan Historians and Their New Jerusalem," *Early American Literature,* vol. 6, no. 2 (Fall 1971), pp. 143, 143–44, discussing Puritan historians' use of biblical metaphors.

4. See, for example, Daniel Bell, "Interpretations of American Politics," in *The Radical Right,* edited by Daniel Bell (Doubleday, 1963), pp. 39, 50. See also Samuel P. Huntington, *American Politics: The Promise of Disharmony* (Belknap, 1981), pp. 240–45.

5. See Louis Hartz, *The Liberal Tradition in America* (Harcourt, 1955), pp. 4–6; Huntington, *American Politics,* pp. 27–30; Sven H. Steinmo, "American Exceptionalism Reconsidered: Culture or Institutions?" in *The Dynamics of American Politics: Approaches and Interpretations,* edited by Lawrence C. Dodd and Calvin Jillson (Westview, 1994), pp. 106, 117–24.

6. Bell, "Interpretations of American Politics," in *The Radical Right,* edited by Bell, pp. 58–59; William Kornhauser, *The Politics of Mass Society* (Free Press, 1959), pp. 121–23.

7. See, for example, Mancur Olson, *The Rise and Decline of Nations: Economic Growth, Stagflation, and Social Rigidities* (Yale 1982), pp. 92–94; Harold L. Wilensky, *The Welfare State and Equality: Structural and Ideological Roots of Public Expenditures* (University of California Press, 1975), p. 52; Phillips Cutright, "Political Structure, Economic Development, and National Social Security Programs," *American Journal of Sociology,* vol. 70, no. 5 (March 1965), pp. 537, 549. But see Harold L. Wilensky and Charles N. Lebeaux, *Industrial Society and Social Welfare: The Impact of Industrialization on the Supply and Organization of Social Welfare Services in the United States* (Free Press, 1958), p. 41.

8. Forum of Federations, "Federalism by Country" (2007) (www.forumfed.org/en/federalism/federalismbycountry.php). The number is twenty-three, according to one count given in Jonathan A. Rodden, *Hamilton's Paradox: The Promise and Peril of Fiscal Federalism* (Cambridge University Press, 2006), p. 39.

9. See, for example, Republic of India, "Public Administration Country Profile" (United Nations, Division for Public Administration and Development Management, January 2006), p. 8 (http://unpan1.un.org/intradoc/groups/public/documents/un/un pan023311.pdf).

10. See, for example, Dele Olowu, "Property Taxation and Democratic Decentralization in Developing Countries," Institute of Development Studies Seminar Paper (2002), p. 19 (www2.ids.ac.uk/gdr/cfs/pdfs/Olowu2.pdf).

11. Rodden, *Hamilton's Paradox,* pp. 9, 31, 93. For a discussion of default risk within the Canadian federal system, see Stuart Landon and Constance E. Smith, "Government Debt Spillovers and Creditworthiness in a Federation," *Canadian Journal of Economics,* vol. 33, no. 3 (August 2000), pp. 634, 636, 653–54 (http://papers.ssrn.com/sol3/papers.cfm?abstract_id=247367). Our argument does not turn on whether the United States is exceptionally different from Canada and Switzerland.

12. The discussion in this section draws on the theoretical statement developed in Paul E. Peterson, *City Limits* (University of Chicago Press, 1981), pp. 68–72. See also Charles Tiebout, "A Pure Theory of Local Expenditures," *Journal of Political Economy,* vol. 64, no. 5 (October 1956), pp. 416, 422 (www.jstor.org/stable/1826343); Wallace E. Oates, *Fiscal Federalism* (Harcourt Brace Jovanovich, 1972), pp. 240–41; Paul E. Peterson, *The Price of Federalism* (Brookings, 1995), pp. 18–19. The contributions of local government to rapid economic growth in China are explored in Gabriella Montinola, Yingyi Qian, and Barry R. Weingast, "Federalism, Chinese Style: The Political Basis for Economic Success in China," *World Politics,* vol. 48, no. 1 (October 1995), pp. 50, 67–78.

13. James Bryce, *Modern Democracies,* vol. 1 (Macmillan, 1921), p. 132 (http://oll.libertyfund.org/?option=com_staticxt&staticfile=show.php%3Ftitle=2084&Itemid=27).

14. See U.S. Census Bureau, *Statistical Abstract of the United States: 2012,* table 30, p. 37 (www.census.gov/prod/2011pubs/12statab/pop.pdf).

15. See Peterson, *The Price of Federalism,* pp. 18–19.

16. Ibid., p. 19.

17. Bryce, *Modern Democracies,* pp. 132–33.

18. Peterson, *Price of Federalism,* p. 19; see also Tiebout, "A Pure Theory of Local Expenditures," pp. 421–22.

19. See Peterson, *Price of Federalism,* pp. 29–30; table 3-3, p. 70; table 3-4, p. 71.

20. 2 US (2 Dall) 419 (1793).

21. Ibid., p. 453.

22. William B. English, "Understanding the Costs of Sovereign Default: American State Debts in the 1840s," *American Economic Review,* vol. 86, no. 1 259, 260 (March 1996) (www.jstor.org/stable/2118266).

23. *Hans* v. *Louisiana,* 134 US 1, 14–15, 21 (1890).

24. See *Monaco* v. *Mississippi,* 292 US 313, 330 (1934).

25. Consider English, "Understanding the Costs of Sovereign Default," pp. 260–61, citing *South Dakota* v. *North Carolina,* 192 US 286 (1904), and *United States* v. *North Carolina,* 136 US 211 (1980).

26. English, "Understanding the Costs of Sovereign Default," p. 261.

27. 514 US 779 (1995).

28. Ibid., p. 838, Kennedy concurring.

29. 505 US 144 (1992).

30. Ibid., p. 175, holding that Congress does not have the authority to force state governments to take title to waste under the Tenth Amendment.

31. 521 US 898 (1997).

32. Pub L No 103-159, 107 Stat 1536 (1993).

33. *Printz* v. *United States,* 521 US at 932–33.

34. Ibid., p. 930.

35. See, for example, *Fitzpatrick* v. *Bitzer,* 427 US 445, 456 (1976). Courts also got around limitations on sovereign immunity by allowing suits to go forward when plaintiffs sued state entities rather than the state itself. For examples of the courts applying this limitation, see *Brown* v. *Board of Education of Topeka,* 347 US 483, 493 (1954); Ex parte Young, 209 US 123, 165 (1908).

36. 527 US 706 (1999).

37. Ibid., p. 712.

38. Ibid., pp. 713, 728.

39. Ibid., pp. 755–56.

40. See, for example, Illinois Constitution, Article 13, § 5.

41. In 1990 the percentage expended by state and local governments from their own resources (that is, excluding federal grants) for elementary, secondary, and higher education was 34.1 percent. See U.S. Census Bureau, *Statistical Abstract: 2012,* p. 273, table 435, and p. 300, table 462.

42. American Presidency Project, "Letter on the Resolution of Federation of Federal Employees against Strikes in Federal Service," from President Franklin D. Roosevelt to Luther C. Steward, president of the National Federation of Federal Employees, August, 16, 1937 (www.presidency.ucsb.edu/ws/?pid=15445#axzz1bRZWSTlq).

43. George Meany, "Meany Looks into Labor's Future," *New York Times Magazine,* December 4, 1955, pp. 11, 38.

44. Paul E. Peterson, *Saving Schools: From Horace Mann to Virtual Learning* (Belknap, 2010), p. 106.

45. Martin Raymond West IV, "Politics, Public Sector Unionism, and Education Policy: Explanations and Evaluations," Ph.D. dissertation, Harvard University, 2006 (on file with authors).

46. For labor-friendly New Deal legislation, see National Industrial Recovery Act of 1933, Pub L No 73-10, 48 Stat 31, codified at 15 USC § 701–10, terminated by Executive Orders 7252 (December 21, 1935) and 7323 (March 26, 1936); National Labor Relations Act, 29 USC § 151 et seq.

47. See U.S. Bureau of Labor Statistics, "Union Members: 2010," press release, January 21, 2011 (www.bls.gov/news.release/union2.nr0.htm).

48. See West, "Politics, Public Sector Unionism, and Education Policy," p. 41.

49. See Clem Brooks and Jeff Manza, "Class Politics and Political Change in the United States, 1952–1992," *Social Forces,* vol. 76, no. 2 (December 1997), pp. 379, 393, figure 1.

50. See West, "Politics, Public Sector Unionism, and Education Policy," p. 55.

51. Ibid., pp. 56–58.

52. Executive Order 10988, 27 Fed Reg 551 (1962). See also West, "Politics, Public Sector Unionism, and Education Policy," p. 64.

53. Peterson, *Saving Schools,* p. 113.

54. Ibid.

55. Marjorie Murphy, "Blackboard Unions: The AFT and the NEA, 1900–1980" (Cornell University Press, 1990), p. 220.

56. See Peterson, *Saving Schools,* p. 113.

57. See Richard C. Kearney and David G. Carnevale, *Labor Relations in the Public Sector* (Marcel Dekker, 2001), pp. 38, 60–61, table 3.2; Randall W. Eberts, "Teachers Unions and Student Performance: Help or Hindrance?" *Future of Children: Excellence in the Classroom,* vol. 17, no. 1 (Spring 2007), pp. 175, 178 (http://futureofchildren.org/publications/journals/article/index.xml?journalid=34&articleid=81). For further research on the growth of teacher unions since 1950, see Joseph E. Slater, *Public Workers: Government Employee Unions, the Law, and the State, 1900–1962* (Cornell University Press, 2004), p. 193, and Hanna Skandera and Richard Sousa, *School Figures: The Data behind the Debate* (Hoover Institution Press, 2003), pp. 106–08. AFT membership includes university faculty, paraprofessionals, and other school employees.

58. Peterson, *Saving Schools,* p. 114.

59. Terry M. Moe, "The Union Label on the Ballot Box: How School Employees Help Choose Their Bosses," *Education Next,* vol. 6, no. 3 (Summer 2006), pp. 58, 60.

60. Peterson, *Saving Schools,* pp. 114–15.

61. Clive S. Thomas and Ronald J. Hrebenar, "Interest Groups in the States," in *Politics in the American States: A Comparative Analysis,* 8th ed., edited by Virginia Gray and Russell L. Hanson (CQ Press, 2004).

62. See Thomas D. Snyder, Sally A. Dillow, and Charlene M. Hoffman, *Digest of Education Statistics: 2009* (U.S. Department of Education, 2010), p. 100, table 64, p. 260, table 181.

63. See Thomas D. Snyder and Sally A. Dillow, *Digest of Education Statistics: 2008* (U.S. Department of Education, 2009), p. 117, table 80.

64. See ibid.

65. Peterson, *Saving Schools*, p. 153.

66. See ibid., p.133.

67. See, for example, the letter from Daniel W. Hancock, chairman of the Little Hoover Commission, to Edmund G. Brown, governor of California, and members of the California Legislature, February 24, 2011 (hereafter "the Hancock Letter"), in Little Hoover Commission, *Public Pensions for Retirement Security*, February 2011 (www.lhc.ca.gov/studies/204/report204.html).

68. See David Stella and Keith Bozarth, "Pension Sustainability: The Wisconsin Example," *Benefits and Compensation Digest*, vol. 47, no. 2 (February 2010), pp. 32, 33.

69. See, for example, the Hancock Letter; Roger Lowenstein, "The End of Pensions," *New York Times Magazine*, October 30, 2005 (www.nytimes.com/2005/10/30/magazine/30pensions.html?pagewanted=print).

70. See Kevin Hassett, "California Leads Nation to Bond Default Abyss," *Tulsa World*, June 2, 2009, p. A12.

71. Daniel J. Nadler and Sounman Hong, "Political and Institutional Determinants of Tax-Exempt Bond Yields," Harvard Kennedy School Report 11-04, p. 3 (www.hks.harvard.edu/pepg/PDF/Papers/PEPG_11-04_Nadler_Hong.pdf).

72. Ibid., p. 15, table 1.

73. Ibid., p. 3.

74. Alan J. Auerbach, "Long-Term Objectives for Government Debt," Swedish Fiscal Policy Council Conference on Fiscal Policy and Labour Market Reforms, February 2008, pp. 10–13. (http://elsa.berkeley.edu/~auerbach/long_term_objectives_govt_dept.pdf).

75. Nadler and Hong, "Political and Institutional Determinants of Tax-Exempt Bond Yields," p. 4.

76. See ibid.

77. In this chapter we ignore defaults by municipalities and other lower-tier governments. Those units of government do not have status in the U.S. Constitution, and their status varies from one state to the next, depending on state law.

78. See English, "Understanding the Costs of Sovereign Default," pp. 261–65.

79. See Rodden, *Hamilton's Paradox*, pp. 59–60.

80. English, "Understanding the Costs of Sovereign Default," p. 265, table 3.

81. Andrew Ang and Francis A. Longstaff, "Systemic Sovereign Credit Risk: Lessons from the U.S. and Europe," Working Paper 16982 (Cambridge, Mass.: National Bureau of Economic Research, April 2011), p. 6 (www.nber.org/papers/w16982).

82. See Paul E. Peterson, *The Politics of School Reform: 1870–1940* (University of Chicago Press, 1985), p. 179.

83. See William J. Grimshaw, *Union Rule in the Schools: Big-City Politics in Transformation* (Lexington Books, 1979), p. 64.

84. See Rodden, *Hamilton's Paradox*, pp. 57, 60.

85. See ibid., pp. 62–63.

86. See ibid., p. 91. See also ibid., pp. 83–87, table 4-1, reporting that the variance in the credit ratings of lower-tier governments in Germany is much smaller than in the United States.

87. Nadler and Hong, "Political and Institutional Determinants of Tax-Exempt Bond Yields," p. 8.

88. See figure 2-4.

89. Nadler and Hong, "Political and Institutional Determinants of Tax-Exempt Bond Yields," p. 8.

90. Ibid.

91. Unlike the simple relationship between union share of the public workforce and bond yield spreads, the simple relationship between yield spreads and the partisan composition of the state legislature does not increase in the wake of the fiscal crisis. The impact of this political factor is detectable only after estimating model 2 in table 2-1.

92. Nadler and Hong, "Political and Institutional Determinants of Tax-Exempt Bond Yields," pp. 6–7.

93. See ibid., pp. 6–7. Since the relationship between decisions to issue state bonds and yield spreads is endogenous, an unbiased estimate of the factors affecting yield spreads cannot be obtained by an ordinary least-squares regression. However, if a change in the size of the deficit is unexpected, the demand for credit changes regardless of the price of the bond, permitting unbiased estimates. The model thus estimates the interaction between deficit shocks and the key political variables included in the models. The model follows those used by James M. Poterba and Kim Rueben, "Fiscal News, State Budget Rules, and Tax-Exempt Bond Yields," *Journal of Urban Economics,* vol. 50 (2001), pp. 537, 539–44.

94. Nadler and Hong, "Political and Institutional Determinants of Tax-Exempt Bond Yields," pp. 6–7.

95. Ibid.

96. Ibid.

97. Ibid.

98. Variations in state expenditures on Medicaid, a "highly redistributive program that might be considered a default risk factor, were not correlated with yield" spreads. Bondholders apparently think that expenditures incurred outside of collective bargaining agreements are more easily managed. See Nadler and Hong, "Political and Institutional Determinants of Tax-Exempt Bond Yields," p. 9, n16.

99. Ibid., p. 9.

100. See ibid., pp. 10–12.

101. See note 12 above.

102. See, for example, *Hans* v. *Louisiana,* 134 US 1, 21 (1890).

103. Rodden, *Hamilton's Paradox,* p. 2.

104. See ibid., p. 8.

105. See ibid., pp. 78–79.

106. See ibid., p. 271.

107. See Rodden, *Hamilton's Paradox,* pp. 62, 67.

108. See figure 2-1.

109. American Recovery and Reinvestment Act of 2009, Pub L No 111-5, 123 Stat 115.

110. See White House, "State Governments Expected to Credit Recovery Act with Creating, Saving at Least 250,000 Education Jobs Nationwide," October 19, 2009, press release (www.whitehouse.gov/the-press-office/state-governments-expected-credit-recovery-act-with-creating-saving-least-250000-ed).

111. See William Murphy, "Stimulus Helps Shrink Deficit," *Newsday,* August 6, 2009, p. A20.

112. See, for example, Douglas Turner, "Serious Budget Troubles Brewing in Many States," *Buffalo News,* January 10, 2011, p. A8.

113. See, for example, Jeb Bush and Newt Gingrich, "Let States Declare Bankruptcy: Reorganization Allowing Breaking of Union Contracts May Be the Best Way for Some," *Baltimore Sun,* January 31, 2011, p. A13.

114. See, for example, Jeff Segal, Martin Hutchinson, and Rob Cox, "California's Only Option," *New York Times,* June 10, 2009, p. B2.

115. Representative Patrick McHenry, *State and Municipal Debt: The Coming Crisis? Hearing before the Subcommittee on TARP, Financial Services, and Bailouts of Public and Private Programs of the House Committee on Oversight and Government Reform,* 112 Cong., 1 sess., February 9, 2011 (www.gpo.gov/fdsys/pkg/CHRG-112hhrg68362/html/CHRG-112hhrg68362.htm).

116. Christopher Edley, "Let Treasury Rescue the States," *New York Times,* July 8, 2010, p. A25.

117. Svea Herbst-Bayliss and Jonathan Stempel, "Buffett: U.S. Can Bail Out States, Insurers Pained," Reuters, May 1, 2010 (www.reuters.com/article/2010/05/01/berkshire-buffett-ratings-idUSN0118355720100501).

118. Ianthe Jeanne Dugan, "Investors Looking Past Red Flags in Muni Market," *Wall Street Journal,* June 14, 2010, p. C1 (http://online.wsj.com/article/SB10001424052748704067504575304782084631368.html).

JONATHAN RODDEN

3

Can Market Discipline Survive in the U.S. Federation?

A rare point of agreement among progressive and conservative ideologues in the United States is that the U.S. system of federalism is dysfunctional. Credit-constrained states are responsible for implementing ambitious federal programs that are funded through inflexible grants that create bad incentives. State taxes are highly sensitive to the business cycle, and federal transfers are not designed to fill the gaps left during recessions. Thus state fiscal policy exacerbates the business cycle, and recessions lead to ad hoc scrambles for additional federal resources. States save very little during booms, and they are tempted to underfund pension programs during slowdowns, leading to a ticking time bomb of unfunded obligations to retirees—which, in the worst-case scenario, will eventually lead to a wave of defaults or federal bailouts or both.

Conservatives believe that the problem lies in the growth of federal programs implemented by states since the New Deal. For the dreamers among them, the solution is a return to a less intertwined form of federalism last seen in the 1920s. For the realists, the answer is another bout of "new federalism" characterized by something like the capped block grants of the Reagan era.

Progressives see the problem differently. They believe that full realization of a centralized system of risk sharing and redistribution has been impeded and that the states have been left with too much authority. The United States, they believe, is trying to solve twenty-first century problems through eighteenth-century institutions. For the dreamers among them, the solution is outright federalization of the programs currently implemented by states. For the realists, the solution is an expansion of conditional grants and perhaps a system through which the federal government borrows on behalf of the states.

The widespread agreement about the failure of U.S. federalism comes as a surprise in Europe and Latin America, where American federalism is often viewed with envy. Argentina and Brazil have experienced macroeconomic crises that can be traced directly to dysfunctional federalism. Spain, Italy, and even Germany have struggled with overborrowing by provincial governments, and the European Monetary Union (EMU) is on the brink of collapse.

A vague, pessimistic view of the United States is gaining traction, especially in the media. The country is thought to have the same underlying problems as Europe, and we are told that it will soon be in the same boat. In this view, in addition to the pathologies of inefficiency and procyclicality, the American system of intertwined federalism also generates growing incentives for fiscal indiscipline that will eventually create a subnational debt crisis. The fiscal crisis of 2008 and the federal response are the last straw, and it is no longer possible to rely on credit markets to discipline the fiscal behavior of state governments.

This chapter argues that the dysfunctions of American federalism are indeed serious and that the problem of unfunded subnational obligations to retirees is one of the largest policy challenges facing the United States today. Yet it is important not to conflate the various pathologies of U.S. federalism. The solution to one problem might exacerbate another.

I argue that since the 1840s, the fiscal decisions of the states have been disciplined by credit markets rather than higher-level governments and that they still are today. That makes the United States quite rare among the world's federations. The death of market discipline has been greatly exaggerated. If anything, the recent fiscal crisis seems to have strengthened rather than undermined market discipline in the states, and state efforts to make politically painful adjustments have far exceeded those of the federal government.

Whether inspired by the right or the left, reforms aimed at correcting some of the basic problems of American federalism should seek to bolster rather than undermine the foundations of market-based fiscal discipline in the states.

The Problem of Fiscal Discipline in Federations

All federations must face up to a basic problem that can be conceptualized in the language of game theory as a dynamic game of incomplete information.[1] When lower-level governments face a serious long-term negative revenue shock requiring fiscal adjustment, they are tempted to avoid the political pain of expenditure cuts or tax increases. That temptation is driven by the belief that the higher-level government can eventually be compelled to assume their debts. Thus, even if lower-level governments know that their fiscal decisions are not sustainable in the long run, they can avoid making the necessary adjustments because of an implicit higher-level guarantee.

The lower-level government generally does not have full information about this implicit guarantee. The higher-level government often makes some sort of formal no-bailout pledge, and its leaders publicly state that bailouts are impossible. However, lower-level governments can often see that those statements are not credible. They look to the final stage of the game, the eve of default for the lower-level government, and attempt to project whether the higher-level government will prefer a bailout to default.

Lower-level officials are not the only ones attempting to make such assessments. Market actors like fund managers, banks, and credit rating agencies also attempt to look down the game tree to evaluate the higher-level government's likely reaction at the moment of default, searching for a variety of clues to the central government's likely behavior. They evaluate the process through which a bailout would be decided and the political incentives of the actors. If the legislature must vote on the issue, what is the probability that the requisite majority would favor a bailout? That probability is determined in part by the number of insolvent lower-level governments and the nature of their legislative representation. If the chief executive has wide-ranging authority to approve a bailout unilaterally, how might the executive contrast the political pain associated with a bailout with that associated with default? This trade-off is shaped by the nature of the chief executive's regional support base.

Some of the most crucial questions are about the creditors. Who are they, and how powerful are they in the political process? If they are a diffuse group of foreign individual investors, perhaps the domestic political costs of default will be sufficiently low to make it a relatively attractive option. On the other hand, if the debt of lower-level governments is an important part of the portfolio of the largest domestic banks, default might be extremely unattractive.

Lower-level officials and market actors also derive clues from the basic architecture of the system of fiscal federalism. When lower-level governments provide some of the most politically sensitive public services, like health care and unemployment insurance, and those services are funded almost entirely by taxes that are levied and collected by higher-level governments, voters are likely to blame the higher-level government for service disruptions. When the political blame for local service disruptions is quickly directed at the central government, the credibility of its no-bailout pledge is undermined, and market actors are more likely to perceive an implicit guarantee.

Perceptions of the credibility of the central government's no-bailout commitment are crucial for local fiscal decisionmaking. If everyone believes with perfect certainty that the central government will not follow through on its commitment, lower-level governments have no incentives to adjust to negative shocks and market actors have only weak incentives to punish them or to distinguish between the creditworthiness of the various lower-level governments.

If lower-level governments and market actors perceive the central government's commitment as perfectly credible, lower-level governments have strong incentives to adjust and market actors face strong incentives to monitor their creditworthiness since default is a very real possibility. Of course, democratically elected governments often avoid making the adjustments needed as long as possible, but eventually the costs of doing so become prohibitive.

While these perfect-information scenarios are instructive, a crucial point is that local officials and market actors often operate under substantial uncertainty. They must base their decisions on bets about the credibility of the higher-level government's no-bailout commitment, using all observable information to inform their evolving beliefs.

Central government policies vis-à-vis lower-level governments are important not only because of the direct incentives that they give and the restrictions that they place on lower-level governments but also because they send valuable signals to players, who are always updating their beliefs in a repeated game. Government policies can bolster or undermine the no-bailout commitment, thus altering the incentives of lower-level governments, creditors, and even voters.

Two Paths to Fiscal Discipline: Hierarchy and Markets

If the higher-level government is unable to refuse to provide bailouts, it faces an obvious and severe moral hazard problem. Consider a typical unitary country in Europe or a highly centralized developing country that has recently made a transition from dictatorship to democracy. Taxation is highly centralized, and the central government has taken on primary responsibility for most public services. Lower-level governments are mere conduits for delivering services that are funded through intergovernmental transfers. In Europe, the central government often makes a formal commitment to provide roughly equal levels of service throughout the country.

In such settings, it is common knowledge that any attempt by the higher-level government to forswear bailouts would lack credibility. It would be politically and in some cases constitutionally impossible to allow a local government to default. Under such conditions, it would be disastrous to allow lower-level governments to approach credit markets and borrow without limits. Thus central governments in fiscally centralized countries typically attempt to regulate the access of lower-level governments to all forms of borrowing.[2] Bond issues and bank loans are strictly monitored and limited by the central government; in some cases, the central government undertakes all borrowing on behalf of local governments and then allocates infrastructure financing according to its own assessments of needs. To the extent that public employee compensation and pension programs provide opportunities for borrowing, they also are regulated.

Any attempts to smooth local government expenditures over the business cycle are clearly in the domain of the central government.

For much of the twentieth century, this type of hierarchical system has been in place in the relatively homogeneous unitary countries of Europe, where there is no pretense of viewing local governments as sovereign borrowers. However, the story is quite different in some federations, where—even after the centralization associated with two world wars and the Great Depression—states and provinces held on to significant authority well into the post-World War II era. When the powers of the central government are limited and the constituent units of the federation possess significant autonomous taxing authority, the central government might be able to credibly commit itself to allow them to default.

In this scenario, lower-level governments can approach credit markets as sovereign borrowers and creditors face incentives to collect information about the sustainability of their finances. The desire to borrow at attractive rates gives governments an incentive to make sustainable choices. Moreover, competition with other states or provinces for taxpaying residents and firms provides additional incentives for exercising prudence and maintaining a sustainable debt burden.

When Federations Fail

The problem with this rosy scenario, however, is that it rarely comes to fruition. Through a series of painful crises, we have learned that it can be very difficult for the central government to fully commit to refusing to rescue defaulting states. In some decentralized federations, a combination of both constitutional and informal political constraints retarded the process of fiscal and administrative centralization that characterized the first half of the twentieth century in much of the world. Those constraints are a double-edged sword. On one hand, by limiting the capacity and incentives of the center to intervene in the fiscal affairs of lower-level governments, a robust federalism can bolster the central government's no-bailout commitment and sow the seeds of market discipline. On the other, it can also prevent the central government from monitoring and regulating the borrowing of lower-level governments.

In such federations, due to the wide-ranging powers of the lower-level governments to tax, spend, and borrow, the stakes are very high if the center's commitment is in any way compromised. In the late 1980s and early 1990s, the Brazilian states and Argentine provinces were on unsustainable fiscal paths, yet they faced weak incentives to undertake politically painful adjustments because they believed that the central government would ultimately step in to bail them out. The central government could not prevent them from continuing to undertake new borrowing and debt rollovers in the face of their very precarious fiscal positions even while they were explicitly waiting for federal bailouts. In both countries the bailouts eventually materialized, and a very costly moral hazard problem played a major role in facilitating a series of fiscal crises. In Argentina, of course, the result was the dramatic default of the federal government.

The European Monetary Union has fallen prey to exactly the same problem, and it seems to be failing in an even more spectacular fashion. Member states and their creditors came to see the debts of the weaker member states as implicitly guaranteed by the stronger member states. Ireland and the Southern European countries were able to borrow at favorable rates, and rating agencies were clearly bolstering their evaluations of the creditworthiness of the weaker member states by assuming an implicit guarantee. Their bailout prophecies eventually became self-fulfilling. The dynamic game of incomplete information reached the final stage, and the European Union confirmed suspicions that it cannot tolerate outright default by a member state.

What lessons are to be learned from these incidents? It is not surprising that these crises are interpreted as failures of market discipline. Unsustainable borrowing took place in part because market actors (correctly) interpreted the higher-level government's no-bailout commitment as not credible. It is just as appropriate, however, to interpret them as failures of hierarchy. As part of the Stability and Growth Pact, the European Union had a formal excessive deficit procedure that, on paper, would be used to punish member states in the early stages of building unsustainable deficits or debt burdens. The Brazilian and Argentine federal systems also had elaborate procedures for monitoring and regulating the debts of the states and provinces.

Unfortunately, however, those regulations and procedures were undone by the politics of federalism. The European excessive deficit procedure proved to be unenforceable. The largest countries had the political power to flout the rules, and smaller countries like Greece engaged in creative accounting without punishment. In Brazil in the 1980s, the senate was responsible for approving and regulating the borrowing of the states, and representatives of insolvent states found that approval of unsustainable borrowing was relatively easy to obtain as part of the game of legislative horse-trading.

Those half-hearted efforts at hierarchical regulation inadvertently undermined market discipline by sending significant signals about the central government's lack of credibility. If officials found it politically impossible to sanction Greece for its accounting abuses or São Paulo for its dubious loans from state-owned banks, how could it possibly summon the political fortitude to allow them to default? Moreover, the very act of attempting to regulate the borrowing of member states signals a certain level of responsibility. Weak or half-hearted regulation may have been worse than no regulation at all.

These failures of market discipline had another crucial common element: externalities associated with the banking system. One of the most important clues to the central government's credibility lies in the identity of the creditors of the lower-level governments, which is in turn shaped by the policies of the higher-level government. The Brazilian states were allowed to borrow directly from large commercial banks that they owned and controlled. Several of them were among the largest and most important banks in Brazil, and by the end, some of their largest "assets" were bad debts to their own state governments. It eventually became clear to everyone that a bailout of states would be necessary to save the banking system from collapse. The crisis of fiscal federalism in Brazil was thus in large part a failure in the organization of the banking system.

Something similar can be said about the European debt crisis. Data about the exposure of large European banks to insolvent member states are sparse, but it is quite clear that concern about bank failures was an important part of the logic of the bailouts of Greece, Ireland, and Portugal, which can be seen as bailouts of troubled German and French banks that had overinvested in ill-fated Southern European real estate developments and bonds.

The European and Latin American episodes demonstrate that in a decentralized federation characterized by strong representation of member states, both market and hierarchical forms of fiscal discipline can easily fail if institutions and incentives are not properly structured. A half-hearted hybrid of market and hierarchical discipline is unlikely to succeed.

A Different Path: Market Discipline in the United States

While difficult, it is by no means impossible for a central government in a federation to make a credible no-bailout commitment. A very costly and credible signal is sent when a crisis arises, the bailout game reaches the final stage, and the central government simply turns its back and allows a default. Such an event would send a strong signal to creditors and other governments, providing a firm foundation for market discipline going forward. That is "the road not taken" in Europe.

However, that is exactly what happened in the United States in the 1840s. After states had engaged in large-scale borrowing in order to build canals, railroads, and other internal improvements, a fiscal panic led to a sudden reduction in tax revenues; without reliable revenues, several states were unable to service their debts. Many of the creditors were British citizens, and Britain threatened military attack if the U.S. federal government did not assume the debts of the states.[3] A coalition of insolvent states assembled a bailout proposal, attempting to buy the support of less indebted states by offering to create a per capita monetary transfer including all states.

However, in a pivotal moment in the history of U.S. federalism, the bailout proposal failed in Congress. Representatives of solvent states constituted a slim congressional majority,[4] and bailout opponents turned public opinion against the proposal in those states. Perhaps another important reason for the decision can be traced, once again, to the identity of creditors, most of whom were foreign individuals rather than important domestic constituencies.

Considerable uncertainty about a federal government payoff in the dynamic bailout game was resolved. Several states repudiated their debts, and the entire federation was cut off from international capital markets. State governments, citizens, and creditors learned a painful lesson: the U.S. states are sovereign debtors. In order to approach credit markets again, states made substantial reforms, including the introduction of direct taxation and the institution of various balanced budget requirements. Creditors learned to carefully assess the states' revenues and obligations.

This episode marked the beginning of a long period of successful market discipline among the U.S. states that was marred only by the repudiation by some Southern states of their debts in the aftermath of the Civil War. Unlike other political unions described above, the U.S. federal government has not endeavored to limit the deficits or debts of the U.S. states. Yet without any hierarchical oversight or regulation, throughout the twentieth century the deficits and debt burdens of the U.S. states have been quite low in comparison with entities in most other federations, especially considering the very large role that they play in providing basic public services and building infrastructure.[5]

The states typically adjust to revenue downturns rather quickly, and most likely because of their balanced budget rules, they do not smooth expenditures over the business cycle through borrowing. In fact, both revenues and expenditures of the U.S. states are extremely procyclical. Negative revenue shocks are met with rapid expenditure cuts.[6] In the most recent downturns, cuts have been so severe as to almost completely offset the impact of any federal government attempts at fiscal stimulus.[7]

Empirical studies suggest that the balanced budget rules that emerged in the 1840s are an important part of the explanation for cross-state variation in the speed of adjustment.[8] While states have devised a variety of tricks and gimmicks to circumvent their balanced budget requirements, including delaying payments into the next fiscal year and underfunding pensions, these rules are probably part of the explanation of the fact that as a share of gross state product, general obligation bond debts of the states have been modest throughout the twentieth century.

State governments have been quite sensitive to credit ratings, and the need to keep debt burdens under control in order to keep borrowing costs down is an important part of political discourse in the states. Credit downgrades are politically costly for governors. The empirical literature suggests that bond yields and credit ratings are quite sensitive to changes in states' debt burdens,[9] more so than in most if not all other federations.

In short, the United States is one of a very small number of federations, perhaps also including Canada and Switzerland, in which the central government has been able to convince market actors that the constituent units should be treated as sovereigns and in which the fiscal decisions of the constituent units have been consistently constrained by credit markets for much of the twentieth century.

The Evolution of American Federalism in the Twentieth Century

This optimistic story about market discipline with roots in the nineteenth century seems increasingly quaint and anachronistic in 2013. A pessimistic view of American federalism is that the growth of federal programs has progressively undermined the fiscal autonomy of the states throughout the twentieth century to such an extent that the no-bailout commitment of the federal government has lost all credibility. In this view, the recent wave of federal bailouts of the private sector, coupled with the recent fiscal stimulus program, has dealt the coup de grâce to the notion of market discipline.

Perhaps the central government was able to ignore the states' bailout demands in the 1840s in part because its powers and obligations relative to those of the states were so limited, as were the economic externalities linking the states. The federal government may have more at stake in allowing California to default today than it had in allowing Pennsylvania to default in 1840. Beginning with the New Deal, the states have increasingly become conduits for the delivery of government programs, like Medicaid, that are conceived and largely funded by the federal government.

Figure 3-1 displays federal grants relative to state and local current expenditures. Federal grants were trivial entering the Great Depression. The federal response to the Depression involved a large increase in grants to the states; entering the 1940s, grants as a share of subnational expenditures reached a new equilibrium of around 10 percent of expenditures.

Figure 3-2 displays real per capita total grants as well as several individual categories of grants. The Office of Management and Budget (OMB) distinguishes between grants that are designated for programs that flow to individuals, grants designated for capital investments, and grants that do not fit into either category. Within the category of grants destined for individuals, it is possible to track Medicaid grants separately.

Figure 3-1. *The Growth of Federal Grants as a Share of State-Local Current Expenditures*

Percent

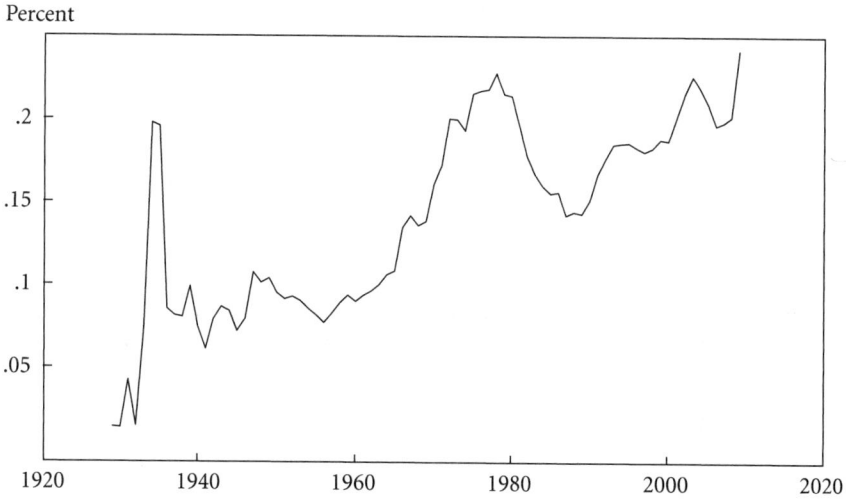

Source: Historical tables archived at www.bea.gov.

Figure 3-2. *Real Per Capita Grants, Various Types*

2005 dollars

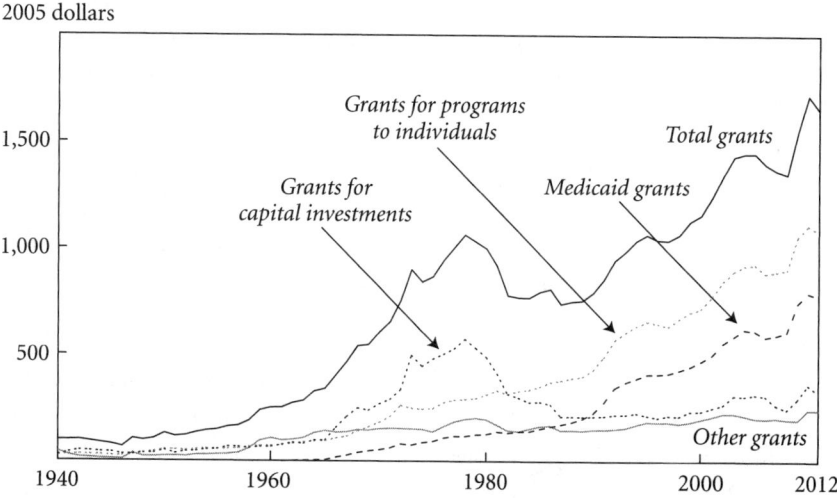

Source: Office of Management and Budget Historical Tables (www.whitehouse.gov/omb/budget/historicals).

The most dramatic growth in transfer dependence in figure 3-1 came about not in the immediate aftermath of the Depression but in the 1960s and 1970s. Figure 3-2 shows that there was sustained growth in the residual category, which was driven primarily by the general revenue-sharing program. The decline in this category tracks the end of revenue sharing. There was also growth in the 1960s and 1970s in transfers to programs for individuals, led by the beginning of the Medicaid program in the mid-1960s.

The Reagan administration saw a leveling off of all grant programs and a precipitous decline in transfer dependence all the way back to pre-Medicaid levels. Since the beginning of the George H. W. Bush administration, transfer dependence has again experienced a steady increase, with especially large spikes during the administrations of George W. Bush and Barack Obama. However, it is important to point out that even after the temporary increase in grants associated with the stimulus program in 2009 and 2010, transfer dependence has returned to roughly the level of the late 1970s. As a share of GDP, grants from the federal government averaged less than 1 percent in the 1940s and reached around 3.5 percent by 1980, returning to around 2 percent by the end of the Reagan era. By 2012 they were approaching 4 percent of GDP.

What has driven the growth of grants since the end of the Reagan era? Figure 3-2 shows that it was driven by the explosive expansion of Medicaid. Real grants for capital investments and virtually everything else have been essentially flat since the 1980s.

In sum, in contrast to those of most federal entities, the vast majority of the expenditures of the U.S. states are still funded by own-source taxes that are not controlled by the federal government. While grants have indeed grown in recent decades, so have state tax revenues. However, among the activities undertaken by state governments, the administration of jointly funded entitlement programs—chiefly Medicaid—has grown steadily.

A danger is that as grants become more important components of subnational budgets and the books of the federal and lower-level governments become increasingly intertwined, the central government's no-bailout commitment loses credibility because it has become politically implicated in service provision in the states.

When faced with a fiscal crisis requiring rapid and politically painful adjustment, elected officials in the states are tempted to avoid adjustment and call upon the central government for additional assistance. The political attractiveness of this strategy is shaped by their ability to make the case to voters that their troubles are not self-induced. Their case is bolstered substantially by a plethora of grant-funded federal programs as well as unfunded mandates. Moreover, states can argue that matching provisions in some grant programs distort their incentives and discourage expenditure cuts that would enhance efficiency.

Moreover, the states have a compelling story to tell about the challenges associated with downturns. Their own-source revenues are highly correlated with the business cycle, and they fall precipitously during recessions just as the pool of individuals eligible for Medicaid increases. Federal Medicaid grants are slightly countercyclical in the aggregate, so that a $1.00 decrease in GDP per capita from the previous fiscal year is associated with a little less than two cents of additional total Medicaid grants per capita. However, grants are positively correlated with the state business cycle. A $1.00 decrease in a state's GDP per capita is associated with a penny or two less per capita in federal transfers over the previous fiscal year.

In other words, in the initial fiscal year of a slump, the states are asked to provide health care and other services for more poor people with less money. Thus, with each fiscal downturn in recent decades, the story has been the same: tax revenues and federal grants fall precipitously, and states are faced with an array of costly new expenditure programs and employee benefits that had been enthusiastically promulgated during the last boom. The states buy some time by borrowing to the extent allowed by their balanced budget rules, engaging in fiscal gimmicks, and, crucially, neglecting to fund their pension programs.

However, those measures are usually not enough to avoid steep expenditure cuts. Declining expenditures in the states easily offset any federal efforts at fiscal stimulus, and a coalition for special assistance to the states begins to form in Washington. Of course, such assistance is not referred to in polite company as a bailout, but it is undeniably an ad hoc, quickly negotiated transfer aimed at filling gaps in state budgets. In the most recent recession, these transfers took the form of special short-term Medicaid supplements and pork-laden stimulus grants for shovel-ready state infrastructure projects.

Figure 3-3 displays total real per capita federal grants to the state and local governments and years of negative per capita GDP growth. It also includes a smoothed Lowess plot. In the recessions of the mid-1970s and early 1980s, there were no obvious spikes in grants associated with downturns. In the recessions of the early 1990s and 2000s, however, while there was no departure from the trend in the initial year of the downturn, there appear to be bumps up from the trend in the years following the recessions.

The most recent recession is especially interesting. Real grants per capita were falling in the two years before the fiscal crisis of 2008 and actually fell in the year of the crisis. They did not recover until the stimulus bill was passed, and after two fiscal years of rapid growth, they are falling once again.

In addition to the inefficiencies associated with delay and political bargaining, a danger of these implicit bailouts is that they send important signals to market actors that the federal government cannot allow states to cut expenditures, much less default on their bond obligations. And they encourage state

Figure 3-3. *Real Federal Grants per Capita*

2005 dollars

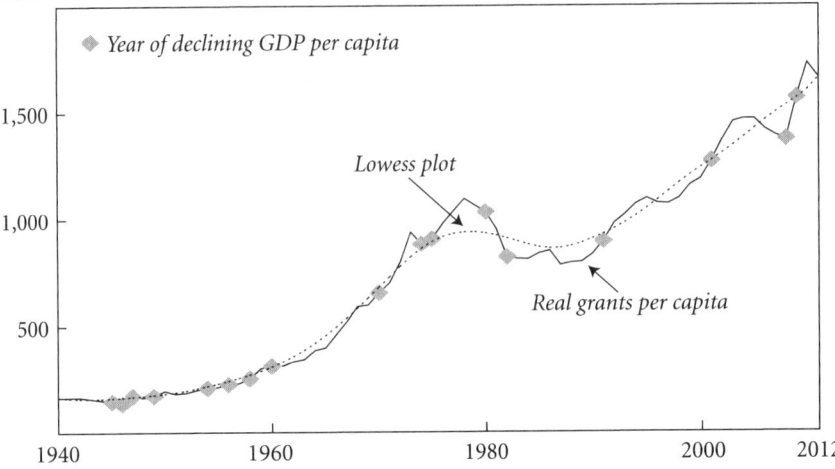

Sources: Office of Management and Budget Historical Tables (www.whitehouse.gov/omb/budget/historicals); Bureau of Economic Analysis, Gross Domestic Product (all industry total) (www.bea.gov); and author's calculations.

governments to believe that the political pain of adjustment might eventually be shifted to the federal government.

In the most recent recession, the federal government has also taken the unusual step of formally subsidizing and presumably guaranteeing a special class of subnational debt known as "Build America Bonds." It was extremely helpful for states to be able to borrow at subsidized rates, but a danger is that market actors view this as yet another sign of the federal government's ultimate responsibility for the obligations of states, another step along the way to a unitary-style system in which the center arranges the borrowing of the lower-level governments but without the concomitant hierarchical borrowing restrictions.

In sum, there is a danger that although a spectacular bailout like that of Greece has not yet happened, the federal government's no-bailout commitment is slowly eroding with each recession. In fact, Nouriel Roubini[10] and Warren Buffett[11] have argued that the central government already provides a strong implicit guarantee, at least to the largest states. They argue that the political importance of California and the externalities associated with default are simply too great to imagine a world in which Congress and the president allow California to default. This argument is bolstered by the fact that the federal government has already revealed its taste for bailouts in the private sector.

Can Market Discipline Survive?

When a string of states defaulted in the early 1840s, expectations of bailouts in future rounds of the game were somewhere near zero. The perceived probability of bailouts is substantially higher today, but the probability is also surely not equal to one. The crucial question is whether the perceived probability is low enough to provide incentives for states to adjust. Faced with the prospect of politically painful tax increases and expenditure cuts, are state governments willing to continue on an unsustainable fiscal path while placing their bets on a federal bailout? Are creditors willing to fund them? If the answer is "no," market discipline can still survive.

First, let us put the growth of federal grants displayed in figure 3-3 into proper perspective. Along with the Canadian provinces and Swiss cantons, the U.S. states are still among the most fiscally autonomous subnational entities in the world, and the vast majority of their expenditures are funded by taxes that they levy and collect themselves. It is not at all clear that a cynical strategy of courting disaster while waiting for bailouts would be politically wise for a state governor.

It is also not clear that a bailout of selected insolvent states would receive a warm reception in Congress given the current political climate. In fact, it is plausible that voters' widespread anger about private sector bailouts would make a bailout of states politically challenging. Even efforts to raise the federal debt limit to avoid federal government default have been exceedingly rancorous and difficult.

Moreover, as in the nineteenth century, at the moment the states that are flirting with insolvency do not come close to constituting a legislative majority. In fact, while it is true that the most troubled states, like California and Illinois, are some of the largest and hence produce the largest externalities, they are dramatically underrepresented in the Senate.

Let us also return to a crucial variable in the analysis above: the identity of the debt holders. Unlike in the Latin American and European cases described above, state defaults would not necessarily threaten the survival of the U.S. banking system. In fact, as purchasers of state bonds, banks are relatively minor players. For the most part, state bonds are attractive to state residents because of their tax-exempt status, so state debts are largely held by the citizens of a state. The externalities associated with the default of a U.S. state might be more limited than those with the default of some other political unions—and hence the federal government's no-bailout commitment more credible—since a significant share of the pain associated with default would be limited to state residents.[12]

How do market actors besides Warren Buffett assess the probability of federal bailouts? If creditors are increasingly reassured by the central government's

Figure 3-4. *Credit Default Swaps for Selected U.S. States and EU Member States*[a]

U.S. dollars, thousands

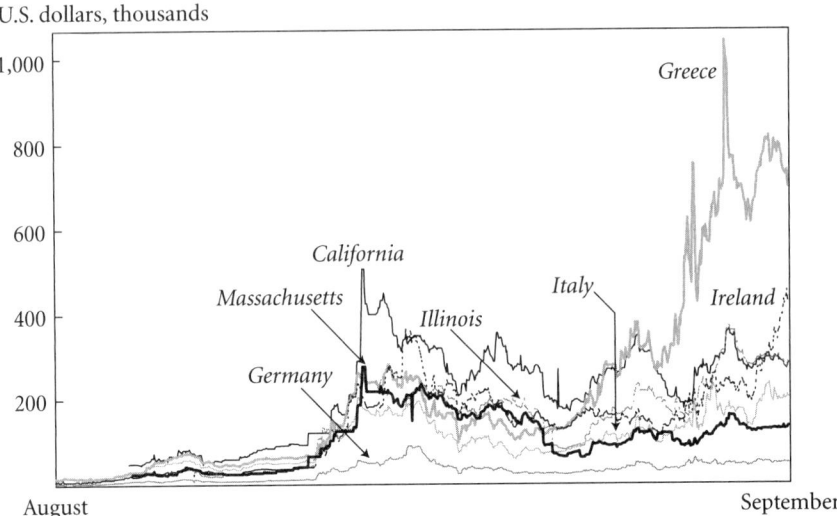

Source: Datastream (Thomson Reuters).
a. Cost of insuring a $10 million bond, in thousands of U.S. dollars.

implicit guarantee, bond yields, credit default swaps, and credit ratings should be converging. Yet the opposite is happening. In the wake of the crisis, markets are behaving as if differences in the creditworthiness of the states have dramatically increased; therefore, spreads have diverged.

Figure 3-4 presents credit default swap (CDS) data for selected U.S. states and European Union member states. The initial pre-crisis clustering of U.S. states and EU member states suggests that creditors underestimated the risks associated with CDS bonds, especially in Europe, where the policies described above allowed creditors to believe that member state debt issues were guaranteed by other member states.

Yet even in the pre-crisis period, there was greater differentiation among U.S. states than EU member states. Moreover, the cost of insuring Greek debt did not surpass that of California debt until very late in the Greek crisis, in spite of a debt burden that was several times higher. Ireland and Illinois were neck and neck until the eve of the Irish bailout.

While market actors may have been asleep at the wheel prior to the crisis, they appear to have awakened with a jerk. In both Europe and the United States, market discipline has returned with a vengeance. In Europe the wake-up call appears to have come too late. Precisely because of the panic at the discovery that the bonds of EU member states were not risk-free instruments, the rapidly increasing spreads among member states depicted in figure 3-4 forced the wealthier member states to step in to stave off Greek default and save their own banks.

In the United States, the increasing bond yield spreads for troubled states did not create a panic, even in 2010 when television analysts began breathlessly predicting a wave of state defaults. Of course, that does not mean that states are not in serious trouble. Debt-to-GDP ratios are manageable in part because balanced budget rules have created incentives to borrow from future public retirees rather than bond markets, and unrealistic accounting assumptions have allowed states to hide the problem. Many state pension programs are clearly on an unsustainable fiscal path, and painful reform is needed.

These are vexing and dangerous problems, but they need not spell the demise of market discipline. The costs of unfunded pension liabilities are finally coming into focus and are informing the assessments of creditors and rating agencies. States are under enormous pressure to find ways to shore up their pension programs. Indeed, markets have punished the most troubled states, which have faced burdensome and increasing borrowing costs. Credit default swaps for the most troubled U.S. states have surpassed those for Latvia and Hungary.

It is worth noting that the states with the largest debt burdens in the United States are not the poor states on the economic periphery, as in Europe. The U.S. states with the largest unfunded pension liabilities, bonded debts, and other obligations are among the wealthiest states—including New Jersey, Connecticut, Illinois, Ohio, and California.

Many of the country's most productive industries and its most well-compensated individuals reside in these relatively large and densely populated states. Yet high income and large size have a downside: these states are called on to subsidize the more sparsely populated and less productive states of the Southern and Western periphery. The wealthy states of the Northeast pay substantially more in federal taxes than they receive in federal expenditures.

The United States does not have a formal revenue equalization program along the lines of programs in Canada, Germany, or Spain, and neither intergovernmental grants nor overall federal expenditures are highly correlated with state income in the United States, as they are in these other federations.[13] In fact, a much better predictor of federal grants is legislative representation: the dramatically overrepresented states of the sparsely populated rural periphery are disproportionately favored in the distribution of federal grants, especially for infrastructure.

The dense, wealthy net contributors to the federal budget must tax their citizens at higher rates in order to provide the same services as the subsidized states of the periphery, and they also have become more reliant on debt. In fact, the gap between federal revenues raised and federal expenditures received in Illinois in a single year is large enough to wipe out its entire bonded debt. As these high-tax states begin to confront their debt and pension problems, benefit cuts and tax increases will be politically unpopular, but at this point there is little to indicate that a career-oriented official would be better off defaulting than simply waiting for a federal bailout that may or may not arrive.

In short, state governments and their creditors may hope for an implicit federal guarantee and assess the probability of an eventual bailout as substantially greater than zero, but their hopes do not appear to be especially high. Governors and treasurers will complain loudly about cuts in federal assistance as the stimulus and Medicaid supplements run out, and they will continue to lobby for increased transfers. However, there is no evidence that they are throwing up their hands, staying the course, and placing all of their bets on a federal bailout. On the contrary, state governments are making serious efforts at reform. Elected officials from both parties are risking their political careers by calling for hard choices. Both Democratic and Republican administrations are asking public employee unions for large concessions. Although they have a long way to go, some states are attempting to make structural changes to pension programs.

Toward a Reform Agenda

The road ahead is rocky, and partisan recriminations and rancor are to be expected. In some states, the battles are between parties, but in others, efforts to achieve fiscal sustainability are creating fissures within rather than between parties. The intensity of the battles reveals that market discipline is functioning quite forcefully.

In fact, in light of draconian and sometimes irrational expenditure cuts in vital areas like infrastructure and especially education, some might argue that it is working all too well. States implement a good deal of federally funded policy, especially through welfare, education, and health programs, where one might hope for some insulation from the business cycle. Yet such programs are funded with highly procyclical revenue sources, and states are not able to smooth expenditures over the business cycle. Therefore every recession is met with draconian cuts that fall disproportionately on the most vulnerable and with calls for implicit bailouts while pension obligations go unpaid.

One might also add that booms are accompanied by fiscal expansions, generous new contracts, and very little in the way of saving. The long-term result is inefficient and procyclical spending, growing debt, and insolvent pension programs.

In one view, market discipline and state sovereignty are the problems rather than the solutions. If the problem is a murky quasi-sovereignty for the states, the solution is hierarchy. In this view, Alexander Hamilton's deep skepticism of independent spending and borrowing by states was warranted, and it is time to implement his vision and turn the states into wards of the federal government. To return to the family analogy, the states should be viewed as children rather than adults. The Civil War and then the New Deal placed the United States on a path of fiscal centralization that was left incomplete because of the outmoded trappings of federalism. As the federal government expanded, the states were left with too much fiscal and political power, and the federal government was forced into an uncomfortable partnership with them.

In this view, the federal government should assume wide-ranging new powers to regulate taxation, expenditures, and borrowing in the states, along the lines of those of European central governments vis-à-vis their municipal governments. Failing that, it should simply federalize existing programs that are implemented by states, which would presumably require a vast buildup of the federal bureaucracy throughout the country. Echoing Hamilton, some might even call for a clean slate, beginning with federal assumption of state debts and pension obligations. Some scholars have called for the Federal Reserve to follow the lead of Mario Draghi and the European Central Bank and bail out indebted states by making massive direct purchases of their bonds.[14]

Leaving partisan ideological debates aside, it is relatively clear that this type of solution is impractical. Above all, it is difficult to imagine such a far-reaching change to the constitutional order. It is not clear where the political impetus for such a major reorientation of American federalism would come from or how it could possibly be achieved without constitutional change. In the current political climate—and with the federal government itself on a precarious debt path—it is also difficult to imagine a solution that relied on a dramatic expansion of the federal government.

The basic structure of American federalism is probably here to stay, and in any case, a hierarchical solution is not promising in such a large and diverse federation. When the higher-level government has just agreed to a large bailout and revealed to the world that it cannot tolerate defaults, as in the Latin American federations and the European Monetary Union, market discipline is impossible in the medium run and hierarchy is the only viable option.

In the European case, there are good reasons for skepticism about the prospects for successful hierarchical control of member state budgets going forward. Europe has reached an unfortunate impasse in which Germany and the other wealthy member states guarantee the debts of the weaker member states. As such, it is crucial that the solvent member states gain new tools with which to control the fiscal decisions of the insolvent members. Yet it is difficult to imagine what such tools might look like in a compact like the European Monetary Union. The history of the excessive deficit procedure suggests the need for an independent enforcement process that is insulated from politics, yet it is difficult to imagine why the weaker member states would voluntarily agree to submit to such a process. Currently, the EMU can only threaten to withhold future tranches of bailouts, but given that it has already revealed that it cannot tolerate default, such threats have no credibility. Fortunately, in contrast to the European Monetary Union or the Brazilian federation, the moment of imminent default has not arrived in the United States, so there is not yet any need to explore second-best hierarchical solutions that would likely run into constitutional obstacles.

The lesson from other failed federations is that it is dangerous to rely on a half-hearted hybrid of markets and hierarchy. Given a choice between pure versions of the two strategies, the best option for the United States is also the most practical: bolster market discipline. There are a number of ways in which a reform agenda can focus on bolstering market discipline while also addressing some of the persistent pathologies of U.S. federalism. One simple goal is to help states manage the business cycle by restructuring existing intergovernmental grant programs so that they are less procyclical. Grants fall off during downturns, along with state taxes; then, after a politicized, ad hoc scramble, some temporary and distortionary relief may or may not be provided by the federal government.

A better option would be for the federal government to come up with a rules-based mechanism for smoothing intergovernmental grants over the business cycle, providing at least some counterweight to the boom-bust pattern of state public finance. That need not imply any change in the size of grants as a share of total state government revenue. It would help firm up the federal government's no-bailout commitment by putting an end to the ad hoc scramble for implicit bailouts and help state governments make more rational expenditure decisions.

Market discipline could also be enhanced by efforts to disentangle the obligations of federal and state governments. Efforts to curb federal unfunded mandates would go a long way to enhance the flexibility of states to solve their budgetary problems, as would reforms to distortionary matching provisions in some federal grant programs. Moreover, if market discipline is to be maintained in the future, the Federal Reserve should not be used to buy bonds of states in order to lower their borrowing costs. That would send all of the wrong signals to investors and state politicians about the obligations of the federal government vis-à-vis state fiscal outcomes.

Another interesting possibility is institution of an orderly default procedure. The federal government can lay out some guidelines about how a default in a state would be handled. One reason why the rising bond yield spreads of Greece and other EU member states quickly turned into a panic was that investors simply had no idea what might be coming next. Not only was there no formal bailout mechanism, but perhaps more important, there was also no sense of how a default or restructuring might be handled.

A good way to send a signal to market actors about the credibility of the central government's no-bailout commitment is to provide a formal set of rules and procedures for dealing with default. After the initial Greek bailout, the German government briefly attempted to propose an orderly default procedure in an effort to rekindle its no-bailout commitment, but that served only to fan the flames of the ongoing financial panic.

It is not yet too late in the United States. In fact, the timing might be quite good to clarify once and for all that states can and will default if they do not achieve fiscal sustainability and to clarify for market actors the rules under which default would take place. Quite simply, an orderly default is preferable to a disorderly default for everyone. By reducing fears of the latter, the federal government can enhance its no-bailout commitment.

As Levitin points out, it is insufficient to rely exclusively on an illusory no-bailout commitment in a modern market economy.[15] Systemic risk cannot be avoided, and no matter how one structures incentives ex ante, a moment might come when the failure of a bank—or the default of a state—would have externalities that are clearly socially unacceptable. Sometimes the costs of allowing an entity to fail are unclear until the moment arrives. In a dynamic situation like the Lehman crisis, the revealed cost of allowing one unit to fail might make it clear that further failures would be unacceptable.

Absolute ex ante commitment may be impossible or undesirable, and the government may eventually find itself deeply involved in the process of loss allocation in the event of a crisis. As the European Monetary Union demonstrates, it is better to be prepared for that moment than to wish it away. By agreeing on a set of rules and procedures now, it might be possible to reduce the possibility of a panic in the future. In order to preserve market discipline, it is important that the loss allocation process be viewed by borrowers and creditors alike as inevitably very painful—something to be avoided under all but the most extreme circumstances.

Finally, reform efforts aimed at bolstering market discipline should focus on bad accounting practices and bad incentives associated with public sector pension programs. It is possible to envision federally imposed accounting standards and information dissemination requirements—and perhaps even funding requirements—that would not send too strong a signal of federal responsibility.

But the most likely path to improved fiscal discipline in the states lies within the states themselves, and it requires that they be treated as adults who ultimately stand on their own. The state governments are currently behaving far more like adults than the federal government. Their shallower pockets and lack of monetary authority have forced them to respond to market pressure and make hard decisions about how to balance their budgets that have eluded the federal government.

This process will continue to be painful, and we have probably not seen the last of street protests like those in Madison, Wisconsin. But the protests in Madison are in many ways preferable to those in Athens. In Madison, the clash is over very different approaches to the question of how the sovereign state of Wisconsin can achieve fiscal sustainability. In Athens, inchoate rage is directed in large part at austerity measures that are viewed as illegitimate foreign impositions from Germany, the EU, and the International Monetary Fund, which have suddenly become responsible for Greek debt.

The United States system of federalism is under stress. Reform is needed both at the federal level and in the states themselves. Yet reformers should be careful to strengthen rather than undermine the system of market discipline that has characterized U.S. federalism throughout the last century.

Notes

1. Jonathan Rodden, *Hamilton's Paradox: The Promise and Peril of Fiscal Federalism* (Cambridge University Press, 2006).

2. Juergen von Hagen and Barry Eichengreen, "Federalism, Fiscal Restraints, and European Monetary Union," *American Economic Review,* vol. 86, no. 2 (1996), pp. 134–138.

3. Benjamin Ratchford, *American State Debts* (Duke University Press, 1941).

4. Erik Wibbels, "Bailouts, Budget Constraints, and Leviathans: Comparative Federalism and Lessons from the Early U.S.," *Comparative Political Studies,* vol. 36, no. 5 (2003), pp. 475–508.

5. Rodden, *Hamilton's Paradox.*

6. Jonathan Rodden and Erik Wibbels, "Fiscal Decentralization and the Business Cycle: An Empirical Study of Seven Federations," *Economics and Politics,* vol. 22, no. 1 (2010), pp. 37–67.

7. Joshua Aizenman and Gurnain Pasricha, "Net Fiscal Stimulus during the Great Recession," Working Paper 16779 (Cambridge, Mass.: National Bureau of Economic Research, 2011).

8. James Poterba, "State Responses to Fiscal Crises: The Effects of Budgetary Institutions and Politics," *Journal of Political Economy,* vol. 102, no. 4 (1994), pp. 799–821.

9. See Tamim Bayoumi, Morris Goldstein, and Geoffrey Woglom, "Do Credit Markets Discipline Sovereign Borrowers? Evidence from the U.S. States," *Journal of Money, Credit, and Banking,* vol. 27, no. 4 (1995), pp. 1046–1059; Rodden, *Hamilton's Paradox.*

10. "Who Will Default First: Greece or California?" *Wall Street Journal,* March 24, 2010.

11. "Buffett Says GM Rescue May Mean U.S. Can't Say No to States," *Business Week* May 5, 2010.

12. The impact of the bond insurance industry on bailout probabilities is unclear. One might argue that as long as the insurers are not viewed as "too big to fail," bond insurance reduces the probability of a bailout since it would be politically easier to impose losses on insurers than individual bondholders, many of whom are voters in the state. In any case, the bond insurance industry essentially collapsed in the wake of the fiscal crisis, and a very small percentage of new issues are now insured.

13. Tiberiu Dragu and Jonathan Rodden, "Representation and Redistribution in Federations," Working Paper 2010/16 (Barcelona Institute of Economics, 2010).

14. Joel Grundfest, Mark Lemley, and George Triantis, "To Lift Economy, Fed Should Buy Munis," *New York Times,* October 23, 2012.

15. Adam Levitin, "In Defense of Bailouts," *Georgetown Law Journal,* vol. 99 (2011), pp. 435–514.

ANDREW G. BIGGS *and* JASON RICHWINE

4 | *Putting a Price on Teacher Pensions*

Public employee pension funds across the nation suffer from unfunded liabilities that are large by any measure, but a growing number of economists, government agencies, and bond raters point out that even so, official figures significantly understate actual liabilities. The movement for "fair market valuation" of pension liabilities argues that financial disclosures must account for the fact that benefit payments are essentially guaranteed and must be paid even if pension investments fail to produce assumed rates of return. When pensions are valued under a fair market approach, state and local pension obligations increase significantly, moving unfunded liabilities from under $1 trillion into the $2 trillion to $4 trillion range. (For perspective, explicit state debt—the value of state-issued bonds—was $2.9 trillion as of 2011.)[1] Four trillion dollars is about 27 percent of total U.S. GDP, making pensions a major contributor to overall government indebtedness. Explicit state, local, and federal government debt combined with total pension debt measured at market value as of 2010 would reach 140 percent of GDP, comparable to debt levels in Greece at the time that the country experienced a financial crisis.

Teachers and other education workers make up 52 percent of total state and local government employment,[2] and the cost of their pensions helps to illustrate larger pension funding issues. Given pensions costs as measured on a market basis, it is unlikely that teacher benefits can continue at their present level. Furthermore, when pension benefits are valued using the fair market approach, average compensation for public school teachers is greater than the amount that the teachers' skills would merit in the private market, indicating that state and local governments have some flexibility in reducing pension benefits without substantially reducing the quality of the public sector workforce.

The traditional "defined benefit" (DB) pension plan is a major factor distinguishing the cost of public school teacher compensation from that of employee compensation in the private sector. According to the Bureau of Labor Statistics, 99 percent of primary, secondary, and special education teachers in the public sector are offered a DB pension, and 94 percent of all teachers take part in the DB pension program.[3] Among white-collar professionals in the private sector, just 25 percent are offered DB pensions and 23 percent participate.[4] In addition, only 17 of the 100 largest U.S. corporations now offer a DB plan, down from 67 in 1998.[5]

With a weak economy playing havoc with state and local government budgets, DB pensions for teachers and other government workers have been thrust into the spotlight. Policymakers are now confronting calls for cost-cutting reforms from voters who perceive—usually accurately—that public employees enjoy retirement benefits that are more generous and secure than those provided by the 401(k) plans that predominate outside of government. "Pension envy" is the tongue-in-cheek term that has been coined to describe their resentment.

In addition, state and local governments face large unfunded public pension liabilities, putting government budgets and bond ratings at risk. Although annual required employer and employee contributions to public pensions have more than doubled since 2001,[6] researchers at the Center for Retirement Research at Boston College project that state and local governments will meet only around 76 percent of required payments in 2013.[7] Because pension funding requirements will gradually incorporate the effects of the poor investment returns in recent years, annual contributions may rise further. For instance, employer contributions for the Teachers' and State Employees' Retirement System of North Carolina are projected to rise from 3.6 percent of payroll in 2009–10 to around 12 percent in 2015.[8]

Disaggregating pension obligations for teachers from those for other state and local government employees is not a straightforward task because both sets of employees often participate in the same pension plan. However, according to the National Income and Product Accounts, teachers and other education employees account for more than half of the state and local government payroll.[9]

As pension funding requirements rise, government resources available for other purposes—including schools—are being squeezed. Pension funding has become front-page news in both national and local newspapers, with increasing emphasis on the size of pension obligations, the funds required to meet them, and the more aggressive investment practices that many pension systems have undertaken in order to achieve their financial goals.

These events have taken place as economists are becoming increasingly critical of the way in which governments estimate the cost of their pension liabilities. In short, the accounting standards favored by financial economists produce liabilities that are several times greater than those shown by government accounting methods.

Public pensions currently report their liabilities as calculated in accordance with accounting rules established by the Governmental Accounting Standards Board (GASB), a nongovernmental organization that promulgates recommended, though nonbinding, accounting standards for state and local government finance. Under GASB rules, a pension plan "discounts" its liabilities using the interest rate that the plan projects that its investments will earn, generally around 8 percent. Applying this standard, the average public pension has fallen to around 75 percent funded in 2011; in 2000, the average was 103 percent funded.[10] Overall, public sector pensions as of mid-2011 were underfunded by at least $783 billion.[11]

To financial economists, however, the picture is much bleaker. Pension benefits for public employees are virtually guaranteed—protected by state laws, legal precedents, and often explicit constitutional provisions. In both economic theory and in private financial markets, the fact that benefits must be paid regardless of how pension investments fare would be reflected in the way that benefit liabilities are valued. But under the pension accounting rules currently promulgated by GASB, the value of pension liabilities is based on the forecast rate of return on pension plan assets. Those assets carry significantly greater risk than the benefits that the assets are used to finance.

Current GASB standards significantly understate the true cost of DB pensions to taxpayers and the true value of pension benefits to public employees. Under fair market valuation, unfunded pension liabilities nationwide would at least triple, placing increased pressure on state and local governments to raise pension contributions and enact more comprehensive pension reforms. Likewise, because the cost of pension liabilities is essentially the value of the pension benefits promised to public sector employees, views on the relative pay of public and private sector workers could change substantially. It is generally perceived that public school teachers receive lower salaries but more generous fringe benefits, including traditional defined benefit pensions, than similarly skilled private sector workers. However, fair market valuation of public pension benefits would increase teachers' pension-related compensation to such an extent that, on average, their overall compensation would significantly exceed that of similar private sector workers. This mismatch between the skills of public school teachers and the level of compensation that they receive has important implications for education policy in its own right, but its most immediate budgetary implication is that reductions in pension generosity may not harm public sector recruiting and retention goals nearly as much as critics fear.

Thus a great deal rides on the outcome of a seemingly arcane accounting issue regarding the proper discount rate to apply to public pension liabilities. In recent years, advocates of fair market valuation have gained considerable ground in the debate as their arguments have made their way from academic journals to reports by federal agencies and bond rating firms.

Background on Teacher Pension Plans

Most state and local governments provide a DB pension plan for public employees as part of their overall compensation. These plans generally provide for retirement, disability, and survivor benefits. DB pension plans either supplement or substitute for Social Security benefits, depending on whether the state or local government has elected to participate in the Social Security system.

DB plans calculate retirement benefits by using a formula based on the employee's earnings and years of service, with most or all investment risk borne by the plan sponsor. For instance, a DB pension might pay a benefit equal to 2 percent of final earnings multiplied by the number of years of service. Under this formula, an employee who begins work at age 25 and retires at age 60 would receive a benefit equal to 70 percent of his or her final salary. Final salary may be defined as the last year of earnings prior to retirement, although three-year and five-year averages have become more common as a means to combat the practice of "spiking" wages just before retirement.[12]

In a survey of teacher plans, Clark and Craig estimated salary replacement rates—that is, pension benefits as a percentage of final earnings—in forty-seven state plans as of 2006 for teachers with thirty years of service. Replacement rates ranged from a low of 43.7 percent in Michigan and Tennessee to a high of 77.7 percent in Nevada, with a mean replacement rate of 58.5 percent of final earnings.[13] Among plans in which teachers were not covered by Social Security, the average replacement rate was 66.4 percent; for teachers who also were eligible for Social Security benefits, the rate was 56.2 percent.

According to the Public Plans Database, as of 2009 the average employee contribution to a teacher pension plan was 5.8 percent of salary.[14] In certain cases teachers and other public employees have their contributions "picked up," or paid for, by their employer, although that would not be reflected in the above contribution rate.

Straightforward comparisons with private sector retirement benefits cannot be made because of differences in structure and accounting that we detail in the next section. Defined contribution (DC) plans—which include 401(k) plans in the private sector and 403(b) plans in the nonprofit sector—carry no protection against market risk. Employers do not promise their employees a fixed benefit at retirement; instead, they make a contribution to each employee's retirement account today. According to the Bureau of Labor Statistics, the median employer contribution for workers defined as "management, professional, and related" was 4 percent of salary as of 2010, with half of employees receiving matches of between 2 and 5 percent of wages and 80 percent of employees receiving matches of between 1.5 and 6 percent of wages.[15]

Employee contributions to DC pensions are generally voluntary, although they are encouraged by tax incentives and employer matching funds. An employer match of 4 percent of wages invested in Treasury securities (to produce a legally guaranteed retirement benefit) yielding 4 percent annually would be sufficient, after thirty years, to allow the employee to purchase an inflation-adjusted annuity replacing roughly 4 percent of his or her final earnings. Adding a 5.8 percent employee contribution would increase the replacement rate to 11.6 percent of pre-retirement earnings. To generate a guaranteed 60 percent replacement rate similar to that paid under a typical public employee pension plan, an employee would have to contribute half of his or her annual earnings.

How Economists Value Deferred Compensation

Measuring compensation is relatively straightforward when limited to salaries and benefits paid today, such as paid time off, health coverage, and employer contributions to DC retirement accounts. But estimating the cost of deferred compensation is more complex, and the accounting rules followed by state and local governments make it more so. For that reason, we first review some basic financial theory.

In the view of financial economists, the value of a future payment—in this case DB pensions, but retiree health coverage can also be included in this category—is a function of how much is promised, when it is to be paid, and how likely the promise is to be kept. Obviously, a larger promised benefit is more valuable to employees and more costly to employers than a smaller one. Likewise, a dollar paid sooner is more valuable than a dollar paid later, due to the time value of money. In addition, a guaranteed payment is more valuable to employees—and more expensive for employers—than an uncertain benefit that might be higher or lower than promised. Therefore, the value of a future payment is largely a function of three questions: How much? When? With what certainty?

Taking risk into account explains how stocks that sell for a given price have the same value as bonds selling for the same amount. Stocks have both higher expected returns and higher risk, while bonds have lower returns and lower risk. Each offers a different package of risk and return, but buyers and sellers in the market judge the packages to have equal overall value.

Perhaps less intuitively, the way in which a future benefit is *financed* says nothing about its *value*. Some governments finance employees' future retirement benefits with larger contributions that are invested in safe but lower-return assets such as bonds. Other governments finance future benefits with smaller contributions invested in riskier assets such as stocks, private equity, and hedge funds. Most governments do not put aside any money toward future retiree health coverage for current workers, making those benefits pay-as-you-go.

But if one assumes that promised pension benefits will in fact be paid, governments' financing choices merely divide the cost of paying retirement benefits between current and future taxpayers.[16] The government's financing strategy does *not* affect the overall value of these benefits, either as a liability of the government or as compensation to employees. With a conservative financing strategy, more of the cost is borne by current taxpayers; with a riskier strategy, a larger share of the cost—technically a contingent liability to pay benefits should investment returns fall short—is borne by future taxpayers. These are important policy choices in terms of intergenerational fairness and potential risks to state and local budgets, but they do not affect how the value of retirement benefits should be measured, either in terms of public sector compensation or in terms of how those liabilities should be placed in an accounting ledger. It can be shown mathematically that the combined value of the upfront contribution and the contingent liability to make good on promised benefits never changes, regardless of the financing strategy chosen by the government.[17]

The fact that the value of a liability is unaffected by how the liability is financed is textbook economics, derived from the classic Modigliani-Miller theorem in corporate finance.[18] It is so well established among economists that it is largely taken for granted. Yet in the public sector, GASB accounting rules allow public employee pension plans to value their liabilities on the basis of the investment strategy of the pension plan. This approach differs from federal requirements with regard to private sector DB pensions and from international standards for pension accounting, under which pension liabilities are generally discounted using corporate bond yields regardless of how the plan itself invests.[19] Since public pensions generally take an aggressive financing strategy based on low contributions invested in risky assets, both the disclosed pension liabilities and the annual payments made to service them do not reflect the full cost of public employee pensions. The contingent liability to make good on pension obligations should investments fail to meet their assumed returns is not incorporated as a cost. That distorts the public's view both of public employee compensation and public sector pension liabilities.

However, sentiment is increasingly shifting toward accounting rules that disclose the full value of public pension benefits. Such rules would provide a very different view of public school teacher compensation and overall government pension liabilities. The following discussion outlines how pension liabilities are valued under GASB rules as well as under the method that most economists advocate.

GASB Accounting Rules Compared with Fair Market Valuation

Under current GASB accounting standards, state and local pensions discount their future benefit liabilities using the expected return on the fund's assets, typically 8 percent. For instance, a $1 million lump-sum payment due twenty years from now would have a present value of less than $215,000 if discounted using an 8 percent interest rate. As of mid-2010, total public pension liabilities measured in this way equaled approximately $3.1 trillion, of which around $783 billion was unfunded; thus public sector pensions were approximately 77 percent funded. Critics of GASB have noted the contradiction in allowing governments to discount pension payments that are intended to be guaranteed—and in practice are guaranteed either by law, constitutional provisions, or the political power of public sector advocates—by using an 8 percent interest rate based on a risky portfolio of investments.

As noted above, both academic economists as well as private financial markets would value a liability by using an interest rate whose risk is similar to that of the liability. Public pension benefits are essentially government-guaranteed payments to individuals and therefore most closely resemble government bonds, which also are government-guaranteed payments to individuals. Therefore, something close to the government bond rate is the appropriate value to apply to public pension liabilities. Even if the guarantee going forward is not as iron-clad as in the past, public pension benefits cannot be even close to as risky as the assets used to fund them. Moreover, the simple intent of the plan sponsor to generate benefits that are riskless suggests that a low discount rate is appropriate.

Accurate accounting for public pension liabilities captures both the cost of upfront investments in risky assets and the value of contingent liabilities to backstop pension finances should assumed investment returns not materialize. One approach to valuing contingent pension liabilities is through the use of financial instruments known as put options, which provide insurance against investments falling short of some guaranteed "strike price."[20] However, a simpler and mathematically equivalent approach is simply to discount the future liability by using a risk-adjusted discount rate. Both methods capture the full cost of pensions to taxpayers and the full value of pensions to public employees.

Some have mistakenly interpreted a riskless discount rate as representing a "worst case scenario."[21] That is clearly not the case. Millions of knowledgeable investors around the world hold U.S. Treasury securities with durations of up to thirty years instead of investments such as stocks, which are riskier but higher yielding. The low yields offered on such safe investments reflect the returns that investors are willing to forgo in order to receive protection against the small—but not zero—chance of doing even worse over the long term. This protection is especially valuable because stock returns are correlated with the state of the economy, meaning that poor investment outcomes would happen at the same time that other sources of income to the individual or firm are likely to be low.

Experts' Views on GASB Pension Accounting Rules

The preceding discussion summarizes the argument in economic theory against the current GASB pension accounting rules and illustrates that they disguise the value of public employee compensation. It is worth noting that the vast majority of academic economists and nonpartisan government agencies take the same position regarding how to value public pension liabilities. In a recent poll of professional economists, 98 percent agreed that "by discounting pension liabilities at high interest rates under government accounting standards, many U.S. state and local governments understate their pension liabilities and the costs of providing pensions to public sector workers."[22] Donald Kohn, then the vice chairman of the Federal Reserve Board, declared in 2008:

> While economists are famous for disagreeing with each other on virtually every other conceivable issue, when it comes to this one there is no professional disagreement: The only appropriate way to calculate the present value of a very-low-risk liability is to use a very-low-risk discount rate.[23]

In a 2009 research paper, Reinsdorf and Lenze, two economists from the U.S. Bureau of Economic Analysis, noted:

> If the assets of a defined-benefit plan are insufficient to pay promised benefits, the plan sponsor must cover the shortfall. This obligation represents an additional source of pension wealth for participants in an underfunded plan.[24]

Beginning in 2013, the National Income and Product Accounts, which are the official ledger books of the U.S. economy, will measure public pension liabilities using a market-based measure that captures the value of benefit guarantees to employees.

In early 2012, the Congressional Budget Office issued a report that was widely taken as confirmation of the market valuation approach.[25] More recently, Moody's Investor Services announced that its ratings of state and local government debt would no longer incorporate pension liabilities as measured under GASB rules. Instead, Moody's would discount pension liabilities by using a corporate bond yield, a method similar to the way in which private pension liabilities are measured.

In response to criticism of its rules, GASB itself recently announced revisions that would lower the discount rate applied to underfunded public pension liabilities, although not nearly as much as most independent analysts would advocate.[26] The State Budget Crisis Taskforce, co-chaired by former New York lieutenant governor Richard Ravitch and former Federal Reserve Board chairman Paul Volcker, stated that even GASB's proposed rules "fall far short of what finance experts argue is appropriate and reported unfunded liabilities will not increase anywhere near as much as they would under a pure finance approach."[27]

In the face of such a strong consensus of expert opinion, it is unclear why GASB's reforms did not go further toward a full market valuation of pension liabilities. Potential explanations could include institutional concerns over how such a large change would affect GASB's reputation, the lack of GASB members with a background in finance or economics, and the board's day-to-day working relationships with public pension administrators who worry that fair market valuation would mean the end of DB plans.

If 8 Percent Is Wrong, Which Discount Rate Is Right?

There is a clear consensus among academics and nonpartisan government agencies that the 8 percent discount rate used by most public sector pension plans in valuing their liabilities is inappropriate. There is less consensus, however, regarding the exact discount rate to use instead. Academic studies have generally discounted pension liabilities using yields on U.S. Treasury securities to reflect the fact that pension benefits are intended to be guaranteed and have continued to be paid even in times of considerable financial turmoil. We have generally used the Treasury yield as the preferred rate for analytical purposes because public employee pensions are intended to be riskless, they are portrayed to employees as such, and they carry constitutional protections that private sector DB pensions—which under federal law are discounted using corporate bond yields—do not. However, other analyses have used different interest rates to value public pensions.

Reinsdorf and Lenze valued pension liabilities using corporate bond yields, although the authors noted that they did so principally because of the convenience of applying similar discount rates to public sector and corporate pension liabilities. The Congressional Budget Office illustrated pension liabilities using a range of discount rates, noting factors that might cause accrued pension benefits to be less risky than explicit municipal government debt, while also noting that future benefits—which are partially accounted for in measures of current pension liabilities—may be riskier than government debt. Reflecting this lack of consensus, table 4-1 illustrates a range of potential discount rates for valuing public pension benefits, based on rates that prevailed in mid-2010.

Table 4-1. *Public Pension Unfunded Liabilities at Various Discount Rates*

Category	Interest rate (percent)	Liability (billions of dollars)
Treasury bond	3.4	4,634
Municipal bond	3.5	4,478
Corporate bond	5.4	2,654
Expected return	8.0	947

Source: Authors' calculations based on Public Plans Database (http://pubplans.bc.edu).

How Does Pension Financing Look under Fair Market Valuation?

As of 2010, public employee pensions in the Public Plans Database were 77 percent funded and faced unfunded liabilities of $783 billion when discounted at an 8 percent average interest rate. When adjusted to account for the roughly 21 percent of public plan liabilities not included in the database, total estimated unfunded liabilities nationwide amount to approximately $947 billion.

When liabilities are discounted by using the 3.4 percent U.S. Treasury yield in mid-2010, plans are only 40.6 percent funded and face unfunded liabilities of around $4.6 trillion.[28] When the slightly higher municipal bond yield is used, total unfunded liabilities would come to just under $4.5 trillion. At the 5.4 percent corporate bond yield, unfunded liabilities as of mid-2010 would decline significantly, to under $2.7 trillion. But all realistic figures are significantly higher than those calculated using an 8 percent interest rate based on risky investments.

The figures cited above indicate the value of pension liabilities in 2010. When interest rates rise or fall, the value of liabilities also changes. This is not a flaw in fair market valuation, as some critics have claimed, but a simple reflection of the fact that as riskless rates of return change, the cost of providing guaranteed future benefits also changes. If a plan wishes to provide a truly guaranteed benefit ten, twenty, or thirty years in the future, the best estimate of the cost of doing so is the yield on riskless investments such as government bonds.[29]

Pension Accounting and Public School Teacher Compensation

While many economists and public policy scholars have pointed out that public pension liabilities should be valued on a fair market basis, our contribution has been to apply that principle to evaluating the total compensation of government workers, particularly public school teachers.[30] In short, market-based valuation of pension liabilities greatly increases the pension benefits—and, by extension, the total compensation—received by teachers.

The compensation question is an essential aspect of the debate on how to confront the high cost of pension obligations. If teachers and other government employees currently receive compensation at or *below* market level, reducing the generosity of public pensions—and, hence, total employee compensation—could prevent state and local governments from hiring or retaining public employees at current levels of employee education and experience. By contrast, if public sector workers currently receive a compensation premium, reducing that premium could be a reasonable strategy for balancing budgets, given that the government compensation package would remain competitive.

To quantify the impact of market-based valuation on the value of teacher pensions, we first measured the cost of benefits that accrue to active teachers for each year that they work. This is called the "normal cost" of benefits, which is distinct from the cost of "amortizing" (gradually paying off) unfunded liabilities from prior years. As mentioned above, public sector pension plans publish their normal costs as calculated by using a discount rate of around 8 percent. But the normal cost calculated at a lower, risk-adjusted rate is the proper measure for both government pension liabilities and the implicit pension compensation received by teachers and other public employees. Unfortunately, most plans do not publish estimates of their normal costs at different discount rates.

The Florida Retirement System (FRS) is an exception, so we use the FRS as our main example. In 2011 the FRS requested that its actuarial firm, Milliman and Company, calculate a variety of system financing measures under a range of discount rates. The FRS assumes an expected return on assets of 7.75 percent, which is slightly below the average nationwide. The Milliman memorandum summarizes plan financing under this baseline discount rate and then under a range of alternative rates going down to 3 percent.[31] Because plan costs follow a linear pattern relative to the natural log of the discount rate, by using the data points provided by Milliman we can accurately estimate plan costs at any given discount rate. Figure 4-1 provides an illustration.

Table 4-2 lists normal costs for FRS regular employees under discount rates ranging from the nationwide average of 8 percent down to the 2010 Treasury yield of 3.4 percent. At the Treasury rate, which reflects the assumption that pension benefits once earned will be paid with certainty, the normal cost of FRS regular pensions rises to 31.50 percent of wages. At the municipal bond yield rate, the normal cost is slightly more than 30 percent of wages; at the corporate bond yield rate, the normal cost is slightly less than 19 percent of pay.

These normal cost figures reflect the percentage of wages that an employee would need to invest in a 401(k) plan holding Treasury securities to generate the same level of guaranteed benefits paid under the FRS. Given that Florida employees contribute only 3 percent of pay to the FRS, the implicit employer

Figure 4-1. *Relationship between Discount Rate and Normal Cost of the Florida Retirement System*

Percent of wages

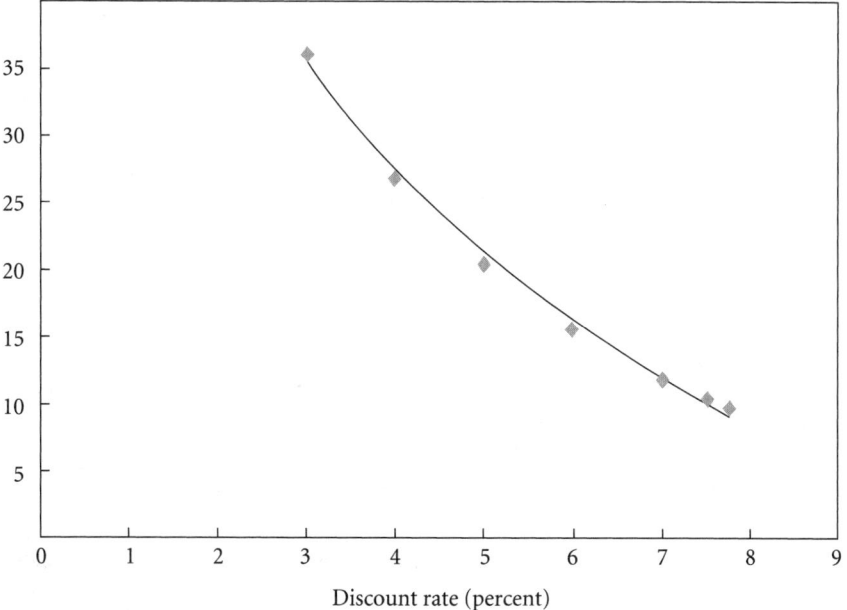

Discount rate (percent)

Source: Authors' calculations based on Robert S. DuZebe, "Study Reflecting Impact to the FRS of Changing the Investment Return Assumption to One of the Following: 7.5%, 7.0%, 6.0%, 5.0%, 4.0% and 3.0%," Milliman, March 11, 2011.

Table 4-2. *Normal Costs of the Florida Retirement System (Regular) under a Range of Discount Rates*

Category	Interest rate (percent)	Normal cost (percent of wages)
Expected return (Nationwide average)	8.0	8.02
Expected return (Florida Retirement System)	7.8	9.84
Treasury bond	3.4	31.50
Municipal bond	3.5	30.44
Corporate bond	5.4	18.68

Source: Authors' calculations based on Robert S. DuZebe, "Study Reflecting Impact to the FRS of Changing the Investment Return Assumption to One of the Following: 7.5%, 7.0%, 6.0%, 5.0%, 4.0% and 3.0%," Milliman, March 11, 2011.

Table 4-3. *Average Benefits as a Percent of Wages, Public School Teachers and Private Workers, 2010*[a]

Percent

Benefit	Public school teachers	Private workers
Paid leave	6.6	11.4
Insurance plans	16.1	13.3
Retirement and savings	11.1	5.4
Total benefits	41.2	41.3

Source: Authors' calculations based on data from the Bureau of Labor Statistics, National Compensation Survey (www.bls.gov/eci). The benefit category "Supplemental Pay" is omitted because those values are included in Current Population Survey wage data.

a. Establishment size = 100+ workers.

contribution is extremely large by private sector standards, under which employers typically contribute only 3 to 4 percent of wages to DC accounts.

These figures are averages. How well an employee fares under a DB pension plan depends critically on career length: short-career workers might actually do better with a DC pension, while full-career employees receive implicit pension compensation that is far higher than the averages presented here. Nevertheless, even the average figures show pension compensation far exceeding typical private sector compensation.

Pension valuation has a critical impact on public-private pay comparisons. The National Compensation Survey (NCS) tabulates teacher benefits and contrasts them with the benefits enjoyed by private sector workers in larger firms (see table 4-3).[32] Under the NCS data, total benefits as a percentage of wages are almost exactly the same for both groups, at around 41 percent.[33] However, the pension compensation measured by NCS is merely employers' current contributions toward pensions, which understates the total pension liability of employers and the total value of pensions to employees. Therefore, we dropped the NCS estimate of pension costs and substituted one of the actual normal costs listed in table 4-2, again using the FRS as an example.

As indicated in table 4-4, measuring pension compensation using Treasury yields would increase pension benefits to 31.5 percent of wages and increase total teacher benefits to 65 percent of wages. Discounting pension benefits at the municipal bond yield rate, as some have advocated, would have a slightly smaller upward effect. Finally, discounting pension liabilities using the corporate bond yield rate—as done by private sector pensions and advocated in Moody's recent discussion draft—would raise total benefits to 52 percent of wages.

Market valuation of teacher pensions, leading to a more than 50 percent increase in listed NCS benefits for teachers when the Treasury rate is used,

Table 4-4. *Florida Teacher Fringe Benefits as a Percent of Salaries, Incorporating Pension Compensation Valued at Different Discount Rates*
Percent

Discount rate	Total benefits/Teacher salaries
Expected return[a]	41
Expected return[b]	43
Corporate bond	52
Municipal bond	64
Treasury bond	65

Source: Authors' calculations based on Robert S. DuZebe, "Study Reflecting Impact to the FRS of Changing the Investment Return Assumption to One of the Following: 7.5%, 7.0%, 6.0%, 5.0%, 4.0% and 3.0%," Milliman, March 11, 2011.
a. Nationwide average = 8 percent.
b. Florida Retirement System = 7.75 percent.

obviously has a substantial effect on how the generosity of teacher benefits in general are viewed. When the value of summer and long holiday breaks (not included in the paid leave category) and retiree health benefits (not considered by the NCS at all) are included, the greater fringe benefits enjoyed by public school teachers easily eclipse any wage penalty that they may incur.[34]

Policy Implications

Valuation of public employee pensions has important implications for state and local government budgets. First, governments will find themselves under greater financial pressure if and when pension accounting standards incorporate market-based liability valuations. Economists Robert Novy-Marx and Joshua Rauh project that for pensions to reach fully funded status over a thirty-year period, contributions must rise from the current level of 5.7 percent of government revenues to 14.1 percent of revenues. Put another way, contributions would need to average 40.1 percent of public employee salaries, considerably increasing the amount that state and local governments must allocate for labor costs.[35]

If forced to fund pension liabilities at market value, state and local governments may not be willing to maintain the present level or structure of teacher pension plans. Future benefits may need to be scaled back—preferably brought fully in line with private sector benefit packages. It is also possible that, lacking an artificial accounting advantage, DB pensions may increasingly be transformed into DC pension plans. Doing so would add transparency to teacher compensation decisions, since the full extent of a DC plan's cost is simply the annual employer contribution to the plan, with no potential for masking benefits or making long-term promises that cannot be kept.

Second, the accurate valuation of teacher pension benefits reveals that the average public school teacher receives greater total compensation than private sector workers with comparable levels of education and work experience. This fact suggests that school administrators do not effectively match teacher compensation with the market value of teacher skills[36] and that teacher compensation is in need of reform. From a budgetary perspective, the compensation premium provides room for state and local governments to scale back future pension benefits without a major impact on recruitment and retention of existing teachers. The premium also means that a hypothetical federal bailout of state and local pension funds could be seen as rewarding poor fiscal management, generating concerns about moral hazard.

Conclusion

Because the cost of retirement benefits for public school teachers and other public employees is a large and growing share of state and local government budgets, policymakers and voters are faced with difficult decisions regarding how to prioritize the uses of taxpayer resources. While almost all teachers participate in DB pensions, in which employers promise a fixed benefit in the future, most private sector employees participate in DC plans, in which employers make a contribution to employee accounts today but make no promises regarding benefits at retirement.

These different forms of retirement compensation require accounting assumptions to make them comparable, but current public pension accounting rules as established by GASB have come under widespread criticism as a way to measure liabilities. An economics-based approach to valuing a guaranteed future benefit captures the full cost to employers and the full value to employees. Compared with government accounting standards, market valuation implies both a much greater budgetary burden from teacher pensions and higher overall compensation to public school teachers. The implication is that legislatures can improve their fiscal situation—and lessen the likelihood of a federal bailout—by reducing pension generosity, without a major impact on the quality of the public sector workforce.

Notes

1. Jeffrey L. Barnett and Phillip M. Vidal, "State and Local Government Finances: Summary: 2011" (U.S. Census Bureau, July 2013) (www2.census.gov/govs/local/summary_report.pdf).

2. "National Income and Product Accounts," table 6.5D, "Full-Time Equivalent Employment by Industry" (www.bea.gov).

3. U.S. Department of Labor, "Employee Benefits Survey," March 2011 (www.bls.gov/ncs/ebs/benefits/2011/ownership/govt/table02a.htm).

4. Ibid.

5. Chris Farrell, "'Pension Envy' Vexes Underfunded Public Workers," *Bloomberg*, January 11, 2011 (www.bloomberg.com/news/2011-01-12/pension-envy-vexes-under-funded-public-workers-commentary-by-chris-farrell.html).

6. Authors' calculations from Public Plans Database (http://pubplans.bc.edu).

7. Alicia H. Munnell and others, "The Funding of State and Local Pensions: 2011–2015" (Center for Retirement Research, Boston College, May 2012).

8. Robert L. Clark, "Evolution of Public Sector Retirement Plans: Crisis, Challenges, and Change," *ABA Journal of Labor and Employment Law* (August 2011).

9. "National Income and Product Accounts," table 6.5D, "Full-Time Equivalent Employment by Industry."

10. Munnell and others, "The Funding of State and Local Pensions."

11. Data from the Public Plans Database indicate that as of 2010 state and local pensions were underfunded by around $783 billion. However, around 21 percent of pension plan assets are not included in the database. Assuming that those pensions are funded at the same level as pensions in the database, as of 2010 total underfunding would be approximately $885 billion.

12. Spiking is a practice in which employees work overtime or use other methods to dramatically increase their salaries in the period immediately preceding retirement in order to boost their pension payments after they have retired.

13. Robert L. Clark and Lee A. Craig, "Determinants of the Generosity of Pension Plans for Public School Teachers: 1982–2006," *Journal of Pension Economics and Finance*, vol. 10, no. 1 (2011), pp. 99–118.

14. Public Plans Database (http://pubplans.bc.edu).

15. U.S. Department of Labor, table 28, "Savings and Thrift Plans" (www.bls.gov/ncs/ebs/detailedprovisions/2010/ownership/private/table28a.txt).

16. This conclusion does not depend on the assumption that benefits will be paid with zero risk; rather, two benefits that will be paid with the *same* level of certainty or risk will have the same value regardless of the risk of the investment strategy used to finance them.

17. See Andrew G. Biggs, "An Options Pricing Method for Calculating the Market Price of Public Sector Pension Liabilities," *Public Budgeting and Finance*, vol. 31, no. 3 (Fall 2011), pp. 94–118.

18. The Modigliani-Miller theorem states that the value of a firm is independent of whether the firm is financed using debt or equity. More broadly, the value of any given asset or liability is a function of the characteristics of the asset or liability itself rather than the way in which it is financed.

19. Aleksandar Andonov, Rob Bauer, and Martijn Cremers, "Pension Fund Asset Allocation and Liability Discount Rates: Camouflage and Reckless Risk Taking by U.S. Public Plans?" May 1, 2012 (http://dx.doi.org/10.2139/ssrn.2070054).

20. Andrew G. Biggs, "An Options Pricing Method for Calculating the Market Price of Public Sector Pension Liabilities."

21. See California Legislative Analyst's Office, "Summary of LAO Findings and Recommendations on the 2011–12 Budget," January 24, 2011 (www.lao.ca.gov/laoapp/budgetlist/PublicSearch.aspx?Yr=2011&KeyCol=305).

22. The one economist who did not agree voted "uncertain" and commented, in reference to GASB's discount rate policy, that he was "not sure why they do that." IGM Economic Experts Panel, "U.S. State Budgets," October 1, 2012 (www.igmchicago.org/igm-economic-experts-panel/poll-results?SurveyID=SV_87dlrlXQvZkFB1r).

23. Donald L. Kohn, "Statement at the National Conference on Public Employee Retirement Systems Annual Conference," New Orleans, Louisiana, May 20, 2008.

24. Marshall B. Reinsdorf and David G. Lenze, "Defined Benefit Pensions and Household Income and Wealth," Bureau of Economic Analysis, *Research Spotlight* (August 2009) (www.bea.gov/scb/pdf/2009/08%20August/0806_benefits.pdf). Also see David G. Lenze, "Accrual Measures of Pension-Related Compensation and Wealth of State and Local Government Workers" (Bureau of Economic Analysis, April 2009).

25. Congressional Budget Office, "The Underfunding of State and Local Pension Plans," May 2011.

26. Andrew G. Biggs, "Proposed GASB Rules Show Why Only Market Valuation Fully Captures Public Pension Liabilities," *Financial Analysts Journal,* vol. 67, no. 2 (March-April 2011), pp. 18–22.

27. "Report of the State Budget Crisis Task Force," July 2012 (www.statebudgetcrisis.org).

28. Unfunded liabilities calculated from the Public Plans Database equal $3.8 trillion; grossing up by 21 percent to account for plans not covered in the database increases total unfunded liabilities to $4.6 trillion.

29. To the degree that public pensions wish to hedge against this volatility, they can easily do so by holding low-risk assets in their investment portfolios. Such investments will rise in value when interest rates fall, thereby hedging against the effects of lower interest rates on the present value of plan liabilities.

30. Andrew G. Biggs and Jason Richwine, "Assessing the Compensation of Public-School Teachers," Center for Data Analysis Report 11-03 (Washington: Heritage Foundation, Center for Data Analysis, November 01, 2011).

31. Robert S. DuZebe, "Study Reflecting Impact to the FRS of Changing the Investment Return Assumption to One of the Following: 7.5%, 7.0%, 6.0%, 5.0%, 4.0% and 3.0%," Milliman Group, March 11, 2011.

32. Note that the Bureau of Labor Statistics reports benefits data based on establishment size, which represents the number of employees at a given location. Establishment size thus differs from firm size, which captures the number of employees at all locations. Most wage data, such as in the Current Population Survey, is reported in terms of firm size. The establishment size of 100+ captures roughly the same percentage of the workforce as the largest firm size category in the survey.

33. The benefits measured by NCS include paid leave, which includes sick time and paid vacation; insurance coverage, which includes health and life insurance; retirement and savings, which include DB and DC plans; and legally required benefits, which include employer contributions to Social Security, Medicare, and other government programs.

34. Biggs and Richwine, "Assessing the Compensation of Public School Teachers."

35. Robert Novy-Marx and Joshua D. Rauh, "The Revenue Demands of Public Employee Pension Promises," Working Paper 18489 (Cambridge, Mass.: National Bureau of Economic Research, October 2012) (www.nber.org/papers/w18489).

36. This is consistent with economist Dale Ballou's finding that many of the most skilled teaching applicants—those who graduate from more competitive colleges, earn higher grade point averages, or hold degrees in specialized areas such as math or science—are turned down in favor of candidates who took the traditional route of majoring in education. Dale Ballou, "Do Public Schools Hire the Best Applicants?" *Quarterly Journal of Economics*, vol. 111, no. 1 (February 1996), p. 120.

CORY KOEDEL, SHAWN NI, *and* MICHAEL PODGURSKY

5

Structural Flaws in the Design
of Public Pension Plans

The cost of retiree benefits in the public sector is under increased scrutiny in states and municipalities across the United States. In a 2010 report, the Pew Center on the States estimates that the unfunded liabilities of state and local governments for retirement benefits total roughly $1 trillion. Novy-Marx and Rauh argue that that is an optimistic assessment because the actuarial reports from the pension funds underestimate the true cost of pension liabilities, primarily by discounting liabilities at the typically assumed 8 percent rate of return.[1] If a more appropriate discount rate is used, the projected unfunded liabilities increase dramatically. Pressure is emerging from credit markets for more accurate accounting. For example, Moody's credit rating agency has proposed using more appropriate discount rates for liability estimates.[2] Pension obligations are also problematic at lower levels of government. Recent municipality bankruptcies, including those in Vallejo and Stockton (both in California), were driven in part by the inability of those municipalities to deliver on promised retiree benefits.

A distinctive feature of public sector pension plans is that they are nearly universally defined benefit (DB) plans. DB pension plans promise a guaranteed benefit at retirement that cannot be changed regardless of the performance of pension investments or shortfalls due to other reasons, such as inadequate contributions from employees or employers. The persistence of DB pension plans in the public sector stands in sharp contrast to what has occurred in the private sector in recent years. Between 1973 and 2005, DB pension coverage in the

The authors acknowledge support from the Center for Analysis of Longitudinal Data in Education Research (CALDER) at the American Institutes for Research and thank Lauren Buller, Mark Ehlert, Angie Hull, and Eric Parsons for valuable assistance in conducting research for this chapter. The usual disclaimers apply.

private sector declined from 88 to 33 percent. In addition, many of the remaining private DB plans have stopped using the final average salary formulas typical in public sector plans, which greatly reward late-career salary increases.[3]

DB plans have not only persisted in the public sector but also become more pronounced in the compensation package for public workers. At the state level, that is the result of legislation enacted in many states in the late 1990s and early 2000s that enhanced public worker pension formulas. The enhancements were enacted toward the end of an extended bull market in stocks, which left many funds with substantial actuarial surpluses. Those surpluses might have been banked against an inevitable run of below-average market returns or at least used for one-time-only payouts to retirees. However, a typical and costly policy response in many states was to enhance pension benefit formulas, thereby transforming a transitory increase in asset values into a permanent increase in liabilities.[4]

We use the pension enhancements to the educator pension fund in Missouri as a case study to illustrate two fundamental structural flaws in subnational public pension plans. First and most important, the enhancement legislation exposes the extent to which these plans are open to rent capture by politically powerful entities. The reason is that promised benefits are not directly tied to contributions and future obligations can be incurred without obtaining immediate financing for expected liabilities. The pension enhancements in Missouri, as in most places, were enacted retroactively, so that senior educators were able to retire with pension benefits that were far more generous than their lifetime contributions afforded. Therefore, senior teachers experienced large windfall gains as a result of the pension enhancement legislation enacted between 1995 and 2002.[5] Today, novice teachers, teachers who have not yet entered the workforce, and K–12 schools have been left with fewer resources because they are required to absorb the costs associated with the benefits that were received but not paid for by now-retired teachers.

A second structural flaw in public DB retirement plans, related to but distinct from the first, is that senior public administrators are typically enrolled in the same pension plans as the larger workforce. Given their length of service within the system and their history of promotions, senior public officials are the largest net beneficiaries of public pension plans. In Missouri, for example, senior education administrators stood to gain the most from the pension enhancement legislation that we examine below. It is unreasonable to expect these individuals to oppose legislation that provides them with large personal gains. The fact that key public administrators are not at arm's length with respect to this type of legislation is problematic given the potentially potent fiscal impact that it can have on the public enterprises that they are charged with managing.

The Politics of Teacher Pensions

Nearly all public K–12 school teachers in the United States are enrolled in a state or local pension plan.[6] Although teachers in a few large cities have municipal plans, over time the trend has been for municipal plans to be folded into the larger state plans; as a result, today most teacher pension plans are statewide plans. In roughly half the states teachers have their own plan (usually shared with other school employees); in the remaining states they and state employees share the same plan. In Missouri, most teachers and other K–12 school employees are in one plan, while state and many local employees are in separate state plans. Another issue is that approximately 30 percent of teachers nationwide are not covered by Social Security. Missouri teachers in the two urban districts (St. Louis and Kansas City) have their own district pension plans and are covered by Social Security. Teachers in the remaining 500-plus Missouri districts—more than 90 percent of the teachers in the state—are enrolled in a statewide plan, the Public School Retirement System (PSRS), and are not covered by Social Security. The latter group is the focus of this chapter.

The governing boards or trustees of state pension plans usually include a mix of appointed and elected members. In PSRS, four of the seven trustees are elected from active and retired PSRS members and three are appointed by the governor.[7] Of the three appointed by the governor, one must be a retired PSRS member. This member-controlled board of trustees reflects the view that PSRS belongs to its members and not to the taxpayers. However, while the board has broad powers over the investment of member funds and selection of the professional staff operating the system, the rules governing the generosity of benefits as well as teacher and district contributions are set by the state legislature.

As in most states, the teacher organizations (there are three in Missouri) have a great deal of influence in the legislature regarding public schools, particularly concerning teacher compensation.[8] The school superintendents have their own organization (the Missouri Association of School Administrators), but by all accounts they have much less political clout than the teacher associations. School administrators belong to the same pension plan as the teachers, and, as we will show, are disproportionate beneficiaries. Our review of available documents finds that school administrators generally supported the pension enhancements that we consider below. They clearly did not publicly oppose the enhancements, and there is no evidence that they have supported general efforts at teacher pension reform (for example, cross-state reciprocity to reduce mobility costs).

Legislatures in several states have recently implemented significant changes to teacher pension plans in an effort to curb their large and growing pension liabilities. The primary opposition to the changes comes from teacher unions.

However, an Internet search of publicly available sources, including newspapers, finds that superintendent associations, to the extent that they are quoted at all, support the traditional defined benefit plans and oppose movement toward defined contribution or hybrid alternatives. In short, labor and management are in the same pension plans and have aligned interests.

Background

As noted above, public workers in the United States are nearly universally enrolled in DB pension plans and their benefits are determined in part by their final average salary. Plans are administered at the state and local levels and share a common structure. The following general formula is used to determine the annual benefit at retirement:

(1) $$B = F * YOS * FAS,$$

where B represents the annual benefit; F is the formula factor, which is usually close to 2 percent for educators; YOS indicates years of service in the system; and FAS is the worker's final average salary, commonly calculated as the average of some number of years of highest earnings. The short time frame over which FAS is calculated in the typical subnational plan plays a key role in our study. It differs markedly from the analogous salary calculation in the federal Social Security program—also a defined benefit pension plan—which uses a thirty-five-year history of earnings to compute the retirement annuity. In PSRS the FAS calculation is based on the three years of highest salary.

It typically takes three to five years to become vested in most state-level educator pension plans; once vested, teachers can collect their pension upon becoming eligible for retirement. The "normal retirement age" is one way that collection eligibility is determined. The age at which a teacher becomes eligible for retirement—typically between the ages of 60 and 65—varies across plans, and eligibility can be based on years of service as well (for example, a teacher may be eligible after thirty years of service). There also are early retirement provisions in most systems that allow individuals to retire and begin collecting benefits before normal retirement. These provisions typically depend on either work experience alone or a combination of age and work experience. An example of the former is the "25-and-out" provision in Missouri, which allows teachers to retire with twenty-five years of system service regardless of age (with a reduced annuity). An example of the latter is Missouri's "rule of 80," which allows for full benefit collection once a teacher's combination of age and experience sums to eighty years. The early-retirement provisions—along with the truncated time

Table 5-1. *Key Parameters of the Missouri Pension System, 1995–2002*[a]

1995	Formula factor was 0.023; early retirement was determined according to 55-25 rule; COLA cap was 65 percent.
1996	Unrestricted 25-and-out rule was implemented.
1997	COLA cap was increased from 65 to 75 percent.
1999	Formula factor was raised to 0.025 for full retirement, with corresponding upward adjustments for early retirement.
2000	Rule of 80 was implemented; final average salary formula was changed to include only the three years of highest salary.
2001	COLA cap was increased to 80 percent.
2002	Formula factor was increased to 0.0255 if years of service was equal to or greater than 31 years (the new factor applies to all service years for eligible individuals).

Source: Authors' compilation.
a. Initial parameters as of 1995 are reported in row 1; there were no changes after 2002.

frame used in calculating *FAS*—are a key source of the backloading of benefits in public sector DB pension plans.

The benefit enhancements to the Missouri pension system occurred primarily between 1995 and 2002. Before that, the formula factor in Missouri was 0.023; final average salary was based on the 5 years of highest earnings; and early retirement was possible through the "55-25 rule," which allowed a teacher to retire and collect benefits without penalty if two conditions were met: the teacher was at least 55 years old, and he or she had accrued at least 25 years of system service. By 2002 the formula factor had been raised from 0.023 to 0.025, the final-average-salary calculation had been changed from the five to the three years of highest earnings, and the 25-and-out and rule-of-80 provisions had been incorporated into the system (the rule of 80 is a more flexible version of the 55-25 rule). In addition, the cap on post-retirement cost-of-living adjustments (COLAs) was raised from 65 to 80 percent of the initial retirement annuity, and a retroactive bonus was added for teachers who reached their thirty-first year of system service.[9]

Table 5-1 lists the plan enhancements in Missouri chronologically. The Missouri system is not unique. Most states enhanced educator pension benefits—and benefits for other public workers—in the late 1990s and early 2000s. The enhancements in many states were substantial, and they appear to have been driven in large part by short-term actuarial surpluses generated by above-average stock market returns.[10]

We had access to administrative personnel records from Missouri, which we initially used to examine the fiscal consequences of the PSRS enhancements across the workforce. To summarize the aggregate fiscal effects, we began by calculating the expected present value of the future stream of retirement benefits for individual educators. Pension wealth at any time s, with collection starting at time j where $j \geq s$, can be calculated as

$$(2) \qquad \sum_{t=j}^{T} Y_t * P_{t|s} * d^{t-s},$$

where Y_t is the annual pension payment in period t, $P_{t|s}$ is the probability that the individual is alive in period t conditional on being alive in period s, and d is a discount factor. We set T to 101. (More details about our pension wealth calculations are presented in an unpublished appendix, which is available upon request.)[11]

Aggregate Fiscal Consequences of the Pension Enhancements in Missouri

Here we summarize our detailed previous analysis of the aggregate fiscal consequences of the Missouri pension enhancements.[12] The enhancement-driven gains in pension wealth were calculated for teachers as the difference in pension wealth under the pre- and post-enhancement rules. That is, for each teacher in the workforce, we calculated pension wealth using the pension rules from 1995 and subtracted that number from pension wealth as calculated under the current (post-2002) rules. When the enhancements were enacted in Missouri, as in other states, they were fully retroactive. So, for example, a senior educator with twenty years of experience at the time when the formula factor was increased could apply the increase to his or her entire service career.

We examined the fiscal costs of the enhancement package in three ways. First, we used estimates of teachers' *current pension wealth* (CPW). The CPW calculations measure immediate changes in pension wealth for teachers, ignoring gains that come through the option value of continued work under the new, enhanced system. The CPW measure understates the total value of the enhancements because teachers' benefits from continued work also are increased. The importance of the option value of continued work in these types of systems has been well documented, which suggests measuring the fiscal costs of the enhancements in terms of teachers' *peak-value pension wealth* (PVPW). The peak-value measure captures the gains in *promised* pension wealth if all teachers retire when pension wealth is maximized. Of course, not all teachers maximize their pension wealth, and for that reason the PVPW measures will overstate the total value of the enhancements. Therefore, we also estimated *expected pension wealth* (EPW), our preferred measure, which incorporates teachers' expected separation behaviors. For example, the expected gain in pension wealth for teachers with five years of experience is unlikely to be well represented by either the CPW or PVPW measures—their gain will fall somewhere in the middle and depends on how long they are expected to stay in the labor force. To calculate EPW, we used personnel files over a two-year span in the pre- and post-enhancement periods in Missouri to create two matrices of separation rates and related statistics for use in our calculations.

Across the teaching workforce, the aggregate, immediate gain in current pension wealth from the enhancements was more than $1.5 billion (in 2009 dollars), or roughly $25,000 per teacher. The gain in peak-value pension wealth was much larger, around $3.0 billion. The gain in expected pension wealth was $2.4 billion. For comparison, the total education budget in Missouri for fiscal year 2000 was $4.8 billion (also in 2009 dollars).

The enhancement legislation generated unfunded liabilities in the pension system because educators who were almost eligible for retirement were able to collect benefits based on the improved pension formula despite paying into the system over the course of their careers at a rate meant to fund benefits at pre-enhancement levels. These unfunded liabilities have increased the costs associated with maintaining the pension system in Missouri. Both public K–12 schools and the current public teaching workforce have sacrificed to offset these previously accrued liabilities. Pension-related labor costs in Missouri today are at least 19 percent higher as a result of the legacy costs of the pension-enhancement legislation (4 percentage points of total teacher earnings). As a practical matter, these costs are evenly split between workers and educators.

It seems difficult to justify the way in which the enhancement legislation was rolled out if the objective was to improve instruction in K–12 schools. For example, the retroactive application of the benefit formula greatly favored senior teachers: *the expected monetary gain for a teacher who was eligible for retirement at the time when the enhancement legislation was enacted was seven times larger than for a new entrant.* Giving large sums of money to teachers as they exit the workforce does not seem consistent with the objective of improving school performance. However, it is consistent with rent seeking by the most politically powerful participants in the pension system—senior educators.

School Administrators

Teachers make up the majority of the public sector workforce; therefore, they are the primary drivers of the total fiscal costs of the enhancement package in

Figure 5-1. *Expected Pension Wealth for Novice Teachers and Same-Vintage Teachers, Principals, and Superintendents*[a]

2009 dollars

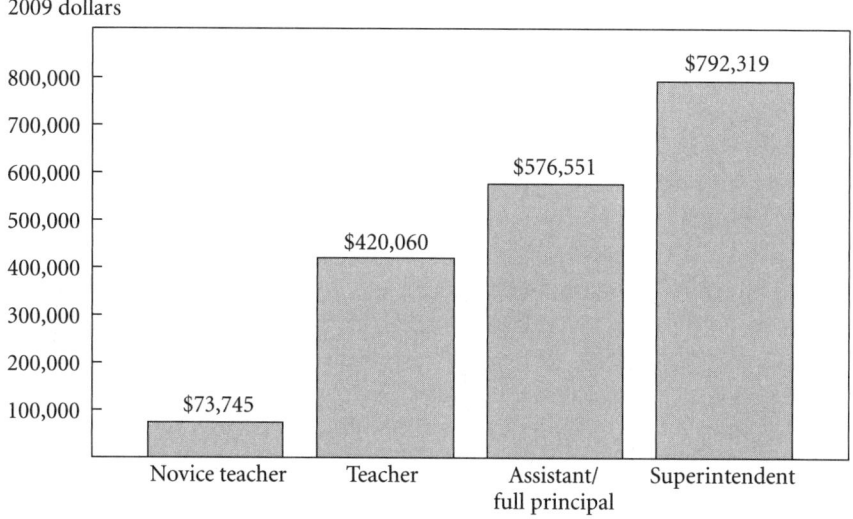

Expected pension wealth

Source: Authors' calculations.

a. Pension wealth is discounted to the current age for each individual and reported in 2009 dollars. The age-experience profiles for teachers and school leaders are set to the average for superintendents in the 2009 cohort in Missouri (age = 50 years; system experience = 21 years). Novice teachers were new entrants in 2009, and the pension wealth calculations for novices incorporate their expected survival probabilities. Calculations are based on the post-enhancement pension rules (2002 and later). Wages for all groups are determined using the Missouri data. The differences between the three groups are driven entirely by promotions.

Missouri. While principals and superintendents do not represent a large enough share of the workforce to have a meaningful fiscal impact in the aggregate, at the micro-level their stake in the enhancement legislation represents an important aspect of the political economy.

A key feature of the benefit formulas in public pension plans is that they rely on a final-average-salary calculation based on late-career earnings. While it is well understood that the final-average-salary DB plans favor long-term teachers over short-term teachers, what seems to have passed largely unnoticed is that the plans also *inherently favor public administrators.* The reason is that public administrators benefit from promotions over the course of their career, with the net result that over time, their earnings growth far outpaces that of most workers.

Figures 5-1 and 5-2 provide some evidence on how promoted and non-promoted individuals differ in terms of their stake in the pension system, again

Figure 5-2. *Ratios of Expected Pension Wealth and System Contributions for Novice Teachers and Same-Vintage Teachers, Principals, and Superintendents*[a]

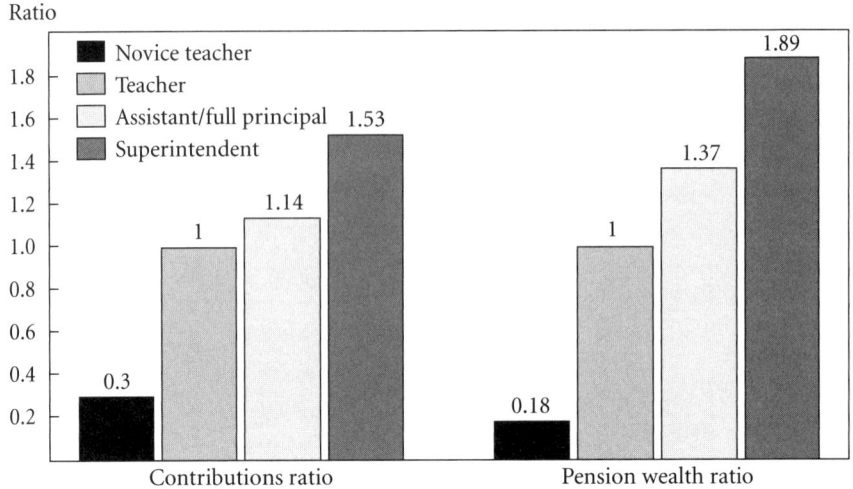

Source: Authors' calculations.
a. Calculations are based on the post-enhancement pension rules (2002 and later).

based on data on Missouri educators. First, figure 5-1 compares the expected pension wealth for four different educator types using the actual Missouri data, based on the post-enhancement pension rules. We began with an average superintendent. In 2009, the average superintendent in Missouri was 50 years old, had 21 years of system service, had been working as a superintendent for 6 years, and had annual earnings of almost $100,000 (2009 dollars). We compared the average superintendent with school leaders and teachers with the same age and experience profiles (that is, similar except with respect to promotions).[13] School leaders with matching age-experience profiles earned, on average, $73,000; teachers earned $55,000. We also compared the three "fixed vintage" individuals to a novice teacher, whose entering wage in 2009 was $31,000.

Figure 5-1 shows that expected pension wealth for the average superintendent far exceeds that for the average same-vintage principal, which far exceeds expected pension wealth for the same-vintage teacher. Put differently, promoted individuals are more heavily invested in the pension system than other workers. Also, of course, the figure shows that pension wealth for all of the experienced educators dwarfs the amount that novice teachers can expect to collect because most novices leave the profession too early to reap substantial rewards from the system.[14]

Next we incorporated contributions into our analysis. Promotions create an additional disconnect between benefits and contributions. For example, during their teaching years, superintendents pay into the system a percentage of their teaching salaries, but years later, after promotions, their benefits are determined independent of that fact. The reliance of the final-average-salary calculation on just the three years of highest earnings rather than on lifetime earnings (as with Social Security) creates disproportionate returns on late-career promotions.[15]

Figure 5-2 illustrates this point. The first four bars on the left show relative contributions over the career cycle for each educator type. Contributions are discounted forward and backward using the same real rate as in the pension wealth calculations (4 percent). Contributions for the age-50 teacher with 21 years of system service are normalized to 1 for the purpose of presentation. Figure 5-2 shows that cumulative superintendent contributions are roughly 50 percent higher than those for the same-vintage teacher, with cumulative contributions for the principal falling in between. Not surprisingly, the cumulative expected contributions for the novice teacher are much smaller than those for the other groups, owing to the fact that many novice teachers do not stay in the system until the late-career stage.

The four bars on the right report total expected pension wealth, again normalized to 1 for the 50-year-old teacher with 21 years of system experience. The difference between the bars on the right and those on the left illustrates that pension returns on contributions are larger for school administrators because administrators spend much of their careers paying into the system at the rate for teachers. Relative to their contributions, the greatest net beneficiaries of the final-average-salary DB plans are principals and superintendents, not senior teachers.

Even viewed in the most favorable light, the enhancement legislation described above should have been seen as an increase in risk for the schooling system moving forward.[16] The way that the enhancements were rolled out seems difficult to justify in terms of improving instruction in K–12 schools. Instead of providing large balloon payments to late-career educators, for example, the funds could have been used on direct instructional expenditures and/or financial incentives to entice new teachers into the profession.[17]

As noted above, we cannot find any evidence of visible opposition to the pension enhancement legislation from school administrators or other senior education officials. The preceding discussion suggests a reason why: the gains from the enhancements for individuals reflect their baseline stake in the system, so school principals and superintendents were the largest beneficiaries from the benefit formula enhancements. For example, the gains from the enhancement package for the average superintendent were essentially twice as large as the gains for same-vintage teachers, owing to their higher late-career salaries.

Novice teachers gained very little from the enhancements. In fact, our calculations show that as a result of subsequent contribution increases required to pay for the benefit enhancements, new teachers were almost certainly made worse off. The reason is that the windfall gains that accrued to experienced educators have become a costly burden on the current pension fund. School districts in Missouri—and the current educator workforce—have been asked to help offset the burden by increasing their contributions to the system. Given the small likelihood that a novice teacher will be in the system long enough to collect substantial benefits, even a small increase in payroll deductions to pay for those benefits turns the benefit-cost ratio negative.

Conclusion

Retirement benefits represent a large and growing cost for the public sector. While the role of DB pension plans in the private sector has greatly diminished over the past 30 years, DB pension benefits have become a more pronounced aspect of worker compensation in the public sector. One reason is that future benefits can be promised without requiring governments to set aside immediate and appropriate funding to cover the corresponding liabilities. Rather than set aside immediate financing, public pension plans count on future investment returns to cover liabilities. History warns us that this strategy is not always successful. Indeed, the recent financial crisis—which was preceded by an extended bull market that prompted many pension funds, in their exuberance, to generously improve participant benefits—has left many plans scrambling to find funding. In Missouri, the short-term solution has been to raise combined employee and employer contributions, which have risen from 21 to 29 percent of earnings over an eight-year period for PSRS members. That approach seems to have provided a temporary resolution to the local crisis, although not all states and municipalities are as well off.

In addition, recent activities by PSRS fund administrators and their actuaries raise concerns that these problems will resurface. Faced with mounting discontent owing to the rapid increase in the system contribution rate, PSRS recently reduced its reported level of unfunded liabilities by $3.7 billion. That reduction was driven entirely by changes in actuarial assumptions per the fund's most recent experience study, which wiped $4.6 billion in liabilities off the books. There were many changes, but some seem untenable. For example, the expected rate of inflation was changed from 3.25 to 2.5 percent. In isolation that estimate may seem reasonable; however, the fund did not change its nominal expected rate of return (8 percent), which in combination with lower expected inflation is equivalent to assuming a *higher real rate of return on investments*.[18]

Mechanically, a higher real rate of return will lower system liabilities, but it is not clear why the fund would expect a higher rate of return over the next 5 years than in preceding decades. It is clear, however, that the new actuarial report has helped to quell discontent arising from eight consecutive years of contribution rate increases.

The pension enhancement period in the late 1990s and early 2000s serves as a recent example of the risk of rent capture inherent in subnational public pension systems. In PSRS, the enhancements were expensive and the benefits accrued primarily to the most politically powerful segment of the workforce— senior teachers. Forward-looking system managers should have been able to recognize that the commitments associated with the enhancements would be risky for public schools. However, it is not reasonable to expect school administrators to forcefully oppose this type of legislation or push for legislation that reduces pension benefits, given their conflicted position as the largest net beneficiaries of these heavily backloaded DB plans.

The structural flaws inherent in subnational public pension plans are likely to ensure that their fiscal condition is continually weak. Without any checks on overextending liabilities, labor organizations will continue to put pressure on education systems for unsustainable benefits. Indeed, a common belief among labor unions and their allies is that if assets reach 80 percent of liabilities, the pension plan is "healthy" and enhancements can begin anew.[19] The large unfunded liabilities created by rent capture present a risk to the federalist model of governance in this area. For example, if a municipality over-commits itself by promising retiree benefits that it cannot deliver, state governments may be asked to step in. Similarly, states in similar circumstances may seek assistance from the federal government. If the federal government serves as the ultimate backer of the liabilities in such pension systems, then at least some federal regulation seems likely. In addition, more centralized regulation might solve some of the most severe political problems plaguing these plans. For example, state and local plans could be made subject to some of the same regulations required of private sector plans by the Employee Retirement Income Security Act (ERISA) or IRS regulations.

Notes

1. Pew Center on the States, *The Trillion Dollar Gap* (Washington: Pew Foundation, February 2010), and Robert Novy-Marx and Joshua Rauh, "The Liabilities and Risks of State-Sponsored Pension Plans," *Journal of Economic Perspectives*, vol. 23, no. 4 (2009), pp. 191–210.

2. Paul Merrion, "Moody's Pension Calculation Changes Could Hit Illinois Hard," *Pensions and Investments*, July 10, 2012.

3. Alicia Munnell, Kelly Haverstick, and Mauricio Sato, "Why Have Defined Benefit Plans Survived in the Public Sector?" (Boston College, Center for Retirement Research, December 2007) (http://crr.bc.edu/wp-content/uploads/2007/12/slp_2.pdf), and Janet S. Hansen, "An Introduction to Teacher Retirement Benefits," *Education Finance and Policy,* vol. 5, no. 2 (2010), pp. 402–37.

4. For example, according to the Delaware Office of Pensions, "The [enhancement] legislation [in Delaware in 2001] was developed to reduce the overfunded position in the State Employees' Pension Plan by granting benefit improvements to active and retired members." Ronald Snell, "Pensions and Retirement Plan Enactments in 2001 State Legislatures" (National Conference of State Legislatures, 2001) (www.ncsl.org/documents/fiscal/2001_pension_summary.pdf).

5. Cory Koedel, Shawn Ni, and Michael Podgursky, "Who Benefits from Pension Enhancements?" *Education Finance and Policy* (forthcoming).

6. The only exception is a relatively small number of teachers in charter schools in a few states. Charter schools are semi-autonomous public schools that are allowed to waive certain state regulations as a condition of their charter. Some states allow charter schools to opt out of the state pension plan, and some of the charter schools that have chosen to do so report no retirement plans for their teachers other than Social Security. See Amanda Olberg and Michael Podgursky, *Charting a New Course: How Charter Schools Handle Teacher Pensions* (Washington: Fordham Institute, June 2011) (http://edexcellence.pub30.convio.net/publications-issues/publications/charting-a-new-course-to.html).

7. This is a slight simplification of an even more complex structure. In Missouri public schools the professional staff (that is, teachers, counselors, and administrators) are in PSRS and are not covered by Social Security, while the nonprofessional staff are covered by Social Security and are in a parallel but less remunerative plan operated by the same board. One of the four elected trustees comes from the nonprofessional staff.

8. James Endersby, Gregory Casey, and James King, "Interest Groups in Missouri," in *Missouri Government and Politics,* 2nd ed., edited by Richard Hardy, Robert Dohm, and David Leuthold (University of Missouri Press, 1995).

9. In 2001 the formula factor was increased to 0.0255 if service years exceed thirty.

10. Information about enhancements in other state pension plans for various years can be found in National Conference of State Legislators, "Pensions and Retirement Plan Enactments in [year] State Legislatures" (www.ncsl.org). For information over a longer time span for educators in particular, see Robert L. Clark and Lee A. Craig, "Determinants of the Generosity of Pension Plans for Public School Teachers: 1982–2006." Working Paper (Vanderbilt University, National Center on Performance Incentives, 2009).

11. The most important parameter that we specify in our calculations, at least in terms of affecting the pension wealth values that we report throughout, is the discount rate. We use a real rate of 4 percent, which is between the rate used in other recent studies, for example, Courtney Coile and Jonathan Gruber, "Future Social Security Entitlements and the Retirement Decision," *Review of Economics and Statistics,* vol. 89, no. 2 (2007), pp. 234–46, and Robert Costrell and Michael Podgursky, "Peaks, Cliffs, and Valleys: The Peculiar Incentives in Teacher Retirement Systems and Their Consequences for School

Staffing," *Education Finance and Policy,* vol. 4, no. 2, pp. 175–211. The pension-wealth values that we report are sensitive to the discount rate, but our findings are qualitatively similar if we choose a different (reasonable) rate.

12. Koedel, Ni, and Podgursky, "Who Benefits from Pension Enhancements?"

13. The system's retirement eligibility rules make individuals' age-experience combinations particularly important determinants of pension wealth. See, for example, Costrell and Podgursky, "Peaks, Cliffs, and Valleys."

14. Koedel, Ni, and Podgursky, "Who Benefits from Pension Enhancements?" provides an extended discussion of new teachers.

15. For the average teacher-to-principal promotion, for example, the single-year wage increase is 30 percent. That increase largely reflects moving from a nine-month to an eleven-month position. The average principal-to-superintendent promotion corresponds to a single-year wage increase of 17 percent. Details are available in an unpublished appendix available from the authors.

16. In fact, the following text was taken directly from the fiscal note attached to the legislation in Missouri that introduced the rule of 80 and changed the FAS calculation from five to three years (Missouri Senate Bill 331, 1999): "There will be a long-term fiscal impact as a result of this legislation, since elimination of the system's surplus and creation of an unfunded actuarial liability will contribute to any need for increased contributions in the future."

17. See Richard Startz, *Profit of Education* (Santa Barbara, Calif.: Praeger, 2010), or Charles F. Manski, "Academic Ability, Earnings, and the Decision to Become a Teacher: Evidence from the National Longitudinal Study of the High School Class of 1972," in *Public Sector Payrolls,* edited by David Wise (University of Chicago Press, 1987).

18. PricewaterhouseCoopers, "The Public School and Education Employee Retirement System of Missouri: PSRS Experience Study" (June 13, 2011), and Public School Retirement System of Missouri, "2011 Comprehensive Annual Financial Report" (2012), p. 93.

19. American Association of Actuaries, "The 80 Percent Funding Standard Myth," Issue Brief (July 2012).

DANIEL SHOAG

6

Past and Present High-Risk Investments by States and Localities

The years between 1824 and 1841 were a period of enormous public investment by state governments.[1] The Erie Canal, completed in 1825, proved substantially more profitable than projected. New York initially set aside revenues from existing sources to meet the canal's financing costs, but to the state's delight, the canal proved to be self-financing. Spurred by that success, Indiana, Illinois, Maryland, Michigan, New York, Pennsylvania, and Ohio financed new canal projects over the next 15 years. Those projects were generally debt-financed and unaccompanied by revenue-raising measures. The estimated proceeds from the projects and the subsequent growth that the projects were assumed to generate factored prominently into state budgets for repayment.

During that time, state governments also invested massively in state-chartered banks and relied heavily on revenue generated from taxes on bank capital and dividends. From 1835 to 1840, bank-related revenue exceeded 20 percent of total state revenue in Massachusetts, Connecticut, Rhode Island, Maine, New Hampshire, Pennsylvania, Delaware, North Carolina, South Carolina, and Georgia. The profitability of banking investments in other states and the winding down of the Second Bank of the United States after President Andrew Jackson vetoed a bill to renew its charter led to large investments in banking by Alabama, Arkansas, Florida, Illinois, Indiana, Louisiana, Mississippi, Tennessee, and Missouri. As with canal building, state governments relied, in part, on the revenue from those investments to service the debt incurred.

This debt-fueled "era of internal improvement" ended ignominiously with the default of eight states and the territory of Florida in 1841 and 1842. By that

This chapter is based on a paper prepared for the conference *The Political Economy of Federalism in Times of Economic Crisis*, sponsored by the Program on Education Policy and Governance at the Kennedy School of Government, Harvard University (2012). I am grateful for comments from Daniel Nadler, Paul Peterson, the conference participants, and an anonymous referee.

time, the combined debt of state governments had exploded to nearly $200 million from a base of $12.8 million in 1825. Indiana, which had annual revenues of approximately $50,000 in 1836, nevertheless authorized $10 million in bonds at 5 percent interest that year for canal development.[2] When land values fell instead of appreciating and revenues from canal and banking investments failed to materialize, the state defaulted on its obligations.

In the aftermath of the wave of state defaults, nineteen states adopted balanced-budget restrictions.[3] Over the years, adoption of restrictions spread, and today every state except Vermont has some form of balanced-budget requirement. Although the rules differ in their structure and severity, with some states requiring only that the legislature submit a balanced-budget proposal and others forbidding the carrying of a deficit into the next fiscal year, the restrictions have been largely successful at limiting formal debt.[4] Formal state debt as a fraction of gross state product ranged from 7 to 25 percent in 2010, with a median value of 17 percent. In contrast, federal debt is equal to nearly 100 percent of GDP. One shortcoming of balanced-budget laws, however, is that they do not cover the full range of state debt-like commitments; for example, they do not cover future obligations to public employees like pension and health benefits.

The seemingly profitable investment opportunities in infrastructure and banking that were offered to state governments in the early nineteenth century are economically similar to the profitable asset market opportunities offered to governments by public employee pension systems today. State and local government retirement systems manage more than $3 trillion in assets on behalf of more than 19 million members. These systems overwhelmingly provide funded defined benefit plans, in which members are promised a stream of benefits that does not depend on trust fund returns. These state commitments mimic economically the formal debt assumed in the nineteenth century in that governments pledge themselves to meet fixed and unalterable liabilities. To fund their commitments, state and local governments contribute money to retirement trust funds, which are invested in the asset markets. Again, state and local governments, not retirees or debt holders, are the residual claimants on these risky investments. While the liquidity of the investments, the identity of the debt holders, and the type of spending financed may differ, the structure of debt-financed risky investment remains the same. Further, as was the case between 1820 and 1840, state governments are staking large sums on potentially profitable, yet risky, outcomes.

Over the past half-century, states have profited enormously from their pension investments. The U.S. Census Bureau's Annual Survey of Public Employee Retirement Systems, a largely complete annual database going back to 1957, contains only the book or cost value of assets before 2002, so annual returns generally cannot be computed. Total earnings for the funds can be approximated,

Figure 6-1. *Earnings as a Percentage of Total Tax Collections,
State and Local Governments, 1958–2008*

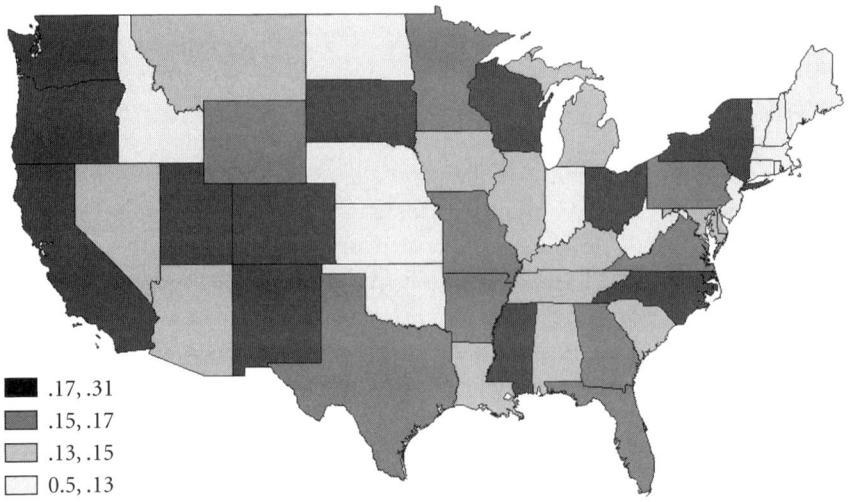

.17, .31
.15, .17
.13, .15
0.5, .13

Source: Data are from the U.S. Census Bureau, State and Local Public-Employee Retirement System Survey, various years.

however, by subtracting the initial balance and the sum of contributions to the fund net of payments from the balance today. Specifically, I calculated total earnings as follows:

$$(2)\ Earnings_{1957,2010} = Balance_{2010} - \sum_{t=1958}^{2010} Contributions_t + \sum_{t=1958}^{2010} Payments_t - Balance_{1957}.$$

In total, state and local governments have earned $3.73 *trillion*. State and local governments in California alone have earned $671 billion, and New York has earned $475 billion. To get a better sense of what these figures mean relative to state tax burdens, I divided total earnings by total state tax collections over the 1958–2008 period. The ratios are presented in figure 6-1, which shows that in many states, pension earnings over those fifty years were a major source of revenue. In the average state, pension earnings amounted to 15 percent of total state and local tax revenues; alternatively, public pensions contributed, on average, a full year of tax revenue every 6 years and 8 months. During that period, pension earnings exceeded 10 percent of total revenue, including transfers from the federal government, for state and local governments in Oregon, Wisconsin, New York, California, Colorado, and Ohio.

Figure 6-2. *Pension Earnings Compared with Liabilities*

Earnings/tax revenue, 1958–2008

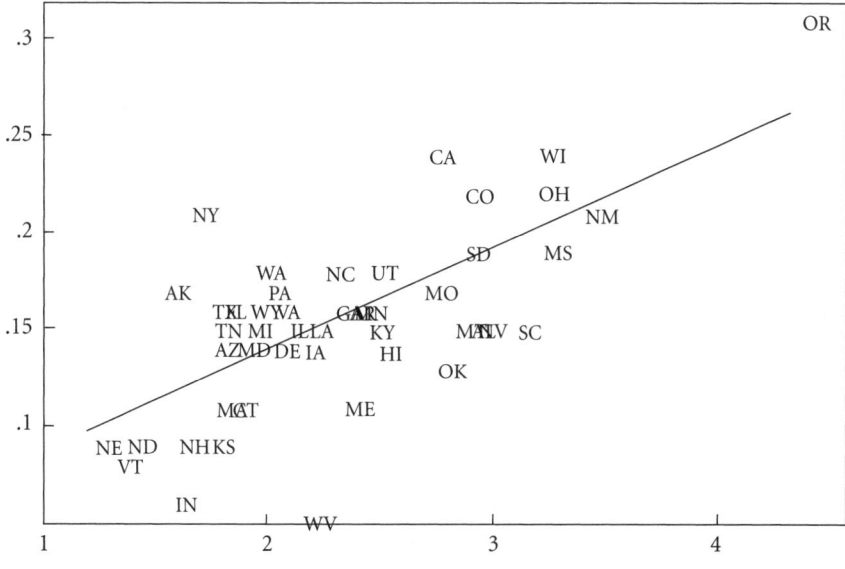

Liabilities/annual tax revenue, 2008

Source: Data are from the Pew Center on the States, "Trillion Dollar Gap: Underfunded State Retirement Systems and the Roads to Reform," February 2010 (www.pewstates.org/uploadedFiles/PCS_Assets/2010/Trillion_Dollar_Gap_Underfunded_State_Retirement_Systems_and_the_Roads_to_Reform.pdf).

Those significant sums were driven by investments in the asset market, which are indirectly financed by the pension obligations assumed by state and local governments. States that have larger pension and associated liabilities also have larger trust funds and investment earnings (see figure 6-2). Measuring the "true" value of those liabilities is complicated, and the figures reported by the plans themselves depend on their assumptions about discount rates, wage and employment growth, and mortality. Novy-Marx and Rauh, for example, argue that the discount rates commonly used by state and local governments are too high and dramatically understate the cost of future retirement benefits.[5] Fortunately, while changing the discount rate generally has a large impact on the size of pension obligations, switching to a low, uniform rate has only a modest effect on the cross-sectional ranking of obligations.[6] For simplicity, I relied on plan-reported numbers in this analysis. Figure 6-2 takes summary measures for each state from the Pew Center on the States, which surveyed the financial reports of the major pension plans. State-level measures of liabilities suffer from an additional problem in that many plans are omitted from existing surveys.[7] Despite the problems, the strong relationship between liabilities and investment earnings can be clearly seen.

Risky investments and pension obligations are not, in themselves, threats to the fiscal health of state and local governments. As discussed, in the 1840s states ran into trouble not because they borrowed to invest in infrastructure but because they depended on the broad returns from their investments to finance their debt. In the remainder of this chapter, I explore which states are most at risk from pension commitments and which common factors predict this risk. I explore these questions using both plan-reported measures of underfunding, such as funding ratios, and measures that the nineteenth-century experience suggests capture fiscal capacity risk. I conclude with a discussion of why managing state and local pension liabilities and risky debt-financed investment in general is important for maintaining sustainable fiscal federalism.

Data and Earlier Literature

In addition to the Annual Survey of Public Employee Retirement Systems and the Pew Center data described above, this analysis draws on three other sources of data on state pensions. The first is the Public Plans Database, assembled by the Boston College Center for Retirement Research.[8] Like the Pew Center data, the Center for Retirement Research data are drawn from the comprehensive annual financial reports (CAFRs) published by the largest retirement systems. These data, which are reported at the plan rather than the state level, are much richer than the Pew Center data.

The second source of data is the Comparative Retirement Studies conducted biannually by the Wisconsin state legislature.[9] The Wisconsin data, which date back to 1982, provide invaluable historical information on the evolution of pension funding. Finally, I used a dataset that I constructed on the historical investment returns of the major state-administered systems, obtained from open record requests and audited financial reports. The data in this set go back through the mid-1980s.[10]

A number of earlier studies have looked at aspects of pension funding across states. Mitchell and Smith (1994), Splinter (2010), and Chaney, Copley, and Stone (2002) find that fiscally stressed states reduced their pension contributions.[11] Munnell, Haverstick, and Aubry (2008) finds that some aspects of plan design and plan governance were correlated with funding outcomes.[12] This study builds on this earlier work by analyzing how plan features, economic outcomes, and state politics are related to plan funding status. It also shifts the analysis to focus on fiscal capacity risks in addition to traditional funding measures and discusses the implications of those risks.

The Distribution of Pension Risk

Measures to quantify states' exposure to pension risks must be developed before the distribution of pension risks is analyzed. The assets and liabilities of defined benefit plans evolve over the course of the fiscal year as fund assets earn investment returns and government agencies hire new workers. The value of those changes is determined through an audit (generally including some smoothing procedure), and new values for plan liabilities and assets are calculated. The difference between the values, or the unfunded actuarial accrued liability (UAAL), is then used in determining the actuarially required contribution (ARC).[13] The traditional metric for evaluating the funding status of a public plan focuses on the ratio of actuarial assets to liabilities, or the actuarial funding ratio. While this metric, analyzed below, is informative, the previous discussion suggests that attention also should be paid to risk measures that refer to the fiscal capacity of state and local governments. Moreover, states' previous experience with risky investments recommends consideration of a measure of the ability of governments to finance their liabilities in the absence of investment returns.

To explore these issues, I constructed two additional risk measures: the ratio of states' UAAL to state population or GDP and the ratio of total actuarial liabilities to population or GDP. The first measure is a rescaling of the funding ratio by the size of liabilities relative to GDP, which allows traditional underfunding to be understood in terms of fiscal capacity. It does not, however, change the traditional assumptions about the value of retirement systems' risky assets. The second measure, which is unquestionably extreme, assumes that those assets are valueless; it can best be thought of as a bounding exercise. What this measure does capture, however, is the notion that a state with 1,000 times its GDP in liabilities and assets is more exposed to pension risk than a state with 10 percent of its GDP in liabilities and assets, even though both systems may be fully funded.

Pension Risk Factors

I now explore what factors explain the variation in funding and risk across states. The analysis can be roughly divided into sections analyzing the effects of state and local government size, state economies, plan features, and state politics. I find that while the size of the government sector, state economic growth, and the generosity of public pension schemes have little impact on funding ratios, they are tightly linked to increases in pension risk relative to state fiscal capacity. In contrast, investment returns on retirement trust funds and state government diligence in meeting actuarially required contributions have big effects on traditional funding ratios. They do not, however, correlate with the measures of capacity. Political variables do not seem to be correlated with either measure.

These facts suggest that, from a fiscal capacity perspective, more weight should be given to risk factors such as a large public sector and sluggish economic growth than to traditional measures of funding status.

Size of the Public Sector

State-administered pension plans provide benefits to former public employees, a fact that suggests that pension risk may be correlated with the size of a state's public sector. The distribution of state government spending varies considerably across regions. Total state and local government expenditures are higher in the Northeast (average of $9,933 per capita in 2008) than in the Midwest ($8,616) and South ($8,352). They are dramatically higher in Alaska (average $18,753) than in other states. Total state and local spending per capita is highly correlated with per capita state and local spending on salaries and wages (0.86), and salaries are generally used in determining pension obligations.

Regression analyses using data from the Bureau of Economic Analysis, the U.S. Census Bureau, and the Pew Center on the States demonstrate that the validity of this assumption depends on the risk measure used. States with high state and local expenditures per capita do not have worse funding ratios or fewer assets for a given dollar of liabilities—rather, states with larger total spending have both higher assets and higher liabilities per capita. The regression of funding ratio on spending per capita yields a coefficient of 0.0008—which is statistically insignificant from zero—with a standard error of 0.008. When combined with flat funding ratios, the greater level of liabilities in states with higher spending means that those states do have higher unfunded liabilities per capita. However, with a coefficient of 0.22 and a standard error of 0.11, the relationship is fairly weak and just barely statistically significant at the 10 percent level. The total liability risk measure, in contrast, is tightly linked to public sector size. A one-dollar increase in total spending per capita increases total liabilities per capita by a little more than one dollar, a relationship with an R-squared value of 0.46. These results demonstrate that states with a larger public sector save roughly the same amount per dollar of liabilities as states with lower overall spending. Therefore, traditional funding metrics would not deem these states to be at greater risk. Risk metrics that measure total liabilities relative to fiscal capacity rather than quantity of risky investments do find that high-spending states face considerably greater pension funding risks.

Given that spending is a function of income, one might imagine that these results are driven by the size of the economy rather than the size of the public sector. Repeating the regressions of funding measures with state government spending scaled as a fraction of state GDP, I find that results are virtually identical in each case. The coefficient for the funding ratio is –0.0002 (0.0006 standard error); unfunded liabilities are no longer significant at the 10 percent level but the magnitude remains the same, 0.22 (0.15 standard error); and the effect of spending on total liabilities when scaled by GDP remains highly significant, with a coefficient of 1.07 and a standard error of 0.24.

Generosity of Benefits

Another factor commonly thought to be correlated with pension risk is the relative generosity of pension benefit payments. There is a significant amount of variation in the generosity of benefits across states and plans. Although benefit formulas often are complicated, the standard benefit measure is determined by the following formula:

(2) *Annual benefit = Benefit factor × Years of service × Final average salary.*

Given this basic formula, it is clear that small differences in the benefit factor can generate large differences in the obligations owed to employees. For example, suppose an employee has a final average salary of $60,000 and retires after 30 years of service. A change in the benefit factor of 0.3 percent (1 standard deviation in the Boston College Center for Retirement Research dataset) changes the annual benefits owed to that retiree by $5,400. Compounded across employees over their lifetime, this represents a major change in the state's liabilities. As I noted before, however, higher liabilities do not in themselves imply higher unfunded liabilities.

Unfortunately, the actual benefit formulas used by states are more complicated than the stylized version presented here, and it is difficult to standardize measures across plans. Therefore, I explored this relationship by creating an average monthly benefit variable that I compared with measures of plan funding status. The average benefit is defined as total benefit payments divided by the total number of retirees (the data are for 2008).

The data from the Pew Center for the States and plan data from the Wisconsin Comparative Retirement Study survey show that for every dollar increase in average benefits, the funding ratio decreases by 0.005 percent, although that estimate is not significant. In other words, an increase of 1 standard deviation in average benefits ($4,786) reduces the funding ratio by 2.4 percentage points (for comparison, a standard deviation in funding status is 13 percentage points). There is only a modest negative relationship between plan generosity and savings per dollar of liabilities. Further analyses show that more generous states do have higher liabilities, however, and once again flat funding ratios imply higher unfunded liabilities per capita. These relationships are statistically significant at the 5 percent level—with coefficients and standard errors of 94.30 and 42.65, respectively, for unfunded liabilities per capita and 267.74 and 66.72 for total liabilities per capita—implying that a dollar increase in average annual benefit increases unfunded liabilities per capita by more than $94 and total liabilities per capita by $268. Similar results hold when scaling by state GDP. As with the total size of the public sector, it does not appear that states with more generous plans save significantly less per dollar of obligations. Their higher overall level of obligations, however, implies that they face more risk relative to their capacity.

The average monthly benefit per retiree is an endogenous variable. Estimates of the benefit may suffer from omitted variable bias if, for example, benefit levels are affected by investment returns or other omitted factors that affect funding rates. To control for this problem, I instrumented for the average monthly benefit payment using the benefit factors of the plans in 1982.[14] Beshears and others (2010) shows that there is a great deal of persistence in benefit levels across plans.[15] I confirmed that finding in my first stage, where the benefit factor in 1982 has an F statistic of 13.3, comfortably above the weak-instrument benchmark advocated by Stock and Yogo (2005).[16] The instrumental variable results of comparing levels of plan generosity with funding status and liabilities indicate somewhat larger effects of generosity on liabilities: the coefficient and standard error increase to 235.58 and 100.22, respectively, on unfunded liabilities per capita and to 523.01 and 166.34 for total liabilities per capita, while the impact on the funding ratio doubles in magnitude but remains statistically insignificant. That would be consistent with benefits growing more slowly in underfunded systems.

Economic Growth

A third possible factor that might influence the degree of underfunding across plans is the economic growth rate of the administering state. For example, a state that experienced poor growth might find itself unable to pay for benefits promised in the past. If that were the case, one would expect to find changes in the funding status of the plans to be correlated with changes in state-level personal income, employment, or population growth. This argument is made in Johnson (1997).[17] In addition, Splinter (2010) and Chaney, Copley, and Stone (2002) find that fiscally stressed states reduced their pension contributions.[18]

This assumption, however, is once again dependent on the pension risk metric being used. Using data from the Bureau of Economic Analysis and controlling for time, I regressed the change in the funding status of the state pension plans from 2006–08 and 2008–10 on the GDP growth rate over those periods. I found no effect of economic growth on state funding ratios (coefficient of –0.002 and standard error of 0.002). In contrast, GDP growth seems to be an important determinant of the ratio of liabilities to GDP, yielding a –1.91 coefficient

(0.256 standard error) significant at the 1 percent level in a regression of the change in the ratio of total liabilities to GDP on the state growth rate. States with faster growth have greater reductions in their ratio of liabilities to GDP. An increase of 1 standard deviation in growth is associated with a reduction of two-thirds of a standard deviation in the ratio of liabilities to GDP.

Of course, economic growth is an endogenous variable. The estimates of the effect of economic growth on funding status may be biased if, for example, better governance leads to both better pension funding and stronger growth. To address these potential issues, I instrumented for state growth rates using Bartik shocks and repeated the tests described above.[19] This procedure, which approximates state-level growth using national industry trends and state industrial composition, yields a first-stage F statistic of 42.9. As before, the coefficients estimated for the funding ratio are statistically insignificant and close to zero. The coefficient on the ratio of total liabilities to GDP remains significant at the 1 percent level and increases in magnitude to −2.646 (0.582 standard error), highlighting the distinction between the two risk measures.

Legal Constraints

In most states, pension liabilities are protected either by statute and case law or explicitly by the state constitution. State constitutions are generally difficult to amend; doing so often requires the approval of successive sessions of the legislature and a public vote. Case law can be similarly difficult to undo. Those provisions, then, commit state governments to honor their pension obligations by making it difficult to legally default on or adjust the benefits promised. Table 6-1 outlines the distribution of protection types across states, as catalogued in Munnell and Quimby (2012).[20]

Much of the recent discussion on the issue of state pension funding has assumed that pension provisions will greatly constrain state behavior going forward.[21] One might assume, then, that states with more stringent provisions would have higher pension funding levels and lower unfunded liabilities. However, that does not appear to be the case. States that provide explicit protections for future, unvested benefits have virtually the same funding status and ratio of liabilities to GDP as states without such protections. Having future benefits protected is not a significant predictor of funding ratio, the ratio of unfunded liabilities to GDP, or the ratio of total liabilities to GDP. Regressing these measures of funding status on an indicator of stringent provisions yields near-zero coefficients that are statistically insignificant from zero. The data give the same result for states with explicit constitutional protections of public pension benefits. Therefore, while such restrictions may constrain future behavior, there is little evidence to date that they have had an effect under any risk measure.

Table 6-1. *Accruals Protected*

Legal basis	Past and future	Past/future uncertain	Past only	None
State constitution	Alaska, Illinois, New York	Arizona	Hawaii, Louisiana, Michigan	
Contract	Alabama, California, Georgia, Kansas, Massachusetts, Nebraska, Nevada, New Hampshire, North Dakota, Oregon, Pennsylvania, Tennessee, Vermont, Washington, West Virginia	Colorado, Idaho, Maryland, Mississippi, New Jersey, Rhode Island, South Carolina	Arkansas, Delaware, Florida, Iowa, Kentucky, Missouri, Montana, North Carolina, Oklahoma, South Dakota, Utah, Virginia	
Property	Maine, Wyoming	Connecticut, New Mexico, Ohio	Wisconsin	
Promissory estoppel	Minnesota			
Gratuity				Indiana, Texas

Source: Alicia Munnell and Laura Quimby, "Legal Constraints on Changes in State and Local Pensions," Research Brief (Boston College, Center for Retirement Research, 2012).

Political Dimensions: Turnover and Unions

A common theme in the political economy literature is that politicians have shorter time horizons than their electorate. When that is the case, they have incentives to borrow from future taxpayers to finance current government consumption. It is possible, then, that differences in funding levels are related to the planning horizons of state officials.

Although term limits for state legislators do not appear to affect funding status, planning decisions may be made at the party rather than the individual level. If so, term limits may be a poor measure of political longevity. The frequency of party changes is a better proxy for determining the effect of political horizons, although this measure may suffer from some endogeneity bias. Regressing measures of pension funding status on the number of shifts in party control of state governorships and legislatures between 1959 and 2007 (using data from the U.S. Statistical Abstract) indicates that gubernatorial changes might have a weakly detrimental effect on funding levels. States with more gubernatorial party turnover have pensions that are less adequately funded: for each additional gubernatorial party change in this time period, the ratio of assets to liabilities decreased by 1.4 percent (0.8 percent standard error), significant at the 10 percent level, suggesting that governors might have greater discount rates in those states. This effect is not present for changes in control of state legislatures, where the same analysis yielded a small positive effect (0.5 percent) that is not significant. Using alternate pension risk measures shows no effect of party turnover in the governorship or state legislature. The coefficients of the ratio of total liabilities to GDP regressed on gubernatorial and legislature party changes are 0.007 (0.004 standard error) and -0.0002 (0.002 standard error) respectively. That indicates that evidence in favor of a gubernatorial discount rate should be interpreted with caution.

The last political influence on the funding status of public sector pension plans that I considered is the strength of state-level public sector unions. There is considerable debate over the extent to which unions are responsible for state budgetary woes, as evidenced by recent legislation to curtail union power in Wisconsin, Ohio, and New Hampshire and the large backlash that those moves engendered. To test the hypothesis that states with stronger unions are more underfunded, I regressed measures of pension funding on proxies for union strength in the state—the percent of the public sector that is unionized and the fraction of 2008 political donations made by public sector unions—using data from the Current Population Survey (through UnionStats.com) and from the National Institute on Money in State Politics. First, I tested the hypothesis that states where a greater fraction of public sector employees are unionized differ in the funding status of their pensions by regressing the usual measures of funding status on this measure of union strength. The results for funding ratio and unfunded liabilities scaled by GDP are nearly zero and statistically insignificant. There is a potential weak positive effect of greater unionization in the public sector on the ratio of total liabilities to GDP returning a 0.069 coefficient (0.04 standard error) significant at the 10 percent level. I tested the same outcomes for states in which a higher or lower fraction of political donations were made by public sector unions and found that increases in that measure did not increase a state's unfunded liabilities scaled by GDP, impair its funding status, or have a significant impact on the ratio of total liabilities to GDP. This finding stands in contrast to the results in Mitchell and Smith (1994), which find that unions do impair public plan funding status.[22]

Investment Returns and Actuarially Required Contributions

More than 73 percent of the receipts for state and local pension funds in 2010 came from investment returns. There is considerable variation in investment returns across plans. Shoag (2010) reports that a within-year standard deviation in returns across plans ranged from 2 to 3 percentage points[23] and that the standard deviation in cumulative returns over a 20-year horizon was nearly 100 percent. Farrell and Shoag (2012) documents that investment returns differed across public pension designs as well.[24] Given this large variation, it is reasonable to assume that differences in returns might explain much of the variation in obligations. I tested this hypothesis by regressing the change in state pension risks from 2001 to 2009 on the annualized cumulative investment return over that period. The data on returns are from the Boston College Public Plans Database. I weighted the plan-level returns by assets in 2001 to calculate state-level averages.

The regression of the change in funding status on investment returns implies that increasing the return by 1 percentage point a year for all 10 years would improve a plan's funding ratio by about 4 percent, a result significant at the 5 percent level. This is a sizable effect given that the standard deviation in annualized returns in this period is 1.04 percentage points (in comparison, a standard deviation for changes in funding status is 11.5 percentage points). Similarly significant effects can be seen for the UAAL-to-GDP ratio, with a coefficient of −1.08 and a standard error of 0.36. In contrast, the relationship between changes in total liabilities and investment returns is less clear. Although the estimated coefficient, −0.40 (0.34 standard error), is negative, it is not statistically significant, and this negative slope is significantly attenuated when outliers are dropped.

In summary, it appears that better investment returns do improve traditional measures of pension funding. There are more assets per dollar of liabilities in the retirement trust funds and a lower ratio of unfunded liabilities to GDP. Investment returns do not, however, seem to be significantly slowing the growth of total liabilities.

Finally, using the plan-level Public Plans Database, I explored the effect that fulfilling the actuarially required contributions has on state pension risk measures. I calculated the percent of the total required contributions actually paid by state and local governments between 2002 and 2009. I then used that measure to predict the same state-level outcomes as in the analysis of investment returns (change in funding ratio, change in ratio of UAAL to GDP, and change in ratio of liabilities to GDP), which measure the change in funding status over that time period.

I find that, like investment returns, meeting ARC targets had a large positive effect on pension funding rates, significant at the 1 percent level, with a coefficient of 0.23 (0.09 standard error). An increase of 1 standard deviation in ARC contributions led to an improvement of one-third of a standard deviation in the change in the funding ratio. A significant negative coefficient, −0.06 (0.02 standard error), from the regression of the change in UAAL on the liabilities ratio shows that meeting ARC targets also decreases the ratio of unfunded liabilities to GDP. In contrast, an increase of 1 standard deviation in ARC contributions was associated with an improvement of less than a 0.17 standard deviation in the total liability-to-GDP ratio, a relationship that is not statistically significant.

Analysis

The upshot of the analysis is twofold: political factors are uncorrelated with pension risk, and the factors affecting traditional metrics of pension funding, like the asset-to-liabilities ratio, are very different from the factors that affect pension obligations relative to fiscal capacity. States that met their required contributions and earned large investment returns tended to see improvements in their funding ratios, though those factors were not correlated with a reduction in the ratio of liabilities to GDP. States can see improvements in the funding ratio and fully meet their ARCs without reducing their reliance on risky returns to meet their obligations. In contrast, states with high economic growth and smaller, less generous public sectors may not see improvements in their asset-to-liability ratio. Those states do, however, have smaller obligations relative to their fiscal capacity.

Conclusion: An Important Issue for Fiscal Federalism

The findings presented in this chapter demonstrate that states today, as in the mid-nineteenth century, rely heavily on risky investments to finance themselves. In the past, excessive reliance on risky investments led to state bankruptcy, and there are fears that similar outcomes could occur today. Certain states are more dependent on revenue from such investments, and many of the factors associated with the resulting pension risk are outlined here. Clearly the reliability of such a revenue source is extremely important to those states. However, it is also important to consider why the risk of bankruptcy or pension defaults for certain states is an issue for federalism and the country as a whole.

The risks of state and local pension obligations for fiscal federalism in the United States are difficult to overstate. The primary concern, obviously, is that the debt holders (or in this case, the pensioners) will not receive the payments that they were promised. Aside from the direct welfare costs, pensioners would likely rely on federal social insurance programs, which are financed in part by taxpayers in other states. Because many members of state and local pension systems are not currently covered by Social Security, these shadow liabilities are rarely considered. Moreover, the utility costs to pensioners might generate political pressure for a bailout by taxpayers outside the defaulting state. In addition to those pressures, the interconnectedness of financial markets opens the door for contagion. Default by one state could lead to a run on the municipal debt market, making it impossible for other states to finance their obligations and forcing them into default as well. The large size of public trust funds (they currently hold roughly 7.5 percent of all U.S. corporate equities) means that a rapid sell-off could force down asset prices, depressing returns and hampering other states. The viability of fiscal federalism depends on the viability of subnational financing and the management of system-wide risk.

Notes

1. Arthur Grinath, Richard Syllas, and John Joseph Wallis, "Sovereign Default and Repudiation: The Emerging-Market Debt Crisis in U.S. States: 1839–1843," Working Paper 10753 (Cambridge, Mass.: National Bureau of Economic Research, 1998).

2. Ibid.

3. James D. Savage, *Balanced Budget and American Politics* (Cornell University Press, 1988).

4. James M. Poterba, "State Responses to Fiscal Crises: The Effects of Budgetary Institutions and Politics," *Journal of Political Economy,* vol. 102, no. 4 (1994), pp. 799–821.

5. Robert Novy-Marx and Josh Rauh, "Public Pension Promises: How Big Are They and What Are They Worth?," *Journal of Finance,* vol. 66, no. 4 (2010), pp. 1207–245.

6. The correlation between plans' reported liabilities and the Novy-Marx and Rauh measure, both in levels and as a fraction of GDP, exceeds 0.99.

7. The Pew Center survey omits the large University of California and state of New York teachers' retirement systems, which I added back in. The Pew survey also omits the large New York City plans for which historical liability data were not available. When the liabilities of these plans are included in the independent variable, New York's earnings better fit the regression line. West Virginia likely underperforms the regression line due to the fact that it was constitutionally prohibited from holding equities until 1997. Data on pension liabilities suffer from yet another complication in that a number of states can transform these liabilities into formal debt through pension obligation bonds. This adds an additional source of noise to the liabilities measure.

8. See Public Plans Database, Boston College, Center for Retirement Research (http://pubplans.bc.edu).

9. See "Comparative Retirement Study, Wisconsin State Legislature, Legislative Council (http://legis.wisconsin.gov/lc/publications/crs.asp).

10. For a detailed description, see Daniel Shoag, "The Impact of Government Spending Shocks: Evidence on the Multiplier from State Pension Plan Returns," unpublished paper, Harvard University Kennedy School of Government, 2010.

11. Olivia S. Mitchell and Robert S. Smith, "Pension Funding in the Public Sector," *Review of Economics and Statistics,* vol. 76, no. 2 (1994), pp. 278–90; David Splinter, "State Pension Contributions and Fiscal Stress," unpublished paper, Rice University, 2010; Barbara A. Chaney, Paul A. Copley, and Mary S. Stone, "The Effect of Fiscal Stress and Balanced Budget Requirements on the Funding and Measurement of State Pension Obligations," *Journal of Accounting and Public Policy,* vol. 21, no. 4-5 (2002), pp. 287–313.

12. Alicia Munnell, Kelly Haverstick, and Jean-Pierre Aubry, "Why Does Funding Status Vary among State and Local Plans?," Research Brief (Boston College, Center for Retirement Research, 2008).

13. This is a misnomer in that governments ultimately have discretion over the amount contributed.

14. Factors are calculated for an individual with 30 years of service prior to retirement.

15. John Beshears and others, "Behavioral Economics Perspectives on Public Sector Pension Plans," *Journal of Pension Economics and Finance,* vol. 10, no. 2 (2011), pp. 315–36.

16. James H. Stock and Motohiro Yogo, "Testing for Weak Instruments in Linear IV Regression," in *Identification and Inference for Econometric Models: Essays in Honor of Thomas J. Rothenberg,* edited by J. H. Stock and D. W. K. Andrews (Cambridge University Press, 2005).

17. Richard Johnson, "Pension Underfunding and Liberal Retirement Benefits among State and Local Government Workers," *National Tax Journal,* vol. 50, no. 1(1997), pp. 113–42.

18. Splinter, "State Pension Contributions and Fiscal Stress"; Chaney, Copley, and Stone, "The Effect of Fiscal Stress and Balanced Budget Requirements on the Funding and Measurement of State Pension Obligations."

19. T. J. Bartik, *Who Benefits from State and Local Economic Development Policies?* (Kalamazoo, Mich.: W. E. Upjohn Institute for Employment Research, 1991).

20. Alicia Munnell and Laura Quimby, "Legal Constraints on Changes in State and Local Pensions," Research Brief (Boston College, Center for Retirement Research, 2012).

21. Jeffrey Brown and David Wilcox, "Discounting State and Local Pension Liabilities," *American Economic Review,* vol. 99, no. 2 (2009), pp. 538–42.

22. Mitchell and Smith, "Pension Funding in the Public Sector."

23. Shoag, "The Impact of Government Spending Shocks: Evidence on the Multiplier from State Pension Plan Returns." The variation in return is even larger for 2009, where the standard deviation across plans with June fiscal years was 5.8 percentage points.

24. James Farrell and Daniel Shoag, "Asset Management in Public DB and Non-DB Pension Plans," unpublished paper, Harvard University Kennedy School of Government and Florida Southern College, 2012.

PART

II

The Federalism Crisis Worldwide

DANIEL ZIBLATT

7

Between Centralization and Federalism in the European Union

In the European Union (EU) today, what are the prospects for the type of decentralized federalism described by Peterson and Nadler in the introduction to this volume? Can a robust multi-tiered political system be created and sustained in which the center and lower-tiered units have constitutionally protected separate spheres of influence and taxing and spending autonomy—and in which subunits have representation in a second chamber, as is standard in federal political systems?[1] In short, can a new supranational federalism save Europe in this age of financial crisis?

In the current context of economic turmoil, proposals for such reforms—previously only wished for by utopian Euro-enthusiasts or decried by conspiracy-theorist Euro-skeptics—have now suddenly entered the world of high politics and serious political discussion. When the European Monetary Union (EMU), which was launched in 1999, collided with the economic crisis of 2008–09, the EU's curiously split personality was exposed. On one hand, the EU is a highly successful, massive free trade zone that has an impressive regulatory reach, an emerging common foreign policy, and a common monetary policy. On the other hand, the European project has left fiscal power in the hands of national governments, and the European Union is, fiscally speaking, a political pygmy; its actual budget is minuscule, and it is arguably the largest political unit in history *without* the power to raise debt for itself. Indeed, it is above all the EU's peculiarly asymmetric sovereignty—marked by the absence of a common fiscal policy to match its remarkable common monetary power—that has, by all accounts, proved devastating to the union's ability to cushion itself against, or even to contain, the financial crisis.[2]

Therefore, the consensus view has become that *fiscal centralization* under the auspices of a federal government is necessary for the monetary union to survive.[3] However, behind the label "fiscal centralization" is a key question: what are the actual prospects of such an institutional arrangement for the EU? After all, unlike in the realm of economic theory, in the real world of politics what is "necessary" or even normatively desirable is no guarantee of any political outcome. Indeed, the European Union's chief political project, its monetary union, may simply dissolve under the weight of impending sovereign debt crises. Or, equally plausibly, even if the European Union's monetary union survives and finds itself increasingly armed with fiscal authority, it is not clear precisely how that institutional authority will be constituted: will the subunits be able to set their own budgets, as subunits do in federal political systems? Will they continue to raise debt? Will they be assured of "bailouts" by the center, or not? Thus, we confront the core question of this chapter: What factors should make us nervous about the viability in the European Union of the competitive federalism that this volume identifies and discusses?

In the following pages I argue that our tendency to view "strong national loyalties" as the major stumbling block to fiscal federalism in the EU is misplaced. All federations form atop local identities. If we look at other instances of forming polities out of formerly sovereign states, federalism represents an effective and normatively attractive method of coping with precisely those sorts of identities.[4] What, then, is the major problem facing the European Union in its aspiration to form a viable competitive federalism?

While recognizing the possibility that the European Union may be *sui generis,* a project without a historical model, I nonetheless argue that it is useful to draw on political theory and past efforts to form larger political unions out of formerly sovereign states—in particular the nineteenth-century cases of German and Italian state formation—to argue that over the long run a potentially bigger problem comes from what might appear to be a counterintuitive and even surprising source: the temptation to engage *unintentionally* in excessive forms of centralization that dismantle the subunit policy autonomy that is a requisite of federalism. Given the uneven histories and levels of institutional capacity across the member states of the European Union, the history of federalism's "failure" in nineteenth-century Italy, and a more general theory of direct and indirect rule,[5] there is reason to believe that a major and largely unanticipated snare for fiscal federalism in the European Union today is that the wrong type of fiscal centralization, a variant of classical *direct rule,* threatens to be unintentionally institutionalized. As EU policymakers repeatedly "rescue" weak states in one-off agreements sealed with centralizing conditions attached (for example, austerity measures), subunit budget autonomy is being usurped. The result is that in the face of economic crisis, the EU is in danger of sliding into a hybrid regime in which a type of direct centralization in certain domains is adopted that paradoxically undermines the core features of a federal, or "indirect," strategy of fiscal centralization.

I first compare two especially revealing historical instances of larger unions developing from sovereign states. Next, I draw out the theoretical lessons of that comparison. Finally, I discuss the implications of my analysis for the European Union today, seeking to find whether the emerging evidence suggests future institutional developments.

What Are the Preconditions of Federalism? Lessons from History

By nearly all accounts, fiscal centralization is necessary for the EU's monetary union to survive. It is now not only politicians—including Euro-enthusiast French and German statesmen who have long aspired to adopt a *gouvernement économique* or *Wirtschaftsregierung*—who make that argument.[6] After all, economic theorists have long emphasized the crucial role of fiscal centralization for the survival of monetary unions, including the European Monetary Union. Economists argue, for example, that the political center must possess the fiscal resources to support a "transfer union" that can cushion citizens against asymmetric economic shocks when a monetary union is laid atop highly diverse socioeconomic regions.[7] It is also widely recognized that the creation of centralized public debt is necessary to contain sovereign debt crises of the subunits as well as bank runs within member states.[8]

While other factors are certainly highlighted by different variants of optimum currency theory as necessary to sustain monetary unions, there is virtual consensus that fiscal centralization is pivotal. It is for that reason that economists, historians, and political scientists all look to the "Hamiltonian moment" in the United States, in which fiscal centralization (that is, public debt and taxing and spending autonomy) within a federal system was crucial for American political development.[9]

But what factors are likely to shape the precise institutional structure of such a fiscal arrangement? To say that "fiscal centralization" is necessary is to leave a series of crucial questions of institutional design unaddressed: Will the resulting polity look more like a federation or a unitary model of governance? Will subunits possess the right to determine their own revenue through taxation and debt? Will they face guarantees of "bailouts" that alter their incentives?[10] Will member state fiscal discipline be achieved, imposed by the EU or by the market?[11] In short, behind the much-vaunted label "fiscal centralization" lies a diversity of institutional forms that call for closer scrutiny.

Turning to past instances of efforts to forge unions out of formerly sovereign states is a powerful way to explore how institutions are coming to be shaped in the European Union today. Furthermore, if we expand our historical repertoire beyond the singular U.S. case that has attracted so much attention[12] to Europe's own multiple experiences with state formation, a richer and more revealing range of institutional outcomes moves to center stage. And more to the point, we move beyond the insight that fiscal centralization has powerful benefits for unions to a second observation: that the institutional makeup of fiscal centralization is not automatic and is itself a product of the caliber of institutions within the *potential* member states of a federation.

Lessons of a Less Familiar History: Germany and Italy in the 1860s

Two distant but similar cases of polity formation—the unification of Italy in 1861 and the unification of Germany in 1871—approximate a natural experiment, and comparing them is an especially fruitful way of examining whether and how federalism emerges when states fuse together in the way that they have in the European Union over the past sixty years.[13] The differences between the contemporary EU and these two historical cases of polity formation are, of course, substantial. But the similarities also are striking, and they reveal a broader logic of how polities institutionalize.

Comparison of nineteenth-century Germany and Italy reveals a great puzzle. In the 1850s and 1860s, two regional states—Piedmont in Italy and Prussia in Germany—undertook the national unification of the Italian and German states, respectively, under similar ideological, cultural, and power-structure conditions that ought to have led to similar institutional outcomes. After the failed democratic "national" revolutions of 1848 in Italy and Germany, the pragmatic political leadership of two militarily powerful states (Prussia and Piedmont) adopted the agenda of nationalism to expand each regional state's zone of political control in Europe. Furthermore, the chief "architects" of national unification in Italy and Germany in the 1860s—Cavour and Bismarck—undertook their political projects with a similar ideological suspicion of the dangers of excessive centralization, and in both cases there was a similar ideological commitment among key intellectual and political leaders to the notion of "federalism" as a solution to the history of division in both regions. Also, the deep-seated cultural and historical regional forces for and against national unification, rooted in uneven economic gradients in both regions, were similar.

Yet, despite these similarities, the two developers of Western Europe adopted very different patterns of territorial governance for each new nation-state. In Germany after 1866, the Prussian leadership, despite support for—and impressive prowess in key sectors of the military that would have allowed for—the conquest of Southern Germany, pursued a negotiated unification to create a system of federalism. By contrast, in Italy, the 1859 Piedmontese leadership, despite substantial support for a federal political order, pursued unification through a strategy of conquest in which Cavour's Piedmont absorbed all fiscal, policy, and jurisdictional authority and shifted power away from the seven Italian states to create a centralized Italian state, with the Piedmontese parliament, constitution, and king at the center.

Before elaborating on what these two historical cases can teach us about the institutional preconditions of federalism that has relevance for the European Union today, it is important to use these cases to dispense with two common claims about the European Union: that a strong federal ideology among policymakers will inoculate the European Union against any prospect of excessive centralization and that the existence of robust national and regional identities likewise are bulwarks that will make centralization beyond federalism utterly impossible. Both arguments, when we look at historical instances of political unions, are flawed and unsustainable.

The Limits of Ideas: Why Wanting Federalism Is Not Enough

First, if we consider the explanation that an ideological predisposition by relevant political elites matters above all else—which might argue that wanting federalism is a sufficient precondition—the two cases raise an empirical anomaly. In both nineteenth-century Italy and Germany the ideology of federalism thrived. Stefan Oeter (1998) has written of nineteenth-century Germany that "for Bismarck and his contemporaries it was utterly self-evident that a union of the German states could only take a federal form."[14] Though most scholars recognize that decentralist ideas were a vibrant part of nineteenth-century German political culture, it is all too often forgotten that, as Binkley (1935) noted of Italy in the 1860s, "the idea of confederation had been present in Italian statecraft for more than generation, not as an exotic political invention but as a seemingly inevitable alternative to the situation established in 1815."[15] One important historian of nineteenth-century European history has written similarly of post-1815 Italy: "The political discussions and proposed solutions returned time and again to the question of unity or federalism in a manner unknown even in Germany."[16]

Indeed, in the nineteenth century at least three consciously federalist intellectual strands existed in Italy: the neo-Guelphs, such as the priest Vicenzo Gioberti, who advocated a confederation of princes under the leadership of the pope; liberals such as Cattaneo and Ferrara, who argued for the creation of a federal and democratic Italy; and regional autonomists, found mostly among prominent political leaders in Sicily and Italy's south, who advocated a decentralized Italy that would protect regional autonomy. In the realm of ideas, federalism was a vibrant part of the political culture of Italy's intellectuals and visionaries.

But not only constitutional scholars and intellectuals advocated federalism in Italy. Important political leaders, first and foremost the Count of Cavour himself, were frequently open advocates of a vague sort of decentralization throughout the 1850s. Prime Minister Cavour made a famous speech in Parliament in

1850 that reflected the Piedmontese liberal-conservative consensus of the era by criticizing France's centralized prefectoral model. Even in the early 1860s, Cavour criticized too much centralization in calling for more regionalist concessions to Italy's south. In his biography of Cavour, Denis Mack Smith (1985) writes that "Cavour had always been a theoretical champion of decentralization and local self- government."[17] And, similarly, the "energetic group of men" that dominated the "Right" and Italian politics after Cavour's death in 1861until 1876, including Ricasoli, La Marmora, Minghetti, Lanaza, Spaventa, Sella, and Peruzzi, were long-time advocates of the confederative principles of Gioberti and Balbo. Yet by 1865, the weakness of institutions in Italy's south triggered a series of events, described below, and federalism in Italy was abandoned. In short, although an ideological commitment to decentralization may be a necessary condition for the creation of federal institutions, the failure of federalism in Italy in the 1860s shows that even a widespread ideological predisposition toward decentralized political organization clearly is not sufficient to guarantee the creation of a federal polity.

Why Strong Regional or National Loyalties Are Not a Problem for Federalism

We confront similar problems when considering arguments that assert strong regional loyalties make federalism more likely to emerge. Here, the Italy and Germany contrast is revealing: we find two similarly historically fragmented societies with different kinds of states. Important scholarship by Umbach (2000), among others, has convincingly made the case that contemporary German federalism is in part a historical legacy of the Holy Roman Empire, a long history of regional autonomy, and the German Reich of 1871.[18] Although accurate in the German context, such accounts cannot explain why a similarly long history of independent city-states, regions, and provinces did not produce federalism in Italy in the 1860s or after 1945. Why did Italian city-states and regions, as the locus of the proud loyalty of their residents since the Middle Ages, not produce the same federal institutional outcome generated by German city-states and regions? Again, we see that explicit comparison of Italy and Germany belies conventional wisdom regarding necessary preconditions for federalism.

The broader point is simple: arguments that use cultural or religious heterogeneity as an explanation for the form of governance tend to play loosely with their concepts and tend to adopt the logic and language of "functional necessity" (the idea that governance assumes a particular form because that form is "required" or "demanded"). Such functionalist reasoning tends to suffer from an underspecified indeterminism. That an institution is "needed" does not mean that it will be created. Rather, as the analysis here shows, the *demand* for federalism will go unmet unless there is a *supply* of "high state capacity" governance structures in place.

Institutional Preconditions: Blocking the Unintended Slide toward Centralization

What determined the adoption of federalism as a strategy of unification in Germany and federalism's failure in Italy? What lessons can be drawn from this? The key difference between the situation confronting Cavour in Italy in 1860 and Bismark in Germany in 1867—the one that generated the divergence in their strategies of unification—was the quality of the governance institutions in the subunits that would have made up the federation. In particular, in the existing states of pre-national Germany, a set of institutions with *high levels of state capacity* at the subunit level assured that the goals of unification (that is, greater fiscal resources, military personnel, social stability, and so forth) would be secure if the states were left intact, staffed by their own personnel, and given distinct areas of taxing and spending autonomy. By contrast, in the preexisting states of Italy, such institutional building blocks were decisively absent. In Italy, state makers believed that if the constituent states were left intact and untouched, the gains of unification would be insecure. That view gave rise to a strategy of "direct intervention" in the other Italian states by Piedmontese state builders, who centralized power by placing Piedmontese officials in Italy's periphery and eliminated completely the taxing and spending autonomy of the formerly sovereign states.

What evidence is there of the claim that this dynamic was driven by preexisting state capacity? First, in table 7-1, which presents three rough measures of governance capacity, we can see that the limited existing evidence suggests that on the eve of national unficiation in Italy, non-Piedmontese states suffered from severe problems of governance. That was the institutional landscape that faced state makers and would prompt a strategy of "unification by direct rule."

As table 7-2 makes clear, the gap between Piedmont and the states that it inherited was much higher than the gap between Prussia and the states that it would inherit several years later. A similar set of measures for the German states shows that on average, the non-Prussian states had equal if not higher levels of governance capacity (compare the last rows in each table). Unlike Piedmont, which was absorbing a series of highly weak states, in Germany, Prussia was absorbing a series of highly effective states.

What difference did that make for national unification? If we examine the unfolding of events in Italy in the 1860s, we can begin to see the parallels with that experience and the European Union today. As national unification was launched in 1859–60, achieving it through Cavour's preferred federal solution

Table 7-1. *State Capacity in Italian Regional States, 1850–60*

State	Measure 1 Extractive capacity (state revenue per capita, in lire)	Measure 2 Conscription rate (military personnel as percent of male population)	Measure 3 Regulative control (percent enrollment of primary school–age children)
Piedmont	32.2	2.3	93
Two Sicilies	14.2	2.0	18
Papal States	14.7	0.7	25–35
Tuscany	19.2	2.0	32
Modena	17.9	1.6	36
Parma	22	1.2	36
Lombardy-Veneto	. . .	. . .	90
Ratio of Piedmont and average of remaining states	1.83:1	1.53:1	2.3:1

Sources: See Daniel Ziblatt, *Structuring the State: The Formation of Italy and Germany and the Puzzle of Federalism* (Princeton University Press, 2006).

became increasingly difficult because of the nature of the governance structures in Italy's central and southern regions. Despite Cavour's own inclinations, the prospects of federalism faded in the face of collapsing states across Italy. The states that Piedmont would inherit with unification were, as the data above suggest, starkly different from the states that Prussia would inherit ten years later in Germany. In all six of the Italian states outside Piedmont, the 1848 parliaments and constitutions had been overturned and absolute monarchs once again ruled without parliamentary restraint.

In addition, especially in Italy's southern Papal States and the Kingdom of the Two Sicilies, public administration suffered. For example, in neither of the two latter states did the central government have a monopoly on taxation; in both cases, there were independent tax zones within the territory, which in theory was controlled by the central government.[19] Similarly, the ability of these states to maintain control over their own territory became increasingly questionable since peasant uprisings began to occur and were subdued only with the assistance of Austrian troops that were called in to bolster the arbitrary and sporadic rule of the central government.

As a result of this institutional landscape—again, one in which we might begin to see parallels with contemporary southern Europe—any Piedmontese inclinations to establish a federation foundered on two fronts. First, efforts to achieve continued autonomy for the preexisting states failed. There exists a

Table 7-2. *State Capacity in the German States, 1850–66*

State	Measure 1 Extractive capacity (state revenue per capita, in thaler)	Measure 2 Conscription rate (military personnel as percent of male population)	Measure 3 Regulative control (kilometers of roads per 1,000 square kilometers)
Prussia	5.5	2.2	66
Bavaria	6.1	4.3	112
Baden	6.2	1.1	136
Württemberg	6.0	1.4	148
Saxony	5.4	2.3	228
Hannover	5.2	2.8	141
Kurhessen	6.0	2.1	143
Darmstadt	5.2	2.8	229
Ratio of Prussia and average of remaining states	1:1.04	1:1.09	1:2.45

Sources: See Daniel Ziblatt, *Structuring the State: The Formation of Italy and Germany and the Puzzle of Federalism* (Princeton University Press, 2006).

massive record of diplomatic correspondence between Cavour and his Piedmontese officials stationed in the central Italian states during the turbulent period of 1859–61.[20] Two types of relevant evidence are found in that correspondence. First, we see repeated efforts by Piedmontese officials to establish working relationships with the Italian states that might have led to a federal bargain. For example, in the period 1858–59, Cavour's diplomatic representative in Tuscany made multiple offers of an alliance between Piedmont and Tuscany. Cavour's envoy called for efforts to fill an institutional vacuum as a result of "revolution" and "anarchy."[21]

Similar dynamics unfolded in the Kingdom of the Two Sicilies. There Piedmontese officials were assigned to the south and reported back to Turin their difficulties in maintaining an orderly system of tax collection. Piedmontese Finance Ministry officials stationed in Italy's south in the early 1860s reported to Cavour the "exhausted" state of public finances and the "collapse" of order and public safety.[22] Cavour received frequent calls mirroring the same sentiments from his officials in the south—"Permit me, excellency, to repeat to you the need for policemen [*carabinieri*] to save this country from ruin!"[23] Also, to the surprised eyes of Piedmontese officials arriving in Naples, another basic government task—elementary school education—was in desperate disrepair. The number of public school teachers employed as a percentage of the population was much lower in the Kingdom of the Two Sicilies than elsewhere in Italy[24] and observers were aghast at the state of the schools, reporting "the system of education did not need reform; it needed to be created."[25] To reassure those in the south, officials in Piedmont promised to provide not only police forces but also more administrative "staff" and "clerks" to maintain order.[26]

The efforts snowballed into the Piedmontese annexation of Italy's southern regions. Agostino Depretis, a Piedmontese official and later prime minister, reported on the unrest, lack of security forces, and unsustainable public finance situation and announced in letters to his colleagues in July 1860 that the only solution for managing the fiscal and social chaos was immediate annexation by Piedmont.[27] As officials and military personnel flowed to the south, all twenty-four governors were replaced on the island of Sicily; the Piedmontese constitution was extended to Sicily in August, as was the monetary system, copyright laws, system of communal administration, military code, and public security law. By the end of the year of 1860, 25,000 troops occupied southern Italy and existing elites and institutions had been dislodged.

Over the course of the next several years, proposals in the Piedmontese parliament to construct federalism were considered but failed for two reasons. First, having dismantled the proto-subunits of a federation, no subunits existed to insist on inclusion in the new constitution. Second, between 1860 and 1865, Piedmontese officials feared a return to revolutionary disorder if power were returned to the old system of governance. By 1865, federalism was dead and the formerly sovereign states of Italy had no administrative autonomy, no discretion with respect to public finance, and no representation in a second national chamber. In short, the institutional weakness of the preexisting states among the Italian states blocked the possibility of federalism.[28]

Whiffs of Smoke? Implications and Evidence for the European Union

What lessons from the Italian experience of state formation can be applied to the European Union? Certainly the two time periods are very different; the role of military conflict in forging unions is different; and the fact that integration today proceeds in a largely democratic environment alters the dynamics of political unions. Nonetheless, the analysis above presents two different modes of integrating sovereign states that Gerring and others (2011) has shown to operate in a variety of contexts, ranging from ancient to modern empires as well as contemporary nation-states.[29] What implications do these modes hold for the European Union? In the first—the "direct," or unitary mode, of political union, illustrated by the Italian case in the 1860s—fiscal coordination was achieved through two steps: first, the political center dismantled formerly sovereign states so that new personnel from the center could supplement and eventually substitute for old personnel; and, second, the political center restricted policy autonomy in the formerly sovereign subunits and gradually usurped greater and greater control of incorporated states. The unitary model in Italy was in large part an *unintentional* result of the efforts of the political elites to cope with weak peripheral states. This represents a unitary model of fiscal coordination or governance in its purest form.

By contrast, in the "indirect" or federal model, found in Germany in the 1860s, fiscal coordination and governance is achieved among formerly sovereign states, which are left intact, and a new parallel "central bureaucracy" is layered *atop* existing bureaucratic institutions; while a new parallel locus of fiscal coordination (concerning, for example, central debt and central fiscal policy) is created atop the formerly sovereign subunits, those units retain policy autonomy with respect to taxing and spending. While systems for sharing public revenue and collaborating were developed among the subunits and the center in Germany through the nineteenth century and in the post–World War II period,[30] the subunits and the center remained constitutionally distinct and autonomous. It is only the latter form of political union that leads to robust federalism.

In which of these two directions is the European Union headed? Of course, in grand historical terms, the European Union project to build federalism—that is, to construct a centralized fiscal system to match its centralized monetary system—is only in its infancy, thus making full-blown analysis of the direction of institutional evolution difficult. Nonetheless, while it may be difficult to find "smoking gun" evidence, whiffs of smoke are visible that suggest the direction of future political development. Initial evidence suggests that not unlike Italy in the 1860s, the European Union is ironically achieving fiscal coordination not through a "federal" model, as one might expect from a loose confederation of nation-states, but is instead gradually institutionalizing itself in some domains along a unitary model of governance to substitute for the *weakness* in some of its member states.

Rather than creating an "indirect," or federal, form of rule, which would add a new layer of fiscal policy at the top of the federation (for example, one involving more robust taxation or pooled sovereign debt) as was done in Germany in the 1860s and in the United States after the 1780s, the EU aims to achieve fiscal coordination by acting like a central finance ministry. In so doing, it rewrites national budgets that violate debt and deficit rules, imposes EU-level limits on member-state spending in the form of budget deficit rules, and provides EU finance personnel the capacity to supersede national-level state personnel. In contrast to developments in the EU, in the U.S. federal system, state-level debt was famously absorbed in the 1780s by the federal government under the financial plan of Alexander Hamilton, the first Treasury Secretary, *without public policy conditions.* And, most decisively, when fiscal discipline among U.S. states emerged over the nineteenth century (in the 1840s and during the Reconstruction era), it emerged "from below" at the initiative of U.S. state legislatures themselves *without any enforcement or even encouragement from the federal government.*[31] In short, in contrast to the pattern in Germany and the United States, in the EU today an incipient unitary pattern is identifiable.

There is, however, an important caveat to be added: the EU's unitary model of governance is being *asymmetrically* introduced in the European Union, in *some* member states only. The result is the emergence of what might be described as an "asymmetrical unitary model" of governance that is in some ways the mirror image of the asymmetrical federalism that has developed in places such as Spain, Russia, and Canada.

Two questions remain. First, what evidence is there that this is being driven by state weakness within member states? Second, is there more concrete evidence about the process of integration that lends support to these claims? On the first question, table 7-3 presents some rudimentary data on contemporary Europe that lends support to the idea that substantial unevenness of governance exists across the European Union, which we would expect to lead to a unitary model of governance. On three major and contemporary proxies of state capacity in the EU—tax evasion rates, scope of the informal/unofficial economy, and historical rates of EU member-state noncompliance with EU law—there appears to be substantial variation between the northern historical "core" and southern historical "periphery."[32]

Indeed, the discrepancy between state capacity at the core and at the periphery in contemporary Europe certainly looks much more like the landscape of pre-unification Italy than of Germany (see tables 7-1 and 7-2). When we think of the relationship of Germany and Greece today, it is quite easy to see parallels with the relationship of Piedmont and the Kingdom of the Two Sicilies. However, as table 7-3 makes clear, several other states (for example, France, the Netherlands, and so forth) in Northern Europe match the "core" state of Germany in terms of governance capacity; in contrast, Piedmont stood out as the only well-developed state in nineteenth-century Italy. This important difference suggests a basis for expecting an asymmetric unitary model of governance in which direct rule is established in the weakest units within the European Union.

The starting conditions may be similar, but what about the process of European integration itself? Is it following the "Piedmontese" model? First, the European Union integration process is long-standing. It began in 1951 with the European Coal and Steel Community, made up of the Benelux countries, France, Germany, and Italy; expanded into the European Economic Union in 1957; and reached a major milestone with the formation of a single market in

Table 7-3. *State Capacity in Largest Member States of the European Union,*
1970s–2010

Member state	Measure 1 Tax evasion rate (concealed consumption as percent of GDP, based on VAT)	Measure 2 Unofficial economy (economic activity not reported in official GDP figures as a percentage of official GDP)	Measure 3 Failure to implement EU directives (annual average noncompliance rate, 1972–93)
Germany	17.9	15.0	1.91
France	25.3	14.9	1.82
Sweden	21.0	18.0	NA
Netherlands	17.6	13.2	1.18
Greece	21.5	27.3	4.30
Spain	27.9	22.8	3.40
Italy	38.5	27.0	7.00
Portugal	30.7	22.3	0.40
Ireland	29.8	15.8	1.11
Ratio of Germany and average of other states	1:1.48	1:1.34	1:1.43

Sources: Tax evasion data are estimates from 2000–03 of what the authors call "concealed con-sumption," based on missing value-added tax (VAT); see Edward Christie and Mario Holzner, "What Explains Tax Evasion? An Empirical Assessment Based on European Data," Working paper 40 (Vienna Institute for International Economic Studies, 2006). The size of the "informal economy" is the average score for 1999–2009 measured for the World Bank through a model that uses data on the labor market, currency in circulation, and several other indicators to predict the share of GDP of economic activity not reported in official GDP statistics; see Friedrich Schneider and others, "Shadow Economies All Over the World: New Estimates for 162 Countries from 1999 to 2007," Policy Research Working Paper 5356 (World Bank Development Research Group, Poverty and Inequality Team, July 2010). Mean scores of member-state noncompliance with EU directives between 1972 and 1993 are reported in Heather Mbaye, "Why National States Comply with Supranational Law," *European Union Politics*, vol. 2, no. 3 (2001), p. 269.

1985. But what is crucial for our purposes is the attempt beginning in the 1970s to try to create a common monetary policy—given special impetus by the col-lapse of the Bretton Woods system in the 1970s, which triggered unprecedented exchange range instability—and a new European monetary system in 1979, in which Germany and France instituted fixed but adjustable exchange rates for all member states except the United Kingdom.[33]

The combination of several major events triggered further monetary coop-eration in this period. First, the Single European Act (1985), which liberalized capital markets, prompted major currency fluctuations in the late 1980s in the context of uncoordinated national monetary policies, making the practical case for coordinated if not centralized monetary policy. Second, German unification in 1989–90 prompted nervousness with regard to national security among British and French politicians, which put major political pressure on Germany's leadership (Helmut Kohl and his foreign minister, Hans-Dieter Genscher) to present itself as committed to the European project and willing to submerge its national currency to tie itself to Europe.[34]

But, crucially for our purposes, the *conditions* attached to the European Monetary Union program as it developed through the 1990s established a new justification for *direct* intervention of the EU's shared standards in national fiscal policy. That represented a decisive juncture—a "parting of the ways"—that in effect established what Peter Hall (1993) calls a "policy paradigm" for future efforts at fiscal coordination.[35] The architects of the monetary union were certainly aware of the need for fiscal coordination to accompany monetary integration. But rather than pursue the undoubtedly politically contentious project of building up the centralized fiscal apparatus of an expanded EU budget through new taxing or spending powers or an EU common debt instrument, the Delors Report in 1989, the Maastricht Treaty in 1992, and the European Stability and Growth Pact (ESGP) in 1997 all sought "fiscal coordination" by stipulating strict compliance with a 3 percent budget deficit ratio and by limiting all national debt ratios to 60 percent. In addition, the pact entailed annual "check-ups" and reports by the EU, accompanied by policy recommendations to ensure compliance.[36] While no concrete policy instruments were introduced to guarantee the enforcement of those terms—and Germany and France were famously the first to violate them—EU officials had developed a general model for trying to cope with fiscal coordination, a model that seemed sustainable during an economic boom.

However, the economic crisis that began in the United States in the fall of 2008 collided explosively with this precarious institutional arrangement in which monetary and fiscal sovereignty was divided between the EU and its member states, arguably giving rise to Europe's current sovereign debt crisis. As a result, new impetus was given to real fiscal coordination. Some serious proposals have been made for what Herman Van Rompuy, the president of the European Council, ambitiously called in his June 2012 report to the Council of Ministers a "genuine economic and monetary union," including often unpopular proposals for "Blue Bonds" (see, for example, Delpla and von Weizaecker 2010), which would in federal or indirect fashion, layer "central" power atop existing nation-states' arenas of power.[37] Equally ambitious would be a new, EU-level, financial transactions tax layered atop existing member-state fiscal structures.[38] However, most measures so far flow largely from the same paradigm as the 1997 European Stability and Growth Pact, which implies a direct or unitary model of governance that simply seeks coordination by removing taxing and spending autonomy from "irresponsible" subunits.

To be sure, the early moves in 2009 to address the crisis were halting and insufficient. The European Commission, for example, initially warned France, Greece, Spain, and Ireland about their debt levels in April 2009, prompted in part by the January 2009 admission by Greece that its budget deficit was 12.7 percent, not 3.7 percent.[39] Later in 2009, the International Monetary Fund hammered out an unused $22 billion safety net for Greece; also in 2009, the European Union created the temporary European Financial Stability Facility (EFSF).

More significant efforts that began in 2010 to provide the EU itself with the tools to impose fiscal coordination have involved three main measures with typically unintelligible Euro-lingo names: the European Semester, the Euro Plus Pact, and the so-called "Six-Pack" measures. They in turn culminated in an alteration of the Lisbon Treaty itself with the formalization of all of these earlier agreements in the Treaty on Stability, Coordination, and Governance, which was signed in March 2012. The European Semester, introduced in March 2010, was conceptualized as a follow-on to the original 1997 European Growth and Stability Pact; it introduced budget "surveillance" procedures in which member states submit their budgets to the EU Commission for assessment and approval. Its aim, which was to increase coordination of member-state fiscal policy, is described in a report by the Bertelsmann Foundation as "significant because member states were previously not obligated to make their economic policies contingent on EU-level influence or approval."[40] The next two measures, the March 2011 Euro Plus Pact and the November 2011 "Six Pack" agreement (so called for its six main articles), gave more "teeth" to previous measures by combining budget surveillance measures with automatic sanctions for violations, a position advocated by Germany, against France's wishes.

All of these measures were then formally incorporated in March 2012 in the Treaty on Stability, Coordination, and Governance. It is true that as of January 2013, all members of the monetary union had committed themselves to adopting national laws (at the constitutional level) by January 2014 to implement balanced budgets, thereby in *principle* ensuring that fiscal centralization is adopted on a formally "voluntary" basis. Beneath the appearance of formal consent, however, the reality was very different: members faced the implicit but serious threat of finding themselves in a situation in which they would have had to withdraw from the monetary union if they had not consented. It is clear that the creation of centralized fiscal power in the EU has been achieved by informally requiring or imposing balanced budget requirements on member states. This remarkable centralizing development is not insignificant. Unlike in the United States, where such state-level balanced budget rules were initiated entirely by the states themselves in the mid-nineteenth century on an uncoordinated basis in response to market pressures, in the EU the impetus has come from richer member states using the power and prestige of the EU to forge fiscal union, in effect, from above.

The developments in Greece can be used to illustrate the "weak states trigger direct rule" logic at work. First, as recent reports and scholarly work have demonstrated in a rigorous and fine-grained way, tax evasion, a key indicator of state weakness, is rampant in Greece.[41] Fiscal problems in Greece are not merely a matter of excessive spending; they also reflect insufficient revenue, a result of the weak state and robust informal economy.[42] The perception of state weakness has prompted European officials, including the German finance minister, Wolfgang Schäuble, to decry Greece as a "bottomless pit."[43] As Greek budgets continued to teeter on the brink of insolvency and the bond spreads never quite made it out of dangerous heights, it was only to be expected that certain northern states might suggest "helping" more directly.

That help—which began even before the March 2012 treaty, in September 2011—involved EU and IMF inspectors, also known as "Troika inspectors." These officials have controlled the Greek government's actions within the framework of the stabilization package and have ensured its correct implementation by making the transfer of each new tranche of the bailout funds contingent on the Greek government's agreement to suggested reforms.[44] As Jean-Claude Juncker put it, "We need [to provide] inspectors or pedagogical assistance, without wishing to insult the Greek people." To Juncker, the ideal solution would be to appoint an EU commissioner tasked with building the Greek economy.[45] That commissioner, who would essentially develop Greece's economic strategy, would have the power to override Greek politicians in hopes of arriving at something compatible with the larger European system. Although that idea was abandoned, it exposes the dynamic underpinning the process. In addition, proposed "solutions" have not been restricted to government circles. One of the boldest initiatives came in the form of an offer from 160 German tax collectors who volunteered to help collect from the nonpaying Greeks, even before the Greek government had requested such "help"![46] In the end, the Germans ran a number of education seminars that petered out by June 2012, mainly due to a lack of Greek enthusiasm.

Most important, however, public policy has been dramatically altered in Greece: major cuts in public sector jobs have been proposed, as has the liberalization of labor laws and the lowering of the minimum wage, along with a whole series of other policy measures.[47] Less remarkable than the nature of these policy changes is this: what has hitherto been only a loose confederation of states, the European Union, may in a sense "leap-frog" beyond federalism to something approaching a unitary pattern of fiscal governance wherein the center dictates subunit taxing and spending in a way that would be unfathomable in a federation.

Conclusion: Broader Lessons

As should now be clear, behind the terms "fiscal centralization" and "fiscal coordination" is a diverse set of institutional formulas for coping with the European Union's currently divided sovereignty. One institutional formula to achieve fiscal coordination that is gaining increased support and currency among key leaders, including the president of the European Council (Herman Van Rompuy) and Germany's chancellor (Angela Merkel), is one in which the fiscal power of the center (including the power to create Euro-bonds) comes only in exchange for the EU being given the authority to monitor and rewrite the budgets of national governments that violate debt and deficit ceilings.[48] While this formula certainly addresses the technical problem of fiscal coordination head on, it is a radical institutional departure from the status quo. To see how radical this proposal truly is, the reader can try to imagine how U.S. state governors or state legislatures would respond if U.S. Treasury officials or members of Congress themselves directly substituted for state officials and, uninvited, tried to write U.S. state budgets.

In contrast to the essentially "unitary" or "direct" form of fiscal coordination that is being carried out in the EU, federalism of the type described by Peterson and Nadler in the introduction to this volume represents an option not being pursued in the EU today: one in which a central government may have massive fiscal and monetary power but that power is *layered atop* subunits that retain sovereignty and significant constitutionally protected control over their own budgets and have important administrative autonomy as well as direct political representation at the "center," usually through second chambers (for example, the U.S. Senate and the German *Bundesrat*). The key question facing Europe today is whether current proposals—to create, for example, a central fiscal authority that directly monitors member states' budgets and personnel—is actually the best way to build a fiscally centralized polity. One may ask how an institutional formula of federal "layering" is applied without removing power from member states. After all, the political reality in Europe today may be that powerful member states, such as Germany, will agree to pool debt only if they gain veto power over other member states' budgets. Indeed, that is probably correct, and it reflects precisely the unevenness of governing capacity in Europe's member states. To put it most sharply, *fiscal coordination is being achieved today in the European Union's own "Hamiltonian moment" at the price of federalism.*

What are the broader lessons of the events unfolding in Europe today? First, the classic trade-off between passing power to a political center and ensuring the robust accountability of that center—a trade-off that American anti-federalists and contemporary European skeptics both have identified as essentially inescapable—can, I would argue, be avoided through the institutional solution of federalism. Here, in effect, I make a normative case for federalism. There are many arguments for why fiscal centralization is necessary for the European Union: to provide for social welfare; to absorb economic shocks in a common currency area; to provide for pooled debt to absorb sovereign debt shocks; and to promote social solidarity. However, contemporary Euro-skeptics as well as American anti-federalists of the eighteenth century thought that those benefits came at a price—that centralization meant the transfer of power without any accompanying instruments for ensuring the accountability and responsiveness of the central government and that it would lead to tyranny. Federalism is in fact a normatively compelling solution to this classic dilemma: by providing local and central representative bodies with *control over* government, the two goals of effectiveness and accountability can be achieved.

Second, however, the viability of the institutional solution of federalism is not automatic or guaranteed. Rather, a key lesson of this chapter is that its viability hinges on very particular institutional preconditions that, for example, nineteenth-century Italy lacked: the subunits themselves must possess similar levels of institutional or governance capacity. Federalism and the normal rules of fiscal discipline hold only when the subunits possess that capacity. The claim here, based on two historical cases of integration, offers a positive theory of federalism.

Finally, without these fundamental institutional attributes of state capacity at the subunit level, we find ourselves ironically back in the world of Euro-skeptics and anti-federalists; indeed, without institutional capacity, federalism cannot be sustained and anti-federalists appear to be correct—centralization comes, but in a different form: *centralization without accountability*. As the European Union intrepidly pursues fiscal centralization without federalism, it is above all this pitfall that the union will encounter.

Notes

1. Arend Lijphart, *Patterns of Democracy* (Yale University Press, 1999); William H. Riker, *Federalism: Origin, Operation, Significance* (Boston: Little, Brown, and Company, 1964).

2. Thomas J. Sargent, "United States Then, Europe Now," Nobel Prize Lecture, Stockholm, Sweden, December 8, 2011; Paul Krugman, "Apocalypse Fairly Soon," *New York Times,* May 17, 2012.

3. Krugman, "Apocalypse Fairly Soon"; Niall Ferguson and Pierpaolo Barbieri, "Merkel Can Achieve Fiscal Union in Europe," *Financial Times,* May 2, 2012.

4. Ugo Amoretti and Nancy Bermeo, *Federalism and Territorial Cleavages* (Johns Hopkins University Press, 2004); Jacob T. Levy, "Federalism, Liberalism, and the Separation of Loyalties," *American Political Science Review*, vol. 101, no. 3 (2007), pp. 459–77.

5. John Gerring and others, "An Institutional Theory of Direct and Indirect Rule," *World Politics*, vol. 63, no. 3 (July 2011), pp. 377–433.

6. See Nicolas Jabko, "Which Economic Governance for the European Union? Facing Up to the Problem of Divided Sovereignty," *Swedish Institute for European Policy Studies*, vol. 2 (2011).

7. Wallace E. Oates, "Fiscal Federalism and the European Union: Some Reflections," unpublished paper presented at a conference sponsored by the Societa Italiana di Economia Pubblica, Pavia University, October 4–5, 2002, pp. 36–57; Krugman, "Apocalypse Fairly Soon."

8. Jacques Delpla and Jakob von Weizsäcker, "The Blue Bond Proposal," *Bruegel*, vol. 3 (May 2010).

9. Sargent, "United States Then, Europe Now"; Kathleen McNamara, "It's the Politics, Stupid," *Foreign Policy* (December 2011); C. Randall Henning and Martin Kessler, "Fiscal Federalism: U.S. History for Architects of Europe's Fiscal Union," Bruegel Essay and Lecture Series (2012).

10. See Jonathan Rodden, *Hamilton's Paradox: The Promise and Peril of Fiscal Federalism* (Cambridge University Press, 2006).

11. One absolutely critical difference between the EU and the United States is that balanced budget rules emerged in U.S. states over time and under no pressure from the federal government or other states, whereas balanced budget rules are being imposed on member states legislatively and constitutionally by the EU and other member states. See Henning and Kessler, "Fiscal Federalism: U.S. History for Architects of Europe's Fiscal Union."

12. See, for example, Sargent, "United States Then, Europe Now"; Henning and Kessler, "Fiscal Federalism: U.S. History for Architects of Europe's Fiscal Union."

13. The following draws directly on Daniel Ziblatt, "Rethinking the Origins of Federalism: Puzzle, Theory, and Evidence from Nineteenth-Century Europe," *World Politics*, vol. 57, no. 1 (October 2004), pp. 70–98; Daniel Ziblatt, *Structuring the State: the Formation of Italy and the Puzzle of Federalism* (Princeton University Press, 2006); and Daniel Ziblatt, "Il perché dell'assenza di federalismo in Italia [Why Is There No Federalism in Italy?]," *Rivista Italiana di Scienza Politica*, vol. 36, no. 2 (2006), pp. 296–308, as well as a range of other secondary sources cited in the text.

14. Stefan Oeter, *Integration und Subsidiarität im deutschen Bundesstaatsrecht: Untersuchungen zu Bundesstaatstheorie unter dem Grundgesetz* [Integration and Subsidiarity in German Federal Constitutional Law: A Study of Federalism Theory in the Constitution] (Tübingen: J.C.B. Mohr Siebeck, 1998), p. 29.

15. Robert Binkley, *Realism and Nationalism: 1852–1871* (New York: Harper and Row, 1935), p. 197.

16. Stuart Woolf, *The Italian Risorgimento* (New York: Barnes and Noble, 1969), p. 7.

17. Denis Mack Smith, *Cavour* (London: Weidenfeld and Nicolson, 1985), p. 249.

18. Maiken Umbach, *Federalism and Enlightenment in Germany, 1740–1806* (London: Hambledon Press, 2000).

19. Luigi Izzo, *La Finanza Pubblica: Nel Primo Decennio Dell'Unita Italiana* [Public Finance in the First Decade of Italian Unification] (Milan: Dottore a Giuffre Editore, 1962), pp. 3–4.

20. See Cavour, *Carteggi di Cavour: La Liberazione del Mezzogiorno e la formazione del Regno d'Italie* [Cavour, The Liberation of the Mezzogiorno and the Formation of the Kingdom of Italy], vol. 2 (Bologna: Nicola Zanichelli, 1961); Carlo Pischedda and Rosanna Roccía, *Camillo Cavour Epistolario* [Camillo Cavour's Letters] (Florence: Leo S. Olschki Editore, 2000).

21. Those were the words of Cavour's envoy in Tuscany in a report in April 27, 1859. See Ziblatt, "Rethinking the Origins of Federalism," p. 85.

22. Ziblatt, "Rethinking the Origins of Federalism," p. 86.

23. Pischedda and Roccía, *Camillo Cavour Epistolario* [Camillo Cavour's Letters], August 2, 1860, Doc. 528, p. 8.

24. Alberto Caracciolo, *Stato e societa civile* [*The State and Civil Society*] (Turin: Giulio Einaudi, 1960), p. 119.

25. James Albisetti, "Julie Schwabe and the Poor of Naples," paper prepared for presentation at the International Standing Conference for the History of Education, Birmingham, England, July 12–15, 2001.

26. Pischedda and Roccía, *Camillo Cavour Epistolario* [Camillo Cavour's Letters], August 17, 1860, Doc. 647, p. 99.

27. Lucy Riall, *Sicily and the Unification of Italy* (Oxford: Clarendon Press, 1998), p. 84.

28. In Ziblatt, "Rethinking the Origins of Federalism"; Ziblatt, *Structuring the State: The Formation of Italy and the Puzzle of Federalism;* and Ziblatt, "Il perché dell'assenza di federalismo in Italia [Why Is There No Federalism in Italy?]." I also analyze the fate of federalism in Germany in this period, which represents a contrasting story of high governance capacity in the subunits generating a federal strategy of polity formation in which existing subunits were preserved in the new larger political entity, maintaining their control of taxing and spending policy, handing the new imperial center control only of tariff revenue.

29. Gerring and others, "An Institutional Theory of Direct and Indirect Rule."

30. See Gerhard Lehmbruch, *Parteienwettbewerb im Bundesstaat* [Party Competition in a Federal State] (Opladen: Westdeutscher Verlag, 2000),

31. Henning and Kessler, "Fiscal Federalism: U.S. History for Architects of Europe's Fiscal Union."

32. On the latter measure, while scholarship has noted several determinants of failure to comply with EU law among EU member states (measured by the EU Commission's opening of a dossier on a member state on a particular infringement), the most consistent predictor of noncompliance is "weak state capacity," typically measured by bureaucratic weakness or corruption. See Heather Mbaye, "Why National States Comply with Supranational Law," *European Union Politics,* vol. 2, no. 3 (2001), pp. 259–81.

33. Barry Eichengreen, *The European Economy since 1945* (Princeton University Press, 2007).

34. Ibid., p. 354.

35. Peter Hall, "Policy Paradigms, Social Learning, and the State: The Case of Economic Policymaking in Britain," *Comparative Politics*, vol. 25, no. 3 (April 1993), pp. 275–96.

36. Ibid., p. 353.

37. Delpla and von Weizsäcker, "The Blue Bond Proposal."

38. Roni Mann, "The Regulatory Road Not Taken," *Wissenschaftszentrum Mitteilungen*, vol. 137 (September 2012) (www.wzb.eu/sites/default/files/publikationen/wzb_mitteilungen/13-16.pdf).

39. "Timeline: The Unfolding Euro-Zone Crisis," BBC News, June 13, 2012.

40. "What Does Europe Want? The Who and How of Resolving the Euro Crisis" (Bertelsmann Foundation, 2012), p. 17 (www.bfna.org/sites/default/files/publications/BF-WhatDoesEurope-eBook%20(18%20Jan%202012).pdf).

41. See, for example, Nikolaos Artavanis, Adair Morse, and Margarita Tsoutsoura, "Tax Evasion across Industries: Soft Credit Evidence from Greece," Chicago Booth Research Paper 12-24 (June 2012) (http://faculty.chicagobooth.edu/adair.morse/research/papers/TaxEvasionWeb.pdf).

42. Harris Mylonas, "Is Greece a Failing Developed State?" in *The Konstantinos Karamanlis Institute for Democracy Yearbook 2011: The Global Economic Crisis and the Case of Greece,* edited by Konstantina E. Botsiou and Antonis Klapsis (Springer, 2011); Evan Liaras and Harris Mylonas, "What Really Went Wrong in Greece?," CNN.com, November 20, 2011.

43. "Greece-Germany Tension Rises, Reflects Wider Euro Rift," Reuters, February 16, 2012.

44. "EU-Kontrolleure sollen Griechen-Krise stoppen [EU Controllers Should Stop the Greece Crisis]," *Handelsblatt,* September 8, 2011.

45. Stefanie Bolzen and Florian Eder, "Überwachen, ohne die Griechen zu beleidigen [Keeping Guard without Offending the Greeks]," *Die Welt,* February 29, 2012 (www.welt.de/politik/ausland/article13893906/Ueberwachen-ohne-die-Griechen-zu-beleidigen.html).

46. "Freiwillige sollen in Griechenland Steuern eintreiben [Volunteers Will Organize Taxation in Greece]," *Focus Money Online,* February 25, 2012 (www.focus.de/finanzen/news/staatsverschuldung/160-freiwillige-deutsche-finanzbeamte-sollen-athen-helfen_aid_717664.html).

47. Indeed, one driver of the austerity measures is the effort to combat public sector unions in Greece. Although northern European public sector unions are among the strongest and most encompassing in the world (see Geoffrey Garrett and Christopher Way, "Public Sector Unions, Corporatism, and Macroeconomic Performance," *Comparative Political Studies,* vol. 32 (1999), pp. 411–34), labor costs have remained contained there, perhaps in large part due to the broader context of institutionalized corporatism, which does not exist in southern Europe and has long been credited with containing labor costs in periods of economic growth.

48. "EU Plan to Rewrite Budget Rules," *Financial Times,* June 25, 2012.

HENRIK ENDERLEIN *and* CAMILLO VON MÜLLER

8

German Federalism at the Crossroads

Germany's fiscal situation in the aftermath of the recent financial crisis and the subsequent "Great Recession" is a paradox. While the debt of the federal government (henceforth the *Bund*) has remained relatively stable in comparison with that of many other industrialized countries and the national outlook is clearly positive, the subnational units in Germany, the *Länder,* face a much more difficult situation. Debt and deficit levels increased rapidly during the crisis and its immediate aftermath. While the majority of the *Länder* have reduced their structural deficits since then,[1] as of 2012 budgetary crises were pending for the *Länder* of Bremen, Saarland, and Schleswig-Holstein.[2] Moreover, as of 2012 an additional number of *Länder* violated thresholds established by the German Stability Council (which represents both the *Bund* and the *Länder*) to measure the fiscal health of public finances in Germany, such as the ratio of interest paid on debt to tax revenues (Berlin), debt per capita (Berlin, Saxony-Anhalt), structural financial deficit per capita (Hamburg), and the loan finance quotient, which measures the percentage of expenditures financed on credit (Hesse, Rhineland-Palatine).[3] Because different *Länder* face varying post-crisis challenges, the financial outlook for the *Länder* is far more mixed than for the *Bund.*

To understand why that is the case, it is important to highlight the differences between the very special type of fiscal federalism that was built into the German Federal Republic after World War II and the other types of fiscally federal regimes discussed in this book. This chapter argues that the German setup has major peculiarities, which add up to what can be labeled the "German problem" in fiscal federalism. The chapter describes that problem and explains the impact of the crisis on the debate surrounding German fiscal federalism in general and the conduct of fiscal policies in the *Länder* in particular.

It is important to single out three key core features of German federalism. First, there is a major asymmetry in the allocation of powers between the

German federation and the *Länder*. While taxes raised at the *Bund* and at the *Länder* level account for equal shares of total German tax revenues (between 40 and 45 percent), the expenditure autonomy of the *Länder* is more limited than that of the *Bund*.[4] *Länder* governments are thus often viewed as "spending" authorities with effectively limited power.[5]

Second, the *Länder* enjoy a de facto bailout guarantee from the *Bund*. This guarantee indirectly derives from a clause in the German constitution (Basic Law) requiring the German federal system to ensure and preserve uniform and equal living conditions throughout the federal territory. If a *Land* faces serious financial difficulties, it can file a complaint with the German Constitutional Court and request funds from the federal government. Two *Länder* (Saarland and Bremen) won their cases in 1992 and 2005 and are still receiving federal money,[6] whereas Berlin lost its case in 2006. However, many market participants still believe that there is a clear bailout guarantee. This chapter discusses this issue in detail.

Third, the *Länder* are very different in terms of their demographics, economics, and fiscal policies. For example, population density is lowest in the state of Mecklenburg–Pomerania, which has 71 people per square kilometer, while the state of North Rhine–Westphalia has 523 people and the state of Berlin has 3,899 people per square kilometer.[7] Differences also apply with respect to economic productivity, which is highest in the state of Hamburg, where GDP per capita as of 2011 was €52,731; in contrast, GDP per capita in the state of Thuringia was €21,608. In terms of fiscal policies, structural differences become apparent in comparing per capita government expenditures, which as of 2011 were highest in the state of Bremen (€8,103) and lowest in the states of Schleswig-Holstein (€3,404), Lower Saxony (€3,435), and Bavaria (€3,469).[8]

The *Länder* vary also in terms of their administration. For example, while most states are administered as political units that comprise both urban and rural areas, there are three "city states"—Berlin, Hamburg, and Bremen—which enjoy *Länder* status for historic reasons. Differences exist also in terms of infrastructure. For example, the former East German states are less developed in structural terms than their counterparts in former West Germany. Less than 10 percent of the geographic area of the states of Brandenburg, Mecklenburg-Pomerania, and Thuringia is used for housing and transportation while 22.4 percent is used in Saarland, 15.5 percent in Hesse, and 14.1 percent in Baden-Württemberg).[9] Table 8-1 presents an overview of the key structural economic features and the debt levels of the *Länder* before and after the recent financial crisis as well as government expenditures before and after the crisis. The table summarizes the burden that the crisis has placed on government budgets and expenditures.

Table 8-1. *Economic and Fiscal Profile of German Länder before and after the Crisis: Current GDP, Pre- and Post-Crisis Government Finances, in Current Prices*

	GDP per capita (euros)	Government expenditures per capita (euros)		Government debt in credit markets (euros, millions)	
Land	2011	2007	2011	2007	2011
Baden-Württemberg	34,943	3,055	3,788	41,710	61,625
Bavaria	35,545	2,700	3,469	22,766	28,713
Berlin	29,153	6,063	6,643	56,645	61,368
Brandenburg	22,051	3,891	4,261	17,280	19,591
Bremen	42,505	6,266	8,103	14,305	18,888
Hamburg	52,731	5,965	7,159	21,619	24,891
Hesse	37,616	3,512	3,846	29,969	38,917
Mecklenburg–Pomerania	21,363	4,000	4,486	10,074	10,176
Lower Saxony	28,306	2,974	3,435	49,446	56,309
North Rhine–Westphalia	31,893	2,766	3,652	114,091	180,019
Rhineland-Palatine	28,311	3,125	3,687	26,825	31,884
Saarland	30,059	3,268	3,947	9,143	12,257
Saxony	22,970	3,673	3,960	11,064	5,623
Saxony-Anhalt	22,336	4,088	4,794	20,082	20,655
Schleswig–Holstein	25,967	3,023	3,404	22,029	27,918
Thuringia	21,608	3,954	4,310	15,704	16,549

Sources: Column 1: Statistisches Landesamt Baden-Württemberg, "Bruttoinlandsprodukt je Einwohner Wirtschaftskraft [GDP per capita]," 2012 (www.statistik-bw.de); columns 2 and 3: authors' calculations based on Statistische Ämter des Bundes und der Länder, "Public Budgets: Expenditures of State and Local Associations of Communities," 2012 (www.statistik-portal.de); Statistische Ämter des Bundes und der Länder, "Area and Population," 2012 (www.statistik-portal.de); Statistisches Bundesamt, "Statistisches Jahrbuch, Ausgabe der öffentlichen Haushalte (Länder) [Statistical Yearbook, Public Expenditures (German *Länder*)]," (Wiesbaden, 2008), p. 562; Statistisches Bundesamt, "Bevölkerung. Kennzahlen nach Ländern [Population. Key Indicators of German Laender]," p. 29; columns 4 and 5: Statistisches Bundesamt, "Schulden der Länder und Gemeinden/Gv. am 31.12.2007 [Debt of German *Länder* and Communities as of 12/31/2007]," p. 589; Statistisches Bundesamt, "Schulden. Schulden der Länder am 31.12.2011 [Debt of German *Länder* as of 12/31/2011]," 2012 (www.destatis.de).

Taken together, these three core characteristics of German fiscal federalism are crucial elements in explaining the largely asymmetric effect of the crisis on fiscal policymaking in Germany. It is not surprising that in the context of the recent crisis German policymakers have realized that it is necessary to rethink the core features of fiscal federalism in Germany. The result has been an intense, ongoing debate on how to reform the German model of fiscal decentralization.

However, this debate is not new. Since the very creation of the German Federal Republic in 1949, when the Allies deliberately sought to "decentralize" Germany as part of their postwar reconstruction strategy, the German approach to fiscal federalism has been facing numerous calls for fundamental reform; the recent crisis is just the latest episode in that saga. Nonetheless, as we argue in the conclusion to this chapter, while the crisis can be viewed as a clear call for reform, any overhaul of Germany's system of fiscal federalism depends on a variety of factors that are beyond purely economic or fiscal considerations.

Hence, the jury is still out on whether Germany will move toward a more "competitive" or a more "centralized" federal fiscal system. If we had to say whether current tendencies point in a particular direction, we would argue that current policies, such as the newly introduced joint issuance of federal- and state-level debt in the form of Deutschland bonds, point toward more centralization and a transfer of powers from the *Länder* to the *Bund* within important policy areas such as debt refinancing of state expenditures. But as long as there is no legal confirmation of that trend—or at least no official political commitments that point toward an overhaul of the system—the current structure of German federalism is likely to remain in place.

The German Approach to Fiscal Federalism

The German federal structure has three levels: national (the *Bund*), state (the *Länder*), and local. The distribution of political authority and legislative powers among these levels is the result of historic and administrative contingencies that are reflected in the current German approach to fiscal federalism.

Historic and Administrative Contingencies

On the national level, the *Bund* operates as the central administrative unit in which national policies are decided. Subnational policies are determined by the sixteen German states, the *Länder,* and their governments. Mirroring the setup of the German Federal Republic, each *Land* represents a political and administrative subunit with its own parliament and elected government, headed by a prime minister or the equivalent. In addition, there is an important local administrative level encompassing 402 counties, of which 107 are independent cities, as well as 11,292 municipalities.[10] The German federal structure was largely determined by historic and administrative contingencies. The allocation of legislative and political powers between national and subnational units reflects two decisive moments in German history.

First, the federal government's status as central legislative authority with respect to major policy areas such as citizenship, defense, and communications infrastructure can be viewed as a result of nineteenth-century developments that turned a loose assembly of sovereign states in the German *Bund* into a unified German state under the leadership of Prussia in 1870.[11]

Second, the limits placed on the central government by checks and balances instituted at the subnational level —for example, in the form of the legislative power of the *Länder* in important policy areas such as law enforcement, education, and culture—can be viewed as a result not only of the pre-1870 situation but also of postwar politics that responded to experiences from the Weimar Republic and the Third Reich:

> This destruction of . . . the old [centralistic] frameworks . . . after the war by the policies of the occupying Western armies, was eventually to make it possible to build the Federal Republic on a much sounder basis than the Weimar Republic of 1918–33, which had been little more than the defeated empire minus the Kaiser.[12]

The robustness and flexibility of the foundation on which the German Federal Republic was built was tested successfully by German reunification in 1990, when the German Democratic Republic was integrated into the German Federal Republic in the form of five new *Länder* plus East Berlin.

Distribution of Legislative Powers: Centralization or Decentralization?

The German Basic Law of 1949 enshrined a very simple allocation of powers between the *Bund* and the *Länder:* it conferred all legislative powers on the *Länder* that were not explicitly conferred on the *Bund*. But from the very beginning of the Federal Republic of Germany, that strongly decentralized model began to be turned into a much more centralized system. Over the years, many powers originally held by the *Länder* were shifted to the federal level, and the requirements of the Basic Law were met through stronger involvement of the *Bundesrat,* the second parliamentary chamber, in decisions at the federal level.

Representing the *Länder* with respect to federal legislation, the *Bundesrat* has to approve all legislation that directly affects *Länder* interests or that changes the federal constitution. Between 1949 and 2009, 52 percent of all federal legislation had to be approved by the *Bundesrat*. Due to changes in the allocation and systematization of legislative powers in the course of the Federal Reform of 2006, that figure was reduced to 39 percent in the 2006–09 period.[13] Today, "most legislation in Germany is passed by the Federation and the Länder under concurrent legislation"[14] and the *Länder* have clear-cut autonomy in policymaking in only a small number of policy areas (for example, regarding the penal system, opening hours of shops, compensation and career schemes for state judges and civil servants, and elements of university regulation and building); thus the *Länder* have limited room for independent legislative maneuver.[15]

Because of the peculiar setup of *political* federalism in Germany, German *fiscal* federalism is characterized by the paradoxes described previously. In formal terms, the *Länder*, which are responsible for almost half of all German public expenditures, enjoy a large degree of spending autonomy. However, their freedom to decide how to allocate money is effectively constrained by the general administrative obligations that they face. Those obligations apply with respect to, for example, tax collection, the judicial system, law enforcement, and education—which are, to varying degrees, also subject to federal and/or joint policies and decisionmaking.

In addition, *Länder* governments are limited in their ability to raise and collect taxes autonomously. With only minor exceptions, most taxes are set at the federal level in joint decisions of the federal parliament and the second chamber, representing the *Länder*. According to recent estimates, approximately 70 percent of German tax revenues come from taxes that are raised jointly by the central and the *Länder* governments, such as valued-added taxes (VAT) and income taxes.[16] Federal taxes account for about 10 to 20 percent of total taxes in Germany, while about 8 percent of total tax revenues come from community taxes.[17] Taxes controlled exclusively by the *Länder* account for less than 5 percent of total German tax revenues, and most of that sum is raised at the level of municipalities since three *Länder*, the "city-states," are also municipalities.[18] Thus the *Länder* have limited room to adopt independent tax policies. That is also due to the fact that rather than remaining in the *Land* of their origin, revenues from taxes are split between the federation and all the *Länder* on the basis of a predetermined allocation rate (generally close to 50:50 between the federation and the *Länder* for the main taxes, but the system can be very complex for each individual tax type).

What is even more important, however, is how tax revenues are redistributed and allocated on the *Länder* level. The amount of actually realized revenues of a given *Land* depends strongly on the number of inhabitants in the *Land,* thus implying that differences in economic performance are reflected to a lesser degree in *Länder* budgets. Variances in per capita differences in financial resources across *Länder* are compressed through a redistribution scheme that guarantees that each *Land* receives at least .995 percent of the overall average per capita tax income.[19] Contrary to the case of neighboring Switzerland, interstate fiscal competition and state-level tax policies are almost nonexistent in Germany.[20] In sum, despite the political significance of the *Länder,* their fiscal independence is rather limited due to legislative structures and the current system for redistribution of tax revenues.

Länder autonomy is greater on the expenditure side, yet limitations to fiscal sovereignty also persist in that regard. According to expert estimates, more than 20 percent of total *Länder* expenditures in 2003–04 was subject to external legislation initiated by the federal government (13.7 percent) or the EU (3.5 percent) or to the terms of joint programs administered by the federation and the *Länder* themselves (4.3 percent).[21] Within the states of former East Germany, approximately 31.9 percent of all expenditures derived from national legislation, the EU, or joint programs. That was more than in the city-states of Berlin, Bremen, and Hamburg, where approximately 21.4 percent of expenditures was allocated on the basis of external legislation and joint programs. It was also more than in the remaining former Western German states, where external legislation and joint programs allocated approximately 15.6 percent of expenditures.[22] Even if these numbers are only an approximation and may vary depending on assumptions and over the years, they show that the sovereignty of the *Länder* with regard to their expenditures is limited.

Limited Fiscal Sovereignty and Bailout Guarantees

As discussed, the German *Länder* enjoy limited fiscal responsibility—in particular in comparison with subnational units of other systems of fiscal federalism, such as the Swiss cantons.[23] Hence, questions emerge as to whether and to what extent German fiscal federalism creates incentives that foster fiscal responsibility at the state level. Does it lead to federal bailouts of German state governments?

The Equalization System as a Disincentive for Budgetary Discipline

A look at the varying levels of state debt invites the assumption that the current framework of fiscal federalism in Germany presents varying incentives for fiscal responsibility at the state level. As of 2010, the states of Berlin and Bremen displayed the highest debt-to-GDP ratio of German *Länder* (> 60 percent) while the states of Bavaria and Saxony displayed the lowest (< 10 percent).[24] In other words, state debt levels in Germany show considerable variation. The fact that some individual states show much higher debt levels than others leads to questions concerning the existence of checks and balances within Germany's framework of fiscal federalism.

From the perspective of investors who aim to determine the default risk of individual *Länder,* the "fact that the *Grundgesetz* [German Basic Law] . . . requires that the 'equivalence of living conditions' be maintained through the federation"[25] is of importance because it limits fiscal responsibility of individual states[26] through the so-called fiscal equalization system discussed above. Because the system is based on burden sharing by states and the federal government and revenue redistribution among states and makes it the responsibility of the federal government to compensate individual states for special burdens,[27] it plays a pivotal role in assessments of the default risk of German state governments.

That is especially the case since the German Constitutional Court decided in 1986 that "the federal supplementary transfers can be used to bail out fiscally troubled *Länder*."[28]

In a separate ruling in 1992 the German Constitutional Court reconfirmed its earlier decision by declaring "that the 'solidarity' obligation contained in the Grundgesetz required that the *Bund* . . . begin using the supplementary transfers to provide [the fiscally troubled states of] Bremen and Saarland with bailouts amounting to 17 billion deutsche marks."[29] With this decision, the Constitutional Court "signaled to the financial markets a high chance of bailout of risky borrowers."[30] The ruling can thus be interpreted as a sign of fiscal centralization as it confirms ongoing interpretations according to which the fiscal health of the *Länder* is directly dependent on the fiscal health of the *Bund*.[31]

A Contrasting View: Limited Bailout Expectations

Nonetheless, not all market participants interpret the 1992 ruling as a clear indication that the German federal government will act as automatic lender of last resort to the *Länder* in the future. For example, the credit-rating agency Standard & Poor's (S&P) has not changed its 2001 interpretation, according to which the constitutional principle of fiscal solidarity guarantees only the financial and political preservation of a state in financial distress without applying automatically to the state's liabilities in capital markets.[32] Hence, S&P reasons that the terms and amount of federal insurance of *Länder* liabilities are contingent on legal and political bargaining if a *Land* should default. Therefore, S&P concludes that ambiguities exist regarding the expected timing and amount of guarantees paid to *Länder* creditors by the *Bund* in the concrete case of a state default.[33] Any bargaining between state and federal governments may, of course, also affect the outcome of claims against *Länder* governments by third parties.

While the Constitutional Court introduced proxies to determine whether a state is in financial distress,[34] S&P argues that the ruling did not install any provision for automatic *Länder* bailouts.[35] Rather, S&P interprets the ruling as confirmation that state bailouts are to be decided on a case-by-case basis. The fact that the court denied bailout payments to the state of Berlin in another ruling in 2006 confirms this view.[36] A 1999 decision of the court further limits bailout guarantees to *Länder* in trouble by holding that the federal and state governments can be expected to assist other states through transfers only if the transfers do not present a threat to the financial viability of the federal and state governments themselves.[37]

In summary, S&P does not believe that an unconditional, universal lender-of-last-resort guarantee exists within the framework of German fiscal federalism.[38] In accordance with the current approaches of major credit-rating agencies such as Fitch and Moody's, S&P therefore deems individual credit ratings of German states to be necessary. That stance implies that the probability of a *Länder* bailout by the *Bund* is neither one nor zero; rather, it is somewhere between those values. Financial markets share S&P's belief in the likelihood of investor losses due to a state default—a belief highlighted by the fact that the *Länder* were confronted with higher borrowing costs as a result of the crisis.

Effects of the Debt Crisis on German Public Finances

The global economic crisis had a notable impact on Germany's export-driven economy. The economic downturn translated into fiscal consequences, which included debt that overshot the "Maastricht criterion," a basic standard of the European Economic and Monetary Union (EMU) that allows EMU members a maximum total debt of 60 percent of GDP. However, while both federal and state governments may be able to remedy the one-time effects of the crisis, it revealed structural imbalances within state budgets that are likely to limit the room for maneuver of fiscal policies undertaken by the *Länder* in the future. These imbalances include off-balance-sheet items in state budget plans, such as future pension claims, which have important effects on the viability of state budgets.

Total Government Debt

As of December 31, 2011, total government debt in Germany was 81.2 percent of GDP;[39] Germany therefore had greatly exceeded the Maastricht criterion. That excess debt was a direct consequence of the crisis. However, the composition of current state liabilities is also the result of past politics. Debt levels increased after reunification in the 1990s, and after a short period of consolidation around the turn of the millennium, they started to grow again.[40] From 2000 to 2010, total government debt climbed from roughly 60 percent of GDP (2000) to more than 80 percent (2010).[41] Debt was thus at a record level, exceeding the level after reunification in the mid-1990s.[42] Significant differences between the mid-1990s and the 2008–10 period exist with regard to the composition of debt. The increasing dependence of Germany's public finances on external funds is signified by the fact that since the 1970s, government net assets have been progressively depleted, as illustrated by the continuous decrease in the ratio of net fixed assets (measured at replacement cost) to GDP—since 1995, to values of less than 50 percent.[43] The differences became further apparent when the ratio of total government net assets to GDP decreased to negative values at the beginning of the new millennium.[44]

Moreover, differences exist with regard to the question of what governments do with the money that they borrow. In the 1990s, the increase in government debt was driven mainly by fixed expenditures, long-term investments such as those for infrastructure, and increased social transfers due to reunification.[45] For the most part, the return on these expenditures is determined endogenously by German economic growth. In contrast, increases in debt levels after the crisis were driven by more than the economic efforts of the federal and state governments to offset the effects of the economic downturn in the private sector by increasing public spending. For example, FMS Wertmanagement, a fund instituted by the federal government to resolve toxic assets of Hypo Real Estate, contributed €192 billion to the €1,312 billion of total federal government debt as of 2010, thus accounting for about 16.5 percent of that sum. In comparison, the national fund for reunification, which had been installed in 2005, contributed 2.9 percent to total federal government debt in the same period.[46]

The fact that in the aggregate, average interest rates halved since German reunification—decreasing continuously from 8 percent in 1992 to 3.25 percent in 2009[47]—blurs the long-term effects and budget risks associated with increasing levels of debt. That is also true for state government debt, for which decreases in the interest burden since 2006 are explained chiefly by low interest rates.[48]

To sum up: As of today, the federal and state governments own fewer net assets than two decades ago and spend smaller fractions of their budgets on long-term investment. Yet they finance their activities by issuing more debt in financial markets, at historically low costs, so that government budgets have higher exposure to those markets.

State-Level Debt

The global financial crisis had a strong effect on the German economy, primarily through limiting exports, which account for roughly half of German GDP. Annual changes in real GDP slowed from 2.7 percent in 2006–07 to 1.0 percent in 2007–08 and to negative 4.7 percent in 2008–09. Overall, changes in *Länder* GDP translated into changes in *Länder* budgets in the form of diminishing tax revenues.[49] Because payroll costs for public employees account for about 40 percent of *Länder* budgets[50] and public labor markets are relatively rigid in Germany,[51] *Länder* governments cannot cut their spending swiftly. Hence, when revenues diminished in the course of the crisis, the reduction affected the sustainability of *Länder* finances immediately.

Between 2008 and 2009, average annual growth of total debt issued by German states amounted to 7.8 percent while average debt reduction for 2006–07 had been 0.6 percent. Also, in 2007 no German state had failed to meet the Maastricht criterion (maximum ratio of public debt to GDP of 60 percent). In 2010, the debt-GDP ratio of both the state of Bremen and the state of Berlin exceeded 60 percent. Table 8-1 provides a conclusive overview of how the crisis affected *Länder* debt.

The states of Berlin and Bremen were not the only ones that reacted to financial pressure by increasing their respective debt levels. As of April 2011, *Länder* parliaments granted net credits (in billions of euros) to the governments of Baden-Württemberg (1.00), Berlin (2.74), Brandenburg (0.44), Bremen (0.91), Hamburg (0.70), Hesse (2.30), Lower Saxony (1.95), North Rhine–Westphalia (7.96), Rhineland-Palatine (2.00), Saarland (0.90), Saxony-Anhalt (0.54), Schleswig-Holstein (1.30), and Thuringia (0.47) for the budget year 2011. Only Bavaria and Mecklenburg-Pomerania abstained from expanding their credit lines, as did Saxony, which even reduced net credits by 0.10 billion euros.[52] Hence, the crisis put severe stress on *Länder* finances, which was reflected in Moody's July 2012 warning of credit-rating downgrades for states such as Berlin, Brandenburg, Saxony-Anhalt, North Rhine–Westphalia, and Baden-Württemberg.[53]

Off-Balance Sheet Items

A full assessment of the impact of the crisis on the financial health of the *Länder* must also account for the burdens following from write-downs of state-owned banks and the continuing development of off-balance-sheet items, such as future pension claims of state employees.

The financial crisis of 2007–09 hit *Landesbanken* (LB), the *Länder*-owned banks, hard.[54] Write-downs that occurred during those years to Bayerische Landesbank (> US$6 billion), Landesbank Baden-Württemberg (LBBW) (> US$4 billion), and WestLB (> US$4 billion) all exceeded the losses of Germany's largest financial institution, Deutsche Bank (> US$2.5 billion).[55] Write-downs and restructurings during the crisis resulted in reductions in the asset base of the *Landesbanken* sector from some €2 trillion in 2007 to €1.5 trillion in 2012.[56]

The fact that the losses of state-owned banks occurred in areas far from their core activities (for example, regionally targeted lending) reflects ongoing changes within the German banking system. The German banking model is traditionally described as a "three-pillar decentralized universal bank-based financial system."[57] The three pillars consist of large private banks (for example, Deutsche Bank, Commerzbank), public sector savings banks (Sparkassen and regional state-owned banks, or *Landesbanken*), and the cooperatives. The three pillars differ in terms of financial structure, legal status, and governance system.[58] LBs assumed a special position within this system since the *Länder* used to act as LBs' formal lender of last resort, which allowed the LBs to borrow at lower costs than competitors in the private sector.[59] The favorable position of LBs was eliminated by a Brussels decision in 2001.[60] Yet *Länder* guarantees still apply for outstanding debt that was issued before 2005. Hence, German states acted as de facto guarantors in the financial crisis for LBs, as became apparent when the responsible

Länder governments bailed out four state-owned banks—Bayerische LB, HSH Nordbank, LBBW (including Sachsen LB, which had been taken over by LBBW in 2008), and WestLB—in the aftermath of the crisis.[61]

While capital injections to LBs by the *Länder* are explicitly listed as items in annual *Länder* budgets, it is currently debated how guarantees to LBs and guarantor liabilities should be accounted for in order to assess the viability of government budgets. For example, the Bavarian Court of Audit showed concern in its 2010 report, observing that together with the Bavarian Association of Savings Banks, the state of Bavaria was holding total guarantor liabilities for Bayerische Landesbank that amounted to more than €89.7 billion at the end of 2009. The guaranteed volume will have been reduced to only €1.9 billion in 2015. Yet its magnitude will continue to pose substantial risk to Bavaria's budget, which comprises €47.4 billion for 2014 and €49 billion for 2015.[62]

Another item that is of direct relevance to the fiscal health of the *Länder* is the issue of future pension claims of public servants. Public pension claims are refinanced on the basis of intergenerational contracting—pay-as-you-go (PAYGO) accounting—in which expenditures for retirees are refinanced substantially by government revenues from the incomes of those who are currently employed.[63] At any given point in time, the expenditure side of the contract is determined by the number of pensioners, which is the product of past employment policies in the public sector and current life expectancies after retirement. The revenue side is dependent on the size of the current working population, which is a product of population growth and life-cycle work behavior. Structural strains on the intergenerational contract exist due to current and foreseeable future expenditure expansions through increases in life expectancy, the growth of the public sector in the post–World War II period, and a "natural decrease" in the working population that will result in a labor force that will be 15 percent smaller in 2035 than it is today.[64]

Implicit budget burdens due to future pension claims vary from state to state. According to University of Freiburg research from the year 2005, present values of current and future pension obligations for the 2001–20 period ranged from 5.9 percent (Saxony) to 27.4 percent (Hamburg) of state tax revenues.[65] Hence they represent significant liabilities that have a direct impact on states' budget policies.

Many *Länder* have begun to undertake measures to cushion future burdens by installing reserve and pension funds. The amounts of funds vary, as do investment strategies. By the year 2017 fund volumes are expected to be between €4 billion (Baden-Württemberg) and €0.24 billion (Bremen).[66] Some *Länder*, such as Bremen and Rhineland-Palatine, have permitted their funds to invest exclusively in German sovereign and subsovereign obligations. The majority of the *Länder,* however, also allowed for investment in obligations of EMU governments, which then were considered risk free.[67] For example, North Rhine–Westphalia invested more than €220 million in Greek government bonds.[68] Compared with the overall volume of core government debt in North Rhine–Westphalia as of year-end 2012, which totaled more than €130 billion,[69] that amount seems to present only minor financial risks to the fiscal health of the *Land,* even if the government receives a haircut on the Greek debt. However, the end of risk-free EMU investments implies the need for strategic changes in the funds' management due to the crisis and thus affects how the *Land* is going to deal with future pension claims in the long run.

Future pension claims are not part of the official budget reports of the *Länder.* Table 8-2 presents an overview of per capita estimates of net present values of future pension claims for the period from 2001 to 2020 and compares them with the volume of *Länder* pension funds as of 2003. Even although the data are dated, the message is clear. As the table shows, future pension claims are a significant factor in the financial planning of the *Länder.* However, they are less of a burden on the former East German states than on the former West German states. The table further shows that per capita volumes of pension funds vary. Hamburg, which is confronted with the highest per capita burden of future pension claims, also runs the largest fund, measured in per capita value. Saxony-Anhalt, which is second to Saxony with respect to relatively low future pension claims, operates the smallest fund, measured in per capita volume. While these differences underline the different approaches that *Länder* take toward the funds, it is notable that the magnitude of the funds represents only a fraction of the net present values of future pension claims. This observation highlights the PAYGO characteristics of the German pension system. Given the previously discussed changes in demographics and future labor markets, it also underlines the need for fiscal reform and consolidation.

In summary: the effect of the crisis on the public pension obligations of the *Länder* is twofold. The crisis and its economic effects in the form of forgone tax revenues have increased pressures on the public pension intergenerational contract. As the contract was already under stress due to long-term trends such as demographic changes and the effects of past public sector employment and labor policies, the challenges brought by the crisis are not new. However, they underline and amplify the need for structural reform. *Länder* attempts to undertake reforms and cushion future pension burdens by installing pension funds have been counteracted by the crisis and the end of zero-risk investments. Compared with U.S. pension funds, German state pension funds are small and only of limited importance in refinancing pension claims. Thus, we estimate that the effects of the crisis in this realm will not lead to abrupt

Table 8-2. *Per Capita Net Present Value (NPV) of Pension Claims 2001–20 against the* Länder *and Per Capita Volumes of* Länder *Pension Funds as of 2003*

Thousands of euros, per capita

Land	Net present value of pension claims as of 2001	Volume of Länder pension funds as of 2003
Baden-Württemberg	26.32	0.023
Bavaria	21.25	0.016
Berlin	36.04	0.023
Brandenburg	20.03	0.008
Bremen	34.85	0.017
Hamburg	42.42[a]	0.025[a]
Hesse	22.06	1.017
Mecklenburg–Pomerania	11.31	0.006
Lower Saxony	23.17	0.016
North Rhine–Westphalia	19.53	0.024
Rhineland-Palatine	23.76	0.016
Saarland	22.49	0.017
Saxony	6.58[b]	N.A.
Saxony-Anhalt	10.01	0.005[b]
Schleswig-Holstein	23.25	0.015
Thuringia	11.57	0.012
Median	22.28	0.016
Mean	22.17	0.016

Sources: Authors' calculations of per capita values are based on the following sources: Column 1: total NPVs as in Daniel Besendorfer, Emily Phuong Dang, and Bernd Raffelhüschen, "Die Pensionslasten der Länder im Vergleich [A Comparison of Pension Claims against German *Länder*: Status Quo and Future Development], 129/05, Institute for Financial Research, Albert Louis University of Freiburg, 2005, p. 27; state population as in Statistisches Bundesamt, "Statistisches Jahrbuch 2001: Bevölkerung nach Bundesländern [Statistical Yearbook 2001, Population in German *Länder*]" (Wiesbaden, 2003) p. 45; column 2: Bundesregierung Deutschland, *Dritter Versorgungsbericht der Bundesregierung* [Third Pension Report of the Federal Government] (Berlin, 2005), pp. 419–25; Statistisches Bundesamt, "Statistisches Jahrbuch 2003: Bevölkerung nach Bundesländern [Statistical Yearbook 2003: Population in German *Länder*]" (Wiesbaden, 2005) p. 29.

a. Minimum.
b. Maximum.

changes but will result instead in a continued search for new alternatives to the current status quo.

Subnational Bond Markets

The crisis has had a further impact on the ability of the *Länder* to finance their budgets through the financial markets; it has thus set the stage for further reforms that are likely to rebalance fiscal powers between state and federal governments. Here we discuss the impact of the financial crisis on subnational debt markets in Germany.

When issuing treasuries, German states access financial markets through private placement and through public issues. The amount of public issues is substantially higher than that of private placements.[70] Bonds issued by the *Länder* differ in terms of amount and structure. Summary statistics for the 1992–2007 period compute roughly €120 million as the mean volume for bonds issued, while the median volume was "slightly less than 30 million euros" in the same period.[71] The largest net issuers were North Rhine–Westphalia, Berlin, and Lower Saxony.[72] Smaller states such as Bremen traditionally access bond markets through joint issues or "federal-state jumbos."[73]

By and large, in the 1990s investors did not differentiate between the default risks of German federal and state bond markets, assuming that the federal government would serve as universal and unconditional lender of last resort to distressed *Länder*.[74] As discussed previously, that is no longer the case. Given the impact of the financial crisis and the limited ability of German states to absorb fiscal shocks, the ability of the *Länder* to sustain debt at zero cost to creditors has come under scrutiny.

This observation is based on examination of daily spreads of bonds issued by the *Bund* and the *Länder* in the 2006–10 period. Figure 8-1 presents yield spreads of bonds with a residual maturity of four to seven years[75] and displays annual minimum and maximum values of *Bund-Länder* spreads as a proxy for annual market volatility and investors' risk perceptions.

As the figure illustrates, bond markets became increasingly volatile over the crisis as the maximum and minimum difference of average spreads widened. In 2006, the difference between the lower-bound value (4.85 basis points) and the upper-bound value (29.16 basis points) of the average *Bund-Länder* spread curve was 24.31 basis points. In 2007, the difference between the lower bound (13.23 basis points) and the upper bound (53.75 basis points) of the curve increased to 40.52 basis points and then climbed to 88.26 basis points in 2008, when the lower bound of the curve was 27.68 basis points and its upper bound was 115.94 basis points (as of December), which was the maximum value observed over the entire period.

In 2009, the difference between lower bound (58.77 basis points) and upper bound (113.05 basis points) decreased to 54.28 basis points. Yet the minimum spread value of 58.77 basis points was still higher than in the years before, depicting persisting market unease with regard to the substitutability of bonds issued by the *Länder* and the *Bund*. In 2010, the difference between lower (39.28 basis points) and upper bounds (77.52 basis points) of the *Bund-Länder* spread curve decreased further, to 38.24 basis points. That value is comparable to the

Figure 8-1. *Annual Minimum and Maximum Values of Average Daily Spreads of* Länder *Bonds over Government Benchmark Paper* (Bund)[a]

Spreads over *Bunds,* in basis points

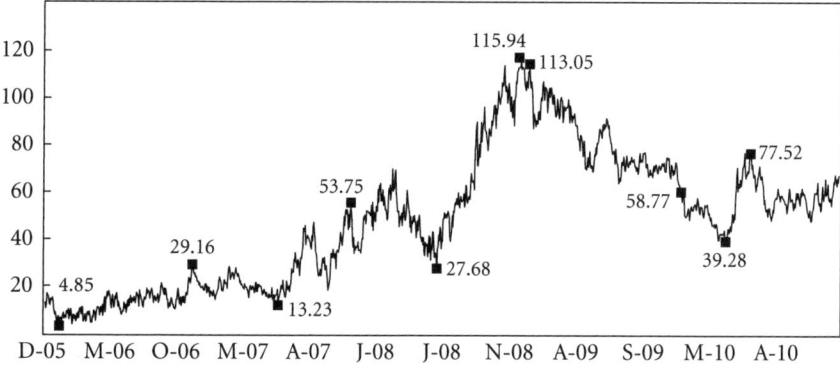

Source: Authors' calculations based on data from Thomson Reuters Datastream; see also Camillo von Müller, "Bond Yields and Bailout Guarantees: Regional Debt Markets in Germany," in Beat Brändli and Sandra Brändli, "Schulden haben und machen: Auswirkungen auf Wirtschaft, Recht und Gesellschaft. Schriften der Assistierenden der Universität St. Gallen (HSG), Band 7 [Being in Debt and Making Debt: Implications for Economics, Law, and Society. Writings of Junior Researchers at University of St. Gallen (HSG), vol. 7]" (Bern: Stämpfli Verlag, 2012), pp.129–47, 138–40; Daniel Nadler, Sounman Hong, and Camillo von Mueller, "Do (German) State Bond Markets Discount Politics?" Harvard University PEPG Research Paper 2012-01 (www.hks.harvard.edu/pepg/research.htm).

a. Bonds with a residual maturity of 4 to 7 years. The numbers signify minimum and maximum values in a given year. Note that maximum values peak in 2009.

minimum-maximum difference computed in 2007. However, it is of note that this value was the result of upper- and lower-bound values of the *Bund-Länder* spread curve that were higher than those computed for the year 2007.

These observations lead us to conclude that bond markets reacted to mounting fiscal pressures during the crisis. Increased relative market prices of *Länder* debt were reflected in widening *Bund-Länder* spreads, which implied that the German *Länder* faced increasing pressures to refinance their expenditures. Even if those pressures were not mounting as in other countries due to the moderate interest rate on German market debt, the increased volatility in debt markets for *Länder* highlighted the ramifications of the crisis and led to debate concerning an institutional overhaul of how *Länder* access financial markets.

Fiscal and Legal Consequences of the Crisis

The *Bund* and *Länder* responded to fiscal burdens resulting from the crisis in 2009 by introducing into the German constitution consolidation rules in the form of a fiscal ceiling ("debt brake"). In particular, successful implementation of the brake should imply that Germany would fulfill the Maastricht criterion before the end of the 2020s. The quid pro quo of the political bargaining process implied that the *Bund* would provide fiscal stimulus if the *Länder* would agree to the implementation of consolidation rules. Thus, the introduction of the debt brake resulted from a combination of macroeconomic reasoning and a political power play that is going to have long-term consequences for German fiscal federalism.

As an instrument of fiscal policy, the debt brake establishes centrally determined rules that apply to all *Länder* equally. It further includes a few emergency provisions that aim to make the system sufficiently flexible to adapt in the face of any unforeseen cyclical downturn that might result from external events. The baseline rule is that both *Bund* and *Länder* are required to balance their budgets; however, the rule has different implications for *Bund* and *Länder*.

The *Bund* is allowed to run a structural deficit of 0.35 percent of GDP. The *Länder,* however, are not allowed to run structural deficits. The fact that stricter budget rules apply to the *Länder* than to the *Bund* can be understood as an indication that the German system might be shifting toward a more centralized model, but only the future can confirm whether this is the beginning of a trend. The German debt brake stipulates that a structurally balanced budget has to be achieved until the end of 2015 for the *Bund* and until the end of 2019 for the *Länder*. By implementing "zero structural deficits" as reference points, the debt brake limits the ability of the *Länder* to build up additional long-term obligations beyond their long-run financial capacity (for example, by increasing the number of state employees beyond certain thresholds). Application of the new debt brake therefore should lead to changes in the fiscal policy in most *Länder,* which have been increasing their levels of structural obligations continuously over the years.

Taken together, the new debt brake regime and the mounting fiscal pressures from the crisis have induced the *Länder* to look for opportunities to consolidate their budgets, as the reform also intended. As a consequence and in the context of volatile capital markets that no longer take a universal federal bailout guarantee for granted, the *Länder* are investigating new ways to decrease their financing costs. The states of Hamburg and Schleswig-Holstein pushed forward in March 2011 for the introduction of bonds jointly issued by the *Länder* and the *Bund*. Other *Länder* and the federal government followed suit. The first Deutschland bond was issued on June 26, 2013, as a fixed-coupon-rate bond (1.5 percent per year) with an issuance volume of more than €3 billion and a time to maturity of seven years. It was issued jointly by the federal government, which accounted for a 13.5 percent share of the issue volume, and the states of Berlin (13.5 percent of the issue volume), Brandenburg (6.75 percent), Hamburg (5.25 percent),

Mecklenburg-Pomerania (3.25 percent), North Rhine–Westphalia (20 percent), Rhineland-Palatine (6.75 percent), Saarland (6.75 percent), Saxony-Anhalt (2.75 percent), and Schleswig-Holstein (8 percent). The issuance conditions stipulate, first, that each party is liable for obligations following from the issuance of the bond in proportion to the share that it accounts for and, second, that no issuing party can be held liable for claims resulting from the default of another issuing party.[76] According to reports in the German press, issuance of the Deutschland bond proved successful as primary market demand exceeded supply.[77] Depending on its further evolution, this new instrument has the potential to contribute to rebalancing fiscal relations between the federal and state governments by tying *Länder* governments closer to the federal government with respect to their financing activities in public markets.[78]

Conclusion: Centralization or Not?

Taken together, the different elements discussed in this chapter indicate that German fiscal federalism is undergoing yet another period of significant change. Established as a strongly decentralized system in 1949, the German federation has continuously shifted toward a more centralized system in most areas of decisionmaking. However, financial decentralization has remained significant, with the *Länder* playing a major role in public expenditures. At the same time, the revenue-generating ability of the *Länder* is very low, as *Länder* have very limited de facto powers to raise taxes independently.

The financial market crises that started in 2007–08 and the crisis in the Eurozone that began in 2010 have added to the problem by increasing pressure on the current structure of German fiscal federalism. The two crises revealed weaknesses in the current institutional design of German fiscal federalism, highlighting suboptimal incentives created by the redistributive tax allocation scheme and the limited credibility of a universal and unconditional federal bailout regime that protects states from a credit default. Yet it appears impossible to abolish these two core components of German fiscal federalism without changing the strongly heterogeneous structure of the *Länder* setup. Consequently, major reform seems unavoidable from a purely functionalist perspective. However, given the political framework of German fiscal federalism, it is unlikely that reform will be implemented in the form of a "big bang." Rather, any fundamental change will have to be the result of mutual bargaining and agreement between the *Bund* and the *Länder*.

Germany still has not decided whether it is a "decentralized" or a "centralized" fiscal federation. There are clearly elements of both in the current design. Quite strikingly, this peculiar setup did lead to acceptable fiscal policy results prior to the crisis and also helped to manage the historically unique task of German reunification. However, there are good reasons to believe that the fiscal and political effects of the financial crisis will put a much more long-term strain on *Länder* finances.

As argued in this chapter, the current crisis puts the viability of the system to the test. While the federation currently has a strong desire to put pressure and control mechanisms in place to constrain the fiscal room for maneuver of the *Länder* (in particular through fiscal ceiling measures such as the debt brake), it is still unclear whether such mechanisms can be sustained. Indeed, as long as the German constitution can be read as requiring the federation to bail out *Länder* in fiscal distress, threats by the federation to allow *Länder* to enter into a default or debt restructuring with private creditors have extremely limited scope. Accordingly, market pressure on *Länder* finances, while having increased slightly in the crisis, is thus likely to remain limited compared with pressure on other federal states in Europe such as Spain. Yet, as the widening of *Länder-Bund* spreads during the crisis showed, increasingly volatile markets are currently creating incentives for the *Länder* to rethink their fiscal policies, for example, by jointly issuing Deutschland bonds with the *Bund*.[79]

It has yet to be determined whether that strategy will prove successful by not only diminishing the borrowing costs of *Länder* but also orchestrating *Bund-Länder* fiscal policies. If it succeeds, the *Bund* would be the clear winner in the ongoing process of change. Debates would then arise on how this change should be accounted for on an institutional level—for example, by redistributing legislative and political powers. In order to guarantee the success of the newly introduced fiscal ceiling, which is intended to decrease the share of debt in the *Länder* budgets, the argument can also be made that it would be more reasonable to allow the *Länder* to control their revenue and spending policies, thus transferring more autonomy to the *Länder*.

To date, predicting the success of either of the two steps seems to be a heroic undertaking, particularly since continuing the current balance of reform and preservation can be a viable strategy as long as fiscal pressures at both the federal and the regional level remain limited. Should the fiscal pressures become too strong (for example, because of continuing pension entitlements that put additional pressure on budgets confronted with shrinking revenues or because of a sudden call on contingent liabilities from state-guaranteed banks during another financial crisis), a more abrupt change would have to take place. Predicting the direction of that change today is a hypothetical and extremely difficult undertaking. In light of the current euro crisis, which asks for the harmonization of EMU member state policies, centralization looks somewhat more likely. If fiscal pressures on the *Länder* were to increase, one route of development could be that the *Länder* slip under the fiscal umbrella of the *Bund* at the cost of a formal loss in sovereignty. That kind of exchange (or similar forms of a quid pro quo) would probably be necessary to rebalance the current equilibrium and make a far-reaching transfer of sovereignty to the federation politically acceptable.

Notes

1. Heinz Gebhardt and Niklas Möhring, "Länderfinanzen 2012 [Länder Finances 2012]," *RWI Konjunkturbericht,* vol. 64, no. 2 (2013), pp. 35–44 (www.rwi-essen.de/media/content/pages/publikationen/rwi-konjunkturberichte/KB_2_2013_laender.pdf).

2. Freie Hansestadt Bremen–Die Senatorin für Finanzen, *Bericht zur Haushaltslage der freien Hansestadt Bremen gemäß § 3 Absatz 2 des Stabilitätsratsgesetzes. Stabilitätsbericht 2012* [Budget Report of the Free Hanseatic City of Bremen on the Basis of Paragraph 3, Clause 2 of the Stability Council Act 2012]; Saarland–Ministerium für Finanzen und Europa, *Bericht des Saarlandes an den Stabilitätsrat gemäß § 3 Absatz 2 StabiRatG. Stabilitätsbericht 2012* [Report of the Saarland to the Stability Council on the Basis of Paragraph 3, Clause 2 of the Stability Council Act. Stability Report 2012]; Finanzministerium Schleswig-Holstein, *Stabilitätsbericht 2012 Schleswig-Holstein. Bericht des Landes Schleswig-Holstein an den Stabilitätsrat gemäß § 3 Absatz 2 StabiRatG* [Stability Report 2012. Report of the *Land* of Schleswig Holstein to the Stability Council on the Basis of Paragraph 3, Clause 2 of the Stability Council Act]. All reports can be downloaded at the Stability Council website (www.stabilitaetsrat.de/DE/Dokumentation/Haushaltsueberwachung/Stabilitaetsberichte/Stabilitaetsberichte_node.html).

3. Senat von Berlin, *Stabilitätsbericht 2012 des Landes Berlin. Beschluss des Senats von Berlin vom 11. September 2012* [Stability Report 2012 of the *Land* of Berlin. Decision of the Senate of Berlin of September 11 2012]; Sachsen-Anhalt–Ministerium der Finanzen, *Bericht an den Stabilitätsrat nach § 3 Absatz 2 Stabilitätsratsgesetz für das Jahr 2012* [Report to the Stability Council for 2012 on the Basis of Paragraph 3, Clause 2 of the Stability Council Act]; Freie und Hansestadt Hamburg–Finanzbehörde, *Stabilitätsbericht der Freien und Hansestadt Hamburg 2012 gemäß § 3 Absatz 2 StabilitätsRatgesetz* [Stability Report 2012 of the Free and Hanseatic City of Hamburg on the Basis of Paragraph 3, Clause 2 of the Stability Council Act]; Hessisches Ministerium der Finanzen, *Stabilitätsbericht des Landes Hessen. Berichtsjahr 2012* [Stability Report of the *Land* of Hesse. Reporting Year 2012]; Rheinland-Pfalz–Ministerium der Finanzen, *Stabilitätsbericht des Landes Rheinland-Pfalz nach § 3 Absatz 2 StabiRatG* [Stability Report of the *Land* of Rhineland-Palatine on the Basis of Paragraph 3, Clause 2 of the Stability Council Act], (2012). All reports can be downloaded at the Stability Council website (www.stabilitaetsrat.de/DE/Dokumentation/Haushaltsueberwachung/Stabilitaetsberichte/Stabilitaetsberichte_node.html).

4. Frank Zipfel, "Finanzen der Bundesländer. Im Schatten des Bundes [Finances of German *Länder*. In the Shadow of the Federal Government]," Deutsche Bank Research, *Aktuelle Themen* 513 (2011), p. 6.

5. Ibid.

6. European Commission, Economic and Financial Affairs, "Fiscal Relations across Government Levels in Times of Crisis: Making Compatible Fiscal Decentralization and Budgetary Discipline," part 4, "Fiscal Decentralization in the EU: Main Characteristics and Implications for Fiscal Outcomes" (2012) (http://ec.europa.eu/economy_finance/events/2012/2012-11-27-workshop/pdf/fiscal_decentralisation_en.pdf), p. 89.

7. Statistisches Bundesamt, *Statistisches Jahrbuch 2012* [Statistiscal Yearbook 2012] (Wiesbaden: Statistisches Bundesamt), p. 14.

8. GDP per capita and government expenditures per capita are computed in table 8-2 in this chapter.

9. Statistisches Bundesamt, *Statistisches Jahrbuch 2012* [Statistiscal Yearbook 2012], p. 14.

10. Statistisches Bundesamt, *Statistisches Jahrbuch 2012* [Statistical Yearbook 2012], p. 29.

11. David Thomson, *Europe since Napoleon* (London: Penguin, 1966), pp. 131, 237.

12. Eric Hobsbawm, *Age of Extremes: The Short Twentieth Century* (London: Abacus, 1994), p. 128.

13. Bundesrat, Statistik, *Verkündete Zustimmungs-bzw.* Einspruchsgesetze [Statistics. Acts of Assent and Objection, respectively] (www.bundesrat.de/cln_320/nn_11012/DE/parlamentsmaterial/statistik/statistik-node.html?__nnn=true).

14. European Commission, "Fiscal Relations across Government Levels in Times of Crisis," p. 80.

15. Roland Sturm, "Kompetenzverteilung zwischen Bund und Ländern bei der Gesetzgebung [Allocation of Legislative Powers at Federal and State Level]," Bundeszentrale für politische Bildung (2009) (www.bpb.de/politik/grundfragen/deutsche-demokratie/39356/kompetenzverteilung).

16. Zipfel, "Finanzen der Bundesländer. Im Schatten des Bundes [Finances of German *Länder*]," p. 6.

17. Ibid.

18. Ibid.

19. Compare European Commission, "Fiscal Relations across Government Levels in Times of Crisis," p. 86.

20. Compare Zipfel, "Finanzen der Bundesländer [Finances of German *Länder*]," pp. 8–10.

21. Helmut Seitz, "Die Bundesbestimmtheit der Länderausgaben [Federal Determinants of *Länder* Expenditures]," *Wirtschaftsdienst* 5 (2008), pp. 340–48, 343.

22. Ibid.

23. Compare, for example, the discussion on tax authority and popular rights with respect to the budgetary process in Gebhardt Kirchgässner, "Fiscal Institutions at the Cantonal Level on Switzerland," University of St. Gallen, School of Economics and Political Science, Discussion Paper 2013-04 (www1.vwa.unisg.ch/RePEc/usg/econwp/EWP-1304.pdf).

24. Zipfel, "Finanzen der Bundesländer [Finances of German *Länder*]," p. 6.

25. Jonathan Rodden, "Soft Budget Constraints and German Federalism," in *Fiscal Decentralization and the Challenge of Hard Budget Constraints,* edited by Jonathan Rodden and Gunnar Eskeland (MIT Press, 2003), pp. 161–86, 163.

26. Jens Rosenbaum, *Der Politische Einfluss von Ratingagenturen. Inaugural-Dissertation zur Erlangung des akademischen Grades eines Doktors der Philosophie am Fachbereich III der Universität Trier im Fach Politikwissenschaft* [The Political Impact of Rating Agencies. Ph.D. dissertation, University of Trier] (Wiesbaden: VS Verlag für Sozialwissenschaften, 2008), p. 111.

27. Rodden, "Soft Budget Constraints and German Federalism," p. 170.

28. Ibid.

29. Ibid., p. 180.

30. Helmut Seitz, "Subnational Government Bailouts in Germany," Research Network Working Paper R-396 (Washington: Inter-American Development Bank, 2000), p. 30 (www.iadb.org/res/publications/pubfiles/pubR-396.pdf).

31. As in Brian Parkin, "Bavaria among Six German States with Outlook Lowered by Moody's," *Bloomberg News,* July 25, 2012.

32. Christian Essers and Alois Strasser, "Ratings der Bundesländer: Zunehmende Bondemissionen lenken Aufmerksamkeit auf Kreditqualität [Ratings of German *Länder:* Increasing Volumes in Bond Issuance Steer Attention toward Credit Quality]" (Standard & Poor's, 2001), p. 5 (on file with authors).

33. "S&P sieht seinen Ratingansatz für Bundesländer bestätigt [S&P Attains Confirmation for Its Rating Approach toward German *Länder*]," *Dow Jones News,* October 19, 2010 (www.finanznachrichten.de/nachrichten-2006-10/7169113-s-p-sieht-seinen-ratingansatz-fuer-bundeslaender-bestaetigt-015.htm).

34. Kristin Heppke-Falk and Guntram Wolff, "Moral Hazard and Bailout in Fiscal Federations: Evidence for the German *Länder,*" *Kyklos,* vol. 61, no. 3 (2008), pp. 425–46, 429–31.

35. Essers and Strasser, "Ratings der Bundesländer [Ratings of German *Länder*]," pp. 5–7, 12.

36. Heppke-Falk and Wolff, "Moral Hazard and Bailout in Fiscal Federations," pp. 426–27.

37. Bundesverfassungsgericht,"Urteil im Normenkontrollverfahren zum Gesetz über den Finanzausgleich zwischen Bund und Ländern vom 23. Juni 1993 zuletzt geändert durch Artikel1 Drittes Gesetz zur Änderung des Finanzausgleichsgesetzes und Gesetz zur Änderung des Gemeindefinanzreformgesetzes vom 17. Juni 1999," BVerfG, 2 BvF 2/98 vom 11.11.1999, Absatz-Nr. (1 - 347) (1999), Section I:2:*c* [Decision of the Constitutional Court on the Norm Control Procedure with Regard to the Financial Equalization Act between the *Bund* and the *Länder* of June 23, 1993, Modified in Its Last Version by Article 1 of the Third Act on the Modification of the Financial Equalization Act and Communal Finances Reform Act of June 17, 1999] (www.bverfg.de/entscheidungen/fs19991111_2bvf000298.html).

38. Essers and Strasser, "Ratings der Bundesländer [Ratings of German *Länder*]," pp. 12–13.

39. Harald Hagn, "Staatsverschuldung in Deutschland [Public Debt in Germany]," *Aufsätze aus den Monatshäften, Thüringer Landesamt für Statistik* (January 2013), pp. 1–2.

40. Deutsche Bundesbank, "Zur Verschuldung und Zinsbelastung des Staates in Deutschland [On the Debt and Interest Burden of the German Government]," *Monatsbericht April* (2010), pp. 15 33, pp. 20–22.

41. Deutsche Bundesbank, "Die Schuldenbremse in Deutschland [The German Debt Brake]," *Monatsbericht Oktober* (2011), pp. 15–41, 16.

42. Compare Deutsche Bundesbank, "Zur Verschuldung und Zinsbelastung des Staates in Deutschland [On Debt and Interest Burden of the German Government]," p. 22.

43. Ibid., p.17.

44. Ibid.

45. Ibid., p. 20.

46. Deutsche Bundesbank, "Die Schuldenbremse in Deutschland [The German Debt Brake]," p. 24.

47. Deutsche Bundesbank, "Zur Verschuldung und Zinsbelastung des Staates in Deutschland [On the Debt and Interest Burden of the German Government']," pp. 27–29.

48. Ibid.

49. Frank Zipfel, "Verschuldungsstruktur der Bundesländer: Kapitalmarkt gewinnt an Bedeutung [Debt Structures of German *Länder:* Capital Markets Gain in Importance]," *Deutsche Bank Research Briefing,* February 2012, p. 2.

50. Seitz, "Die Bundesbestimmtheit der Länderausgaben [Federal Determinants of *Länder* Expenditures]," p. 5.

51. Katharine G. Abraham and Susan N. Houseman, "Does Employment Protection Inhibit Labor Market Flexibility? Lessons from Germany, France, and Belgium," Working Paper 4390 (Cambridge, Mass.: National Bureau for Economic Research, 1993).

52. Ibid., p.7.

53. Parkin, "Bavaria among Six German States with Outlook Lowered by Moody's." Bavaria was an additional state on the Moody's list. The fact that it was subject to Moody's warning along with the federal government while being also a net payer in the system of fiscal transfers within the German fiscal equalization system can be interpreted as sign of Moody's general distrust of the financial viability of German public finances at that time.

54. Ian Hardie and David Howarth, "Die Krise but Not La Crise? The Financial Crisis and the Transformation of German and French Banking Systems," *Journal of Common Market Studies,* vol. 47, no. 5 (2009), pp. 1017–039, 1028.

55. Ibid.

56. James Wilson, "German Public Banks Still Face Problems," *Financial Times,* June 28, 2012 (www.ft.com/cms/s/0/4f51fe3a-c104-11e1-853f-00144feabdc0.html#axzz2YZt 3ZHLy).

57. Hardie and Howarth, "Die Krise but Not La Crise?," p. 1019.

58. Ibid., p. 1019.

59. Markus J. Fischer and others, "Government Guarantees and Bank Risk Taking Incentives," AFA 2012 Chicago Meetings Paper, p. 2 (http://papers.ssrn.com/sol3/papers. cfm?abstract_id=1786923).

60. Ibid.

61. Compare Christoph Kaserer, *Staatliche Hilfen für Banken und ihre Kosten—Notwendigkeit und Merkmale einer Exitstrategie. Gutachten im Auftrag der Inititative Neue Marktwirtschaft* [Measures of Government Support for Banks and Their Costs—The Necessity and Features of an Exit Strategy. Expertise for the Initiative New Market Economy] (München: Technische Universität München, Lehrstuhl für Finanzmanagement und Kapitalmärkte, 2010), pp. 36–40.

62. Bayerischer Oberster Rechnungshof, *Jahresbericht 2010* [Annual Report of the Bavarian Court of Auditors for the Year 2010] (München, 2010), p. 40; Gesetz über die Feststellung des Haushaltsplans des Freistaates Bayern für die Haushaltsjahre 2013–2014 [Budget Act Affirming the Budget Planning of the State of Bavaria for the Budget Years of 2013–2014] (www.stmf.bayern.de/haushalt/staatshaushalt_2013/haushaltsplan/Haushaltsgesetz.pdf).

63. Axel Börsch-Supan, "Germany: A Social Security System on the Verge of Collapse," paper presented at the 1997 Kiel Week Conference "Redesigning Social Security" (1997), pp. 1–4.

64. Axel Börsch-Supan, "Labor Market Effects of Population Aging," Working Paper 07-26 (Universität Mannheim, Sonderforschungsbereich 504, 2001), p. 1 (http://mea.mpisoc.mpg.de/uploads/user_mea_discussionpapers/dp11.pdf).

65. Daniel Besendorfer, Emily Phuong Dank, and Bernd Raffelhüschen, "Die Pensionslasten der Bundesländer im Vergleich: Status Quo und zukünftige Entwicklung [A Comparison of Pension Claims against German *Länder:* Status Quo and Future Development]," Working Paper 129/05 (Institut für Finanzwirtschaft der Albert-Ludwigs Universität zu Freiburg im Breisgau, 2005), p. 27.

66. Bundesregierung Deutschland, "Dritter Versorgungsbericht der Bundesregierung [Third Pension Report of the Federal Government]," (Berlin, 2005), pp. 419–25.

67. Ibid.

68. Handelsblatt, "Staatsanleihen: Griechenland-Absturz würde NRW hart treffen [Government Bonds: Greek Default Would Hit NRW Hard]," June 26, 2011 (www.handelsblatt.com/politik/deutschland/staatsanleihen-griechenland-absturz-wuerde-nrw-hart-treffen/4324590.html).

69. Landesrechnungshof Nordrhein-Westphalen, *Jahresbericht 2013* [Annual Report 2013] (www.lrh.nrw.de/LRHNRW_documents/Jahresbericht/LRH_NRW_Jahresbericht_2013.pdf), p. 43.

70. Alexander Schulz and Guntram B. Wolff, "The German Subnational Government Bond Market: Structure, Determinants of Yield Spreads, and Berlin's Forgone Bailout," *Jahrbücher für Nationalokonomie und Statistik,* vol. 229, no. 1 (2009), pp. 61–83, 64–67.

71. Ibid., pp. 66.

72. Deutsche Bundesbank, "The Market for Federal State Bonds," *Monthly Report* (June 2006), pp. 31–46, 36 (www.bundesbank.de/Redaktion/EN/Downloads/Publications/Monthly_Report_Articles/2008/2008_06_state_bonds.pdf?__blob=publicationFile).

73. Ibid.

74. Klaus-Peter Fox, "Das Rating von Ländern bei der Kreditaufnahme ist verzichtbar [Separate Ratings of German *Länder* Are Not Necessary]," *Wirtschaftsdienst,* vol. 6 (2002), pp. 357–63.

75. For a detailed description of the data, see Daniel Nadler, Sounman Hong, and Camillo von Mueller, "Do (German) State Bond Markets Discount Politics?" Harvard University PEPG Research Paper 2012-01 (www.hks.harvard.edu/pepg/research.htm).

76. Bundesrepublik Deutschland, Finanzagentur GmbH, "Emissionsbedingungen. 1,50% Bund-Länder-Anleihe von 2013 (2020) [Issuance: Terms and Conditions of the 1.50% Deutschland-Bond of 2013 (2020)]" (www.deutsche-finanzagentur.de/fileadmin/ Material_Deutsche_Finanzagentur/PDF/Informationsmaterial/Emissionsbedingungen_ Bund-L%C3%A4nder-Anleihe.pdf).

77. Handelsblatt, "Gelungene Premiere für Deutschland-Bond [Successful Placement of Deutschland-Bond]," June 26, 2013 (www.handelsblatt.com/finanzen/boerse-maerkte/anleihen/anleihe-gelungene-premiere-fuer-deutschland-bond/8411718.html).

78. Handelsblatt, "Bund plant offenbar 'Deutschland-Bonds'" [The Federal Government Seems to Plan "Deutschland Bonds"]," November 19, 2012 (www.handelsblatt. com/finanzen/boerse-maerkte/anleihen/gemeinschaftsanleihe-mit-laendern-bund-plant-offenbar-deutschland-bonds/7411300.html).

79. The "Deutschland bond" received favorable comments by institutions such as Moody's, which said that "the issuance of the Deutschland Bond by the German federal and regional governments is credit positive for German Laender as it reinforces the cohesiveness of the institutional framework, reduces the risk premiums and enhances the investor base and liquidity" (https://www.moodys.com/research/Moodys-Deutschland-bonds-are-credit-positive-for-German-Laender--PR_276665?WT. mc_id=NLTITLE_YYYYMMDD_PR_276665).

CÉSAR COLINO *and* ELOÍSA DEL PINO

9

Spanish Federalism in Crisis

Spain has been hit very hard by the current fiscal crisis. Although Spanish federalism has faced a number of challenges before—for example, in accommodating territorial and ethnic differences and promoting economic efficiency—today it is having to deal with a combination of fiscal and political problems that were previously unknown: economic stagnation and fiscal crisis, increasing economic divergence among regions, and the strengthening of traditional centrifugal forces in some autonomous communities (ACs). Discussion of the demise or radical reform of the system has now entered the public sphere and the government agenda.

While some of the literature on Spain has pointed out several centralizing trends within the territorial model, not much of it has been able to convincingly show any formal shift of authority toward the center over the last decades. In the wake of the first stage of the crisis, little formal change or shift of authority was observed, since the central government had plenty of financial and regulatory powers to deal with the crisis.[1] During the second phase, however, the government's austerity policies exposed the system to centralizing pressures that resulted in some formal changes that are already having an impact on the autonomy of the ACs; those changes have in turn exacerbated some centrifugal tensions, such as secessionism in Catalonia.[2]

In this chapter we seek to contribute to the growing discussion on the effects of the current crisis on the stability and fiscal sustainability of federal systems.[3] In particular, we look at whether, after a period of sweeping decentralization in most of them, these systems are experiencing strong pressures to centralize and if so, how. We examine how the Spanish system is evolving and how it has reacted to the imperatives of the economic and fiscal crisis, whether through

The authors acknowledge support from the Project CRISAUT, CSO2012-33075, funded by the Spanish Ministry of Economy and Competitiveness.

159

formal reform, cooperation among government tiers, the central government's use of previously unused formal powers, or centralization of powers. We explore the scope and severity of the crisis in central and regional government finance and some of the main structural and contextual factors that have generated or aggravated it, looking, for example, at the role of social security and welfare benefits and public employees' salaries. In addition, we also seek to establish whether the fiscal crisis has implied or will imply any major shift of authority toward the central government.[4]

We also discuss whether the Spanish system confirms a growing literature[5] that suggests that the fiscal governance regime in the Spanish variant of federalism—based mostly on revenue and tax sharing, transfers by the central government, and little taxing autonomy of subnational units—leads to both recurring fiscal indiscipline and an increase in regional spending and debt in times of crisis. This literature also would expect to find centralizing tendencies in response to the crisis, which could occur within a stimulus phase as well as an austerity and adjustment phase.[6] We argue that, partly confirming the literature and the previous experience of similar federal systems, the crisis has produced fiscal problems and centralizing pressures that have reinforced the primacy of the central government in economic and fiscal policymaking. Even if sometimes warranted for the management and coordination of policies to combat the crisis, this centralization has met resistance, of different degrees, from the constituent units, producing increased political and jurisdictional tensions and conflicts that seek to restore the former balance of power or give additional leeway to regions.

As the historical data show, the potential problems of the Spanish system of fiscal federalism, well known to experts and covered by the literature, did not manifest themselves seriously before 2008. They seem to have been latent or disguised by the preceding long period of economic expansion and rising public revenues. After the onset of the crisis, however, all the wrong incentives built into the system finally produced a "perfect storm." One could argue, therefore, that rather than resulting from excessive or irresponsible spending or borrowing in the past, the current problems with deficits and debts are largely a product of the sharp reduction in regional revenues produced by the bursting of the real estate bubble and the resulting collapse of tax yields combined with the sovereign debt crisis from 2009 onward.

That revenue shock and the restriction of credit in the sovereign debt markets produced a sustainability problem that has forced both informal and formal centralization: informal, through the use of existing rules not previously enforced; formal, through amendments of regulations that give the central government more regulatory authority over regional fiscal policies and borrowing. At the same time, the central government has had to relinquish part of that authority to the European Union, which has also strengthened its fiscal and budgetary rules through the recent EU Fiscal Compact. The central government has thus mimicked the EU's attempts to strengthen coordination of its member states' finances by keeping their deficits and debts under control. This double upward shifting of authority has exacerbated the vertical and horizontal tensions traditionally present within the Spanish system and has been used by some regional politicians to shirk or to shift blame, pretty much as the Spanish government has done in the European context.

The Spanish central government faced a dilemma: either let the market discipline regional governments and allow some to default or guarantee basic public services and avoid the negative electoral implications and the consequences of default for the country's international creditworthiness. It has finally opted for a middle way, increasing regulation and control of regional spending and borrowing as well as providing an implicit guarantee and bailout in the form of liquidity loans with strict fiscal conditions attached. The consequences of those measures for fiscal adjustment and future sustainability are still unknown. Given the central government's also dismal financial situation, which has made its role as a debt guarantor doubtful, markets and rating agencies have indirectly helped with the task of disciplining the regions by increasing yield spreads of regional bonds to the point of expelling Spanish ACs from the credit markets. Apart from the centralizing trend, the effects of the crisis on the system are more complex. It has also promoted some cooperative tendencies and even some decentralizing tendencies in the realm of regional taxes.

The Spanish Territorial System before the Crisis

The so-called "autonomic state" was devised by the 1978 Spanish constitution, which allowed for the establishment and development of various autonomous communities by way of extensive decentralization of government power and responsibilities along with the constitutional recognition of certain regions' particular characteristics. The model was based largely on both the principle of autonomy for nationalities and regions and some constitutional provisions about how it had to be exercised. The constitution legally recognized and protected the existence of different regional languages, political traditions, and civil law traditions; special fiscal arrangements in some regions; and the insular condition of other regions.[7]

A Bit of History

The initial institutional design of and some social forces within the system operated in favor of diversity, and some de jure asymmetries were entrenched in the constitution—primarily with respect to fiscal arrangements, language, culture, and civil law. But the Spanish autonomic state increasingly evolved—through the repeated adaptation of some regional charters of autonomy, through political practice, and through judicial interpretation—in the direction of a virtually homogeneous or symmetrical cooperative federal model, with shared responsibilities and finances as its prevailing *modus operandi*. This decentralized distribution of powers, largely accomplished through the repeated intervention of the Constitutional Court over several years, became increasingly coherent and clear to political actors. To understand recent developments, it is useful to refer to several unique characteristics of the system that existed when the crisis began:[8]

—Strong nationalist movements and parties existed in two of the autonomous communities, and they were continually demanding increased powers and recognition.

—The territorial system was relatively decentralized with respect to public spending and legislative authority. Sharing of regional and central government powers and revenues predominated, and the tendency toward greater decentralization of resources and powers was growing.

—In its political dynamics, the Spanish model had simultaneously produced a centrifugal and differentiating tendency in some regions and a centripetal and equalizing one in others, articulated by regional governments and parties through their policies and demands for reform and manifested in intergovernmental relations.

The evolving model, despite some relative success, was never without its opponents. There always had been discontent and criticism regarding its operation as well as frustration among regional nationalist parties and governments that had, paradoxically, been the main beneficiaries of the system. In recent years, some initiatives to reform regional statutes of autonomy have been discussed or enacted by regional parliaments in eight ACs. Most of the reform initiatives have been triggered and influenced by discussion of the reform of the Catalan autonomy statute. The initiatives have entailed further devolution of competencies, redistribution of resources, introduction of regional charters of rights, and some other symbolic issues, such as recognition of the historical identities of regions.

Division of Powers

The constitutional distribution of responsibilities and powers in Spain was not clear cut, showing elements of both dual and cooperative federal systems. Some powers are reserved exclusively for the central government (for example, those regarding defense, social security, criminal law, external trade, telecommunications, immigration, and coordination of economic activity) and some for the

ACs (for example, those regarding agriculture, industry, spatial and urban planning, culture, social services, and tourism). However, in most sectors of public activity, powers are concurrent or shared. Hence, one finds an increasing interlocking of powers and some type of intervention by the central government in most sectors. In health, education, environmental protection, local government organization, and the media, the central government has a framework legislative power, which concurs with regional legislative competencies, by which it sets some minimum standards for regional legislation. It may thus limit their discretion in order to achieve national policy objectives or establish national regulatory standards.

According to the constitution, in some policy areas the central government may intervene to guarantee the "coordination of the general planning of economic activity," thus potentially encroaching on exclusive regional powers in agriculture, industry, trade, and so forth. In others, it may intervene to guarantee the "equality of all Spanish citizens," thus potentially encroaching on powers in social services, health care, and education. In still others, it may impose obligations or unfunded mandates on ACs, which have to implement some central regulations—for example, regarding labor relations, criminal law, and immigration. In practice this interlocked distribution of responsibilities generates many conflicts before the Constitutional Court, which on several occasions has supported central intervention but in others has clearly limited the central government's use of its spending powers and legislative powers.

Some asymmetric powers, constitutionally entrenched, remain. Apart from the special economic-fiscal regime for the Canary Islands, the most consequential asymmetry in the system is the constitutional recognition and protection of special economic-fiscal arrangements—for example, enhanced tax autonomy, independent tax collection systems, and exemption from the equalizing scheme—for the Basque Country and Navarre.

The Institutionalization and Capacity of AC Governments

All autonomous communities have established a parliamentary system of government with proportional representation, in which the government is politically responsible to the regional assembly. Parliaments at the regional level play an important role in shaping regional politics and policies. Their role is, however, limited by the predominance of presidents and ministers that is typical of parliamentary systems. A regional political class has developed, although the high turnover rate of regional members of parliament (MPs) has impeded the consolidation of a class of regional parliamentarians. This reflects a pattern of career mobility in which politicians move between the regional and the national governments. The Spanish system of territorial governance has also given rise to considerable influence of AC prime ministers, and one can observe the presidentialization of regional governments. The fact that prime ministers usually are the leader of their party in their AC has made them the main representative of their territory's interests. Besides that, they may acquire a political role in national politics, especially when their party is not in power in Madrid. In that case, they obtain additional influence within their national party's organization.

The process of decentralization was naturally accompanied by the establishment of regional civil services, most of which were built with personnel transferred from the central or local governments—a total 1.85 million public employees were transferred through the process. Each AC developed a regional administration to implement regional policies and to coordinate national policies with the central government. Most of them followed the national bureaucratic model. ACs with a greater number of powers at the beginning developed a more stable and professional civil service, and some have more civil servants per capita or more career civil servants than others. From 1999 to 2004, the number of regional public employees increased 70 percent, a total of half a million people, while the number of those working for the central government decreased by half. Now the central level represents around 20 percent of all public employees—half of whom are in the armed forces, the police, and the judicial system. Regional government employees, of whom 76 percent are teachers and health employees, represent 50 percent of the total number.[9]

ACs spend 74 percent of their budgets on health, education, and welfare services and 12 percent on transport, infrastructure, and agriculture. While ACs have concentrated on very labor-intensive social policies and services, they also take care of other basic policies related to economic productivity and growth (such as those on infrastructure and R & D).[10] Despite this notable decentralization process, the central Spanish government has maintained an important role in many policies and services besides economic policy. It still has its own country-wide implementation network for some policy sectors and programs, such as unemployment and social security, public order, infrastructure, and tax collection. It also holds a strategic position in all intergovernmental relations networks, being a permanent intermediary for the EU and for the AC and local governments.

Fiscal Federalism: Taxation and Spending

Fiscal federalism in Spain has evolved from a system based on conditional transfers to a system that increasingly relies on tax sharing, own-source tax revenues, and some unconditional equalization grants that affect various regions differently. There have been continuous improvements in resources and spending autonomy of ACs. In 2007, 34 percent of AC revenues came from own-source taxes, 21 percent from revenue sharing, 24 percent from equalization grants, and

21 percent from conditional grants (mainly Spanish and EU regional structural funds).[11] Almost half of public expenditures in Spain are currently managed by regional and local governments. The share of the central government is around 20 percent, and 31 percent is managed by the social security system, which is a central competence but is calculated separately. A large share of central government public spending—more than 40 percent—consists of money transfers to the other tiers of government.

Currently, regional governments receive a fixed percentage of revenues collected by the central government through several taxes. Regional governments have the power to increase the personal income tax rate in their territories and full power (over collection, base, and rate) on certain taxes: the asset transaction tax, stamp duty, inheritance tax, transport tax, tax on the sale of certain hydrocarbons, gambling tax, and fees related to particular services (for example, tuition fees).

The fiscal equalization scheme, through several funds, supplements the gap between the funding needs of ACs and their tax capacity. This system seems to have fairly redistributive effects. Criticism of the system has come from the wealthiest regions, which argue that the system is far too redistributive and lacks clear distributive criteria and incentives for subsidized regions to improve their performance. The 2009 reform of the funding system resulted in an increase in revenues from shared taxes (raising the regions' share of personal income tax from 33 percent to 50 percent, their share of value-added tax from 35 percent to 50 percent, and their share of the excise tax from 40 percent to 58 percent). Of those revenues, 75 percent is allocated to the Fund to Guarantee Public Services, which is divided among the ACs according to adjusted population criteria. The remaining 25 percent is allocated among the ACs in which the revenues were generated. The equalization system has thus slightly changed to a system that equalizes only partially (80 percent of needs), but it is frequently adjusted.[12]

For many observers, this funding formula is excessively dependent on revenue sharing and central transfers. Following a rational strategy, AC governments have consistently preferred to increase their percent of revenue sharing with the center rather than use their discretion to raise revenues by taxing their citizens. While ACs have some leeway to change tax credits, tax deductions, and tax rates for the shared taxes and may also establish surcharges on central taxes, they have to use the same tax base and definition as the central government. The funding formula guarantees funds to ACs irrespective of their fiscal performance and of whether they decide to establish new taxes or increase tax pressure on their citizens to obtain more revenue.[13] That leads to lack of responsibility on the part of regional politicians and to the well-known soft budget constraint, which gives ACs no incentives to raise their own revenues through taxes. Regional governments resort to a permanent state of bargaining and bilateralism with the central government, horizontal competition, and blame shifting.[14] Moreover, the existence of the special charter system for the Basque Country and Navarra, which produces more per capita funding for them, and the frequent renegotiation of the system has led to ACs' continual expectations of further resources from the central government and therefore to incentives to overspend.[15]

Fiscal Rules on Regional Borrowing and Debt: An Implicit Guarantee of the Central Government?

Budget stability rules and limits on borrowing have become increasingly strict due to EU and national regulations. The 1997 Stability and Growth Pact of the EU and the approval of the Spanish budget stability laws in 2001, amended in 2006, led to some intergovernmental decisionmaking and controls with regard to regional budget balances and some limitations on regional borrowing. Before new regulations were introduced in 2010, regional borrowing and fiscal deficits were subject to regulation and multilateral approval by the Spanish intergovernmental body known as the Council of Finance and Fiscal Policy Ministers. When an AC breached its fiscal target, it had to submit an economic-financial rebalancing plan to this body, including measures to reach budgetary stability in a three-year period. These regulations have been strengthened in the wake of the recent austerity measures and constitutional amendment, discussed below.[16] Some regions questioned the stability regulations before the Constitutional Court for eroding their constitutionally protected financial autonomy.[17]

By law, ACs cannot declare bankruptcy. In principle, they have autonomy to manage their finances, and if an AC cannot service its debt or repay bondholders, the central government is not legally obligated to assist it. However, there are numerous legal mechanisms that allow the central government to rescue ACs with financial problems, through loans or through authorization of new debt issuance. So, as the Spanish prime minister recently confirmed in parliament, it seems that there is an implicit guarantee that the central government will not let any region or local government default on the service of its debt, as has been recently demonstrated with the autonomous community of Valencia. In practice, that means that under normal circumstances credit markets do not see the subnational units as sovereign, so the markets do not serve to discipline the units' borrowing behavior. Instead, they expect an implicit guarantee of the units' debt from the central government, and bond yields of regions tend to converge with the yields of Spanish treasury bonds. Currently, however, the funding costs of regional governments show that the markets and the rating agencies are clearly distinguishing between the debt of the Spanish treasury and the regions through increasing yield spreads.

In sum, the Spanish model of fiscal federalism is funded mainly by tax sharing and equalization grants, and regional taxes are heavily regulated and inflexible. That produces considerable autonomy for regional spending, low autonomy with respect to revenues, and no incentives for regions to use their tax autonomy. Under these circumstances sanctions and controls on deficits and debts cannot be strictly applied and do not seem to work in either a period of growth or an economic downturn. According to some recent studies, the Spanish system features, together with the implicit guarantee of regional debt that existed until the onset of the crisis, what is deemed the most dangerous combination in terms of fiscal discipline in a federal system: a central government that dominates taxation and revenues but that is politically constrained for electoral or partisan reasons (for example, having to favor certain stronghold regions or to ally with some regionalist parties in the central parliament) and cannot control the spending and borrowing of the subnational units.[18] If they have the legal capacity and they perceive the center's no-bailout stance as having low credibility, many regions, both wealthy and poor, may follow what for them is a rational strategy when a crisis comes: namely, to delay adjustment and initiate a new cycle of heavy borrowing, bailout demands, and blame shifting. According to the evidence in the literature, under such circumstances the central government can restore some discipline only by controlling borrowing. That has been the Spanish central government's path, following the German example.

The Crisis in Spain: Scope, Effects, and Conditioning Factors

Two distinct periods in the development and effects of the crisis can be identified: the first, one of economic stagnation with decreasing economic growth and rising unemployment; the second—in part a result of government action during the first period combined with a crisis in the international credit markets—one of strict requirements for governments to adjust through budget consolidation and debt reduction. In these two phases the responses of the Spanish government and regions have been similar to those in other countries. However, the severity of the crisis, in both the first and second phase, seems to have been unique in Spain.

Budget Deficits and Increasing Regional Debt Problems

Like Italy and the three rescued countries (Greece, Ireland, and Portugal), Spain faced particular funding problems as a result of the institutional design of the Eurozone, which was not prepared to deal with asymmetric shocks.[19] Membership in the Eurozone may thus have contributed to the deepening of Spanish crisis. In the Spanish case, however, unlike in some of the other cases, previous irresponsible fiscal behavior did not seem to contribute to the financing problems. Over the last decade Spain had one of the best records in achieving the Maastricht criteria. In 2007, regional finances were close to being balanced and the central government had a surplus. Until the 2008 crisis, ACs had reasonable aggregate deficit and debt levels and spending increases were underwritten by the soaring tax base. However, in three years the Spanish economy went from having a surplus of 1.9 percent in 2007 to a deficit of 9.2 percent in 2010, which peaked at 11.1 percent in 2009. Total public debt increased from 36.1 percent in 2007 to 60.1 percent in 2010.[20]

Adjustment and spending cutbacks have mainly concentrated on capital expenses and intermediate consumption. Social benefits have increased due to demographic changes and increases in spending on pension and unemployment benefits. Interest on debt reached €38 billion in the 2013 budget, a 33.7 percent increase since 2008. Interest, the second-largest category of spending after pensions, represents a quarter of all expenditures, and it is likely to grow in the coming years.

In 2010 regional deficits amounted to 2.83 percent of GDP, out of a national deficit of 9.24 percent. The central government accounted for 76 percent of all public debt in 2010. The regional debt-to-GDP ratio has increased from 5.7 to 12.6 percent, with strong differences across ACs. The most indebted are Valencia, Catalonia, Castile–La Mancha, and the Balearic Islands; the less indebted are the Basque Country and Madrid. Part (20 percent) of the regional public debt originated in public corporations created by regional governments;[21] the deficit and debt limits established by the central government thus seem difficult to meet.

Before the markets were closed to them, ACs borrowed close to €30 billion in 2011; in contrast, the pre-crisis annual average was €6 billion. With the crisis in sovereign debt markets, ACs began to face growing divergence of their risk premiums. Whereas a couple of years ago the yield spread with the central government was minimal, there is evidence that credit markets increasingly discriminate among regions, not only on the basis of credit ratings but also on the basis of variables such as degree of commitment to and compliance with budget targets, size of debt, market experience and access, and liquidity of debt issues. In 2011, the spread ranged from 80 basis points over Spanish treasury bonds for the best-rated regions to more than 300 basis points for the most poorly rated regions. In the secondary market in 2012, bonds of the Andalusian government maturing in October 2013 and those of the Catalan government maturing in July 2013 were offering yields of more than 10 percent, while the Spanish treasury bond due in October 2013 had a yield of only 2.6 percent. In those secondary markets, Catalonia would have to pay a yield of 12 percent for ten-year bonds. That represents a spread of 600 basis points over debt issued by the central government and 1,100 basis points over the German treasury bond. It is still worse for the bonds of other regions, which means that credit markets are closed to the ACs.

What Systemic Factors Have Contributed to the Crisis in Regional Finance?
Social Security Entitlements and the Public Sector Wage Bill

As in other federal countries, in Spain there is evidence that some long-term structural and institutional factors such as social security entitlements and public sector collective bargaining have aggravated the fiscal crisis of the regional governments and the fiscal sustainability and funding capacity of the Spanish federal model, thus distorting the role of the central government and endangering the autonomy of the lower tiers of government.[22] However, while those two factors play a really important role in public expenditures in Spain, the Spanish social security system—which is based on a public pension scheme and a different division of powers between tiers of government—has led to outcomes that differ from those in the United States, for example. While the inflexible public employee wage bill and spending on health care are very relevant to the incremental evolution in regional expenditures and current regional deficits, pension entitlements have affected only central government finances.

The Spanish pension system consists of state-financed and -administered pensions and voluntary privately funded and managed pensions. The former include pay-as-you-go financed and earnings-related retirement, permanent disability, and survivor benefits. Contributions to the social security system are compulsory for all employees; private pension plans are voluntary and intended primarily to supplement public pensions.[23] Economic benefits provided by the social security system are managed by the INSS (Instituto Nacional de la Seguridad Social [National Social Security Agency]). Apart from the public pension scheme, the central government has an occupational pension fund created in 2004 to supplement central government employees' public pensions. This pension fund includes 605,432 participants. Regional governments such as that of Catalonia have also created occupational pension funds for their employees. These are voluntary defined contribution schemes. In the wake of austerity measures, the central government has prohibited itself, ACs, and local governments from making contributions to occupational pension plans.

With the crisis, the ratio between workers and pensioners has decreased to 2.41, the worst figure since 2002. While in 2002 the number of employed was similar—about 16.8 million—today's workers have to bear the cost of an additional 1 million pensioners and more than an additional 1.7 million unemployed. That means that currently there are sixteen people to pay for every ten recipients of social security benefits.[24] The gap between contributions and benefit payments is also apparent in the 2013 budget, in which about €105 billion in revenues from employer and employee contributions but more than €106 billion in expenditures on pension benefits were forecast. Pension benefits have not posed special problems for regional finance.

A different issue is the weight of regional public employee salaries in Spain. While the central government spends 11 percent of its budget on salaries, the AC governments spend a third of their budgets, with differences across regions (ranging in the middle of the first decade of the 2000s from 38.9 percent in the Canary Islands, 35.8 percent in Valencia, and 17 percent in Catalonia to 13 percent in the Basque Country). Regional personnel expenses increased in real terms by nearly 60 percent between 1995 and 2010. Between 1999 and 2009 public sector staff increased by 463,356 employees (24.53 percent). While the number of central government employees has fallen by 302,655 employees (55.85 percent), the ACs have had an increase of 558,990 employees (93.01 percent) due to the devolution of responsibility for administering education and health care and the establishment of new welfare services. According to Eurostat data, the civil service wage bill in Spain increased 59.2 percent, rising from €1,608 per capita in 2000 to €2,560 in 2008. During the same period, the increase in the EU was around 31.4 percent, to €2,629 per capita.[25]

That increase in the wage bill clearly indicates several dysfunctional dynamics at play in the way that collective bargaining works in the Spanish public sector. In Spain, Law 7/2007 formally recognized the right of public employees to engage in collective bargaining and to participate in determining their working conditions. That right is restricted by the principles of rule of law and availability of public funds. There is evidence that the way in which salaries are negotiated with public employees has led to an incrementalist dynamic and to competition among regions and different public sector professionals to raise salaries.[26] Due to differences in regional employment policies regarding civil servants' regulatory regimes and pay, regions raise their salaries to attract employees, in the end causing sustainability problems without necessarily improving regional public services.

How the Spanish Government Responded to the Crisis: Strategies and Centralization Tendencies

As predicted by most of the literature on the role of central governments in financial crises—and as was to be expected from the Spanish model of fiscal federalism—the central government has had a dominant role in fighting the economic crisis in Spain. Two different strategies can be seen in the two distinct phases of the crisis.

Phase 1: Demand Management through Stimulus Packages
(August 2008–April 2010)

In the first phase the central government pursued countercyclical demand management through stimulus packages. It was able to do so because at the beginning of the crisis both levels of government had a good fiscal surplus. The central government allowed regions to borrow and pursue deficit spending to implement the countercyclical measures recommended by the EU and the G-20; it also injected more monies into regional finance through the 2009 reform, which also increased the regions' autonomy to raise taxes. The central government, as in other federal countries, also used its spending power to stimulate spending by local governments, especially on public works and social services, through conditional and matching grants. Other central government monies were used to help subsidize regional industries and bail out some ailing regional savings banks.[27]

None of those measures, which were taken in cooperation with ACs in multilateral intergovernmental bodies, raised significant opposition or jurisdictional conflict. In this phase, regional governments followed the countercyclical measures set by the central government. Neither the central government nor the credit markets disciplined the fiscal behavior of regions by punishing irresponsible spending or borrowing behavior, so the regions did not have many incentives to adjust by cutting back on spending or by raising their taxes. ACs continued to increase their spending in 2008, 2009, and 2010 by increasing public hiring and welfare services. Some of the regions even borrowed recklessly, expecting future bailouts by the central government. Only the EU, when it opened an excessive deficit procedure in 2009, signaled that there were problems.

Some of the measures had a clear centralizing effect, which sometimes reinforced previous centralizing pressures in the system and sometimes led to jurisdictional conflicts. The first phase of the crisis provides three examples:

—The reinforced use by the central government of its spending power for subsidies and conditional grants for local governments (for public works or social services) bypassed the AC governments without letting them participate in the assignment or management of these central grants in aid. Until 2008, although they did not have much power regarding these subsidies, regions had participated in the management and distribution of grants to local governments.

—The central government's matching grants to aid ailing industries (for example, the automotive industry) also limited the autonomy of regions.[28]

—The promotion of reform of the financial sector indirectly brought about centralization since most regional savings banks (a regional jurisdiction) were forced by the Central Bank of Spain to merge and transform into banks (a central competence) and consequently excluded AC governments from their boards.

Phase 2: Austerity and Budget Consolidation through Expense Cuts and Structural Reforms (May 2010–July 2012)

In the second phase, the situation changed completely because of external factors such as new EU requirements and the sovereign debt crisis in the Eurozone.[29] The central government was forced to change its strategy by seeking to boost fiscal coordination and impose firmer limits on the rising levels of regional expenditures and debt while at the same time avoiding the default of some ailing regions. Strict budget consolidation goals set by the EU, the liquidity problems of ACs due to credit restriction, and soaring bond yields led the central government to reform the constitution and establish tighter controls on regional spending and borrowing. It also tried to force ACs to raise their regional taxes or cut spending on personnel and public services and at the same time signaled its intention to avoid defaults through different conditional loans of around €40 billion to help them service debt and pay for public services. At that point, credit markets also began to discipline regions and distinguish among them, since for the first time a regional default seemed a real possibility.

The first austerity measures of the Socialist central government in the spring of 2010 consisted of cuts in public spending (salaries of senior political officials, civil servants, and other public employees) and pension reform. But the most significant measure was the amendment of Article 135 of the constitution to set limits on public spending and borrowing. The amendment, to which the main opposition party agreed, was to be implemented through the Fiscal Stability and Financial Sustainability Act, passed on April 27, 2012. The act followed the German model and the European Fiscal Compact in introducing strict monitoring, enforcement, and sanctions for noncompliance with deficit and debt targets, unilaterally set by the central government—no longer, or only formally, through the Council of Finance and Fiscal Policy Ministers.[30]

Under the new conservative government elected in November 2011, the central government raised personal income and value-added taxes and sought to ease, through its framework legislation, cutbacks in regional education and health care services. Measures were adopted on April 20, 2012, to rationalize regional public spending on the National Health Service and on education, seeking savings of €10 billion. To alleviate the regions' dismal liquidity situation, the central government also established the Fund for Financing Payment to Suppliers and the Regional Liquidity Fund, the latter holding up to €18 billion, to enable centralization of public debt issuance and provide liquidity to ACs (eight of which had applied for it as of the end of 2012) through less costly loans. This mechanism is also based on strict fiscal conditions and monitoring of regional rebalancing plans.

The centralizing consequences on the system of the measures taken in the second phase have been more obvious than those of the measures taken during the first, in particular the following:

—The imposition of cuts in public employees' wages and salaries, which has affected the autonomy of ACs to organize their public bureaucracies.

—The unilateral imposition of procyclical policies on all ACs and the abandonment of countercyclical policies in some of them (for example, Andalusia).

—The exclusion of the ACs in the process of establishing budget consolidation and debt limit goals. Under the new regulations, the agreement of the Council of Finance and Fiscal Policy Ministers is no longer necessary.

—The enhanced powers of the central government since 2010 to authorize regional borrowing, limit debt issuance, monitor and enforce compliance, and sanction noncompliance.

—The refusal to mutualize or explicitly guarantee regional debt and the insistence of the central government on favoring loans achieved through the centralization of public debt issuance and those with strict fiscal conditions attached. These measures give the central government further control of regional budgetary policies.

—The decisions to set the additional margin of the adjustment burden conceded by the EU in favor of the central government consolidation targets and not to offer financial relief to the regional governments. Those decisions have been criticized as unfair by the regional governments.

Conclusions: Toward Centralized Control?

Before the crisis, ACs had a certain autonomy to borrow and spend without fearing sanctions and without depending on the central government for their liquidity. They had plenty of revenues, and for electoral or partisan reasons, such as alliances with some regionalist parties, the sanctions in existing stability regulations were not actually applied. That led to the too-common practice of failing to comply with budget stability and debt goals.

From that pre-crisis situation, over the last five years Spanish ACs have slowly entered a period in which revenues have plummeted, credit markets have been virtually closed, and ACs have become completely dependent on central government equalization grants and liquidity loans to fund deficit spending and to service maturing debt. Without changing the constitutional division of powers, the centralization of the system implied by these developments has affected the autonomy of elected regional governments and their accountability to their citizens. Through the combined effects of the credit markets and the centralization measures of the central government (unilateral fixing of budget deficit targets, increased control of borrowing, and conditions attached to liquidity loans), ACs have lost most of their financial autonomy and discretion, which was already limited. Paradoxically, in other cases regions have resorted for the first time to raising revenues through their own taxes. This current fiscal situation has been used by some regional governments to avoid or shift blame and to justify further irresponsible fiscal behavior. Especially in some wealthy regions, it has been used to justify new fiscal asymmetries and special fiscal treatment or to bolster separatist demands, putting a strain in the stability of the Spanish political system.

Although the central government has sought to ameliorate the fiscal situation of ACs by injecting more resources into the regional funding system and increasing both revenue sharing and the possibility of own-source taxes for regions, those measures have been offset by austerity requirements and problems in the credit markets. However, so far the measures pursued have not been able to stop the growing indebtedness of regional governments, and most of those governments have not been able to meet the fiscal consolidation goals that would confirm their fiscal responsibility and allow them to regain their credibility in the credit markets. It seems as if the delayed response and the diverse adjustment paths of the regional governments, along with the delayed regulatory response of the central government, have prevented the effective coordination of spending and borrowing among governments. It will take some time to translate central government measures into reduced spending, fiscal discipline, and international creditworthiness.

Given the now apparent failure of austerity policies to boost job creation and growth, it will be a while before budget consolidation and debt goals are met by the regions and the central government. Centralized fiscal decisionmaking and conditional central transfers may become a common feature of the system for some years into the future. Lack of regional autonomy will parallel the Spanish government's loss of sovereignty in determining its own budgetary and borrowing policy. Not until, at the very least, the economy recovers and the credit markets reopen to the regional governments, which still may take years, will regions be able to determine, in part, their own level of spending and borrowing. Meanwhile, they may begin to reform their administrations, rationalize their spending, and use all of their autonomous taxing potential. Not until then will Spanish federalism be able to regain its true identity, combining both solidarity and diversity.

Notes

1. See Carles Viver, "Impact of the Global Economic Crisis on the Political Decentralisation in Spain," *L'Europe en formation,* vol. 4, no. 358 (Winter 2010), pp. 61–90 (www.cairn.info/resume.php?ID_ARTICLE=EUFOR_358_0061).

2. César Colino, "The State of Autonomies between the Economic Crisis and Enduring Nationalist Tensions," in *Politics and Society in Contemporary Spain: From Zapatero to Rajoy*, edited by Bonnie N. Field and Alfonso Botti (New York: Palgrave Macmillan, 2013), pp. 81–100; Julio López-Laborda, "Nuevas reglas fiscales para las comunidades autónomas [New Fiscal Rules for Autonomous Communities]," in *Informe Comunidades Autónomas 2011,* edited by Joaquín Tornos (Barcelona: Instituto de Derecho Público, 2012), pp. 771–95; Violeta Ruiz-Almendral, "Curbing the Deficit in Spain and Its Autonomous Communities: A Constitutional Conundrum," presented at the Center for Constitutional Studies, Madrid, October 2012; Carles Viver, "Impact of the Economic Crisis on the Crisis of the State of the Autonomies in Spain," in *Federalism and the Global Financial Crisis: Impacts and Responses,* edited by John Kincaid and Sonja Wälti (Oxford University Press, forthcoming).

3. See Paul E. Peterson and Daniel Nadler, "Freedom to Fail: The Keystone of American Federalism," *University of Chicago Law Review,* vol. 79, no. 1 (2012), pp. 253–91 (https://lawreview.uchicago.edu/sites/lawreview.uchicago.edu/files/uploads/79_1/10%20Peterson%20Nadler%20SYMP.pdf); Dietmar Braun and Philipp Trein, "Economic Crisis and Federal Dynamics," in *Federal Dynamics: Continuity, Change, and Varieties of Federalism,* edited by Arthur Benz and Jörg Broschek (Oxford University Press, 2013); John Kincaid and Sonja Wälti, *Federalism and the Global Financial Crisis: Impacts and Responses* (Oxford University Press, forthcoming).

4. For a similar attempt in the American federal system, see Peterson and Nadler, "Freedom to Fail."

5. For this literature, which encompasses a number of findings on financial intergovernmental transfers, multilevel fiscal adjustments, soft budget constraints, and bailout expectations, see Jonathan Rodden, Gunnar S. Eskeland, and Jennie Litvack, "Introduction and Overview," in *Fiscal Decentralization and the Challenge of Hard Budget Constraints,* edited by Jonathan Rodden, Gunnar S. Eskeland, and Jennie Litvack (MIT Press, 2003), pp. 3–32; Jonathan Rodden, *Hamilton's Paradox: The Promise and Peril of Fiscal Federalism* (Cambridge University Press, 2006); Peter Claeys, Raúl Ramosand, and Jordi Suriñach, "Fiscal Sustainability across Government Tiers," *International Economics and Economic Policy,* vol. 5, no. 1(2008), pp. 139–63 (http://econpapers.repec.org/article/kapiecepo/v_3a5_3ay_3a2008_3ai_3a1_3ap_3a139-163.htm); Jonathan Rodden and Erik Wibbels, "Fiscal Decentralization and the Business Cycle: An Empirical Study of Seven Federations," *Economics and Politics, vol.* 22, no. 1 (2010), pp. 37–67.

6. Rodden, *Hamilton's Paradox*; Braun and Trein, "Economic Crisis and Federal Dynamics."

7. See for example, César Colino, "The Spanish Model of Devolution and Regional Governance: Evolution, Motivations, and Effects on Public Policymaking," *Policy and Politics,* vol. 36, no. 4 (2008), pp. 573–86; César Colino and Eloísa del Pino, "Spain: the Consolidation of Strong Regional Government and the Limits of Local Decentralization," in *The Oxford Handbook of Local and Regional Democracy in Europe,* edited by John Loughlin, Frank Hendriks, and Anders Lindström (Oxford University Press, 2011), pp. 356–83.

8. For these characteristics, see César Colino, "The State of Autonomies between the Economic Crisis and Enduring Nationalist Tensions," in *Politics and Society in Contemporary Spain: From Zapatero to Rajoy,* edited by Field and Botti.

9. See Colino and del Pino, "Spain: the Consolidation of Strong Regional Government and the Limits of Local Decentralization."

10. Jesús Ruiz-Huerta, Carmen Vizán, and Myriam Benyakhlef, "Crisis Económica y Tensión Fiscal en las Comunidades Autónomas [Economic Crisis and Fiscal Stress in Autonomous Communities]," in *Informe Comunidades Autónomas 2011,* edited by Tornos, pp. 51–74.

11. See Julio López-Laborda, Javier Martínez-Vázquez, and Carlos Monasterio, "The Practice of Fiscal Federalism in Spain," in *The Practice of Fiscal Federalism: Comparative Perspectives,* edited by Anwar Shah (McGill-Queen's University Press, 2007), pp. 287–316.

12. On the 2009 reform of the system, see Antoni Zabalza and Julio López-Laborda, "The New Spanish System of Intergovernmental Transfers," *International Tax and Public Finance,* vol. 18 (2011), pp. 750–86; Santiago Lago, "El nuevo modelo de financiación autonómica: luces y sombras [The New Model of Regional Finance: Lights and Shadows]," in *Informe sobre Federalismo Fiscal en España '09,* edited by IEB (Barcelona: IEB, 2010), pp. 62–73; Hansjörg Blöchliger and Camila Vammalle, "Spain: Reforming the Funding of Autonomous Communities," in *Reforming Fiscal Federalism and Local Government: Beyond the Zero-Sum Game,* OECD Fiscal Federalism Studies (OECD Publishing, 2012), pp. 113–21.

13. Violeta Ruiz-Almendral, "Sharing Taxes and Sharing the Deficit in Spanish Fiscal Federalism," *eJournal of Tax Research, vol.* 10, no. 1 (2012), pp. 88–125.

14. On the funding arrangements and Spanish fiscal federalism, see López-Laborda, Martínez-Vázquez, and Monasterio, "The Practice of Fiscal Federalism in Spain"; Sandra León, "The Political Rationale of Regional Financing in Spain," in *The Political Economy of Inter-Regional Fiscal Flows: Measurement, Determinants, and Effects on Country Stability,* edited by Nuria Bosch, Marta Espasa, and Albert Solé (Cheltenham: Edward Elgar, 2010), pp. 249–70; Ruiz-Almendral, "Sharing Taxes and Sharing the Deficit in Spanish Fiscal Federalism."

15. León, "The Political Rationale of Regional Financing in Spain."

16. Alain Cuenca, "Estabilidad Presupuestaria y Endeudamiento Autonómico en la Crisis 2008–2011 [Budget Stability and Regional Debt in the 2008–2011 Crisis]," *Cuadernos de Derecho Público,* vol. 38 (2012), pp. 161–75.

17. López-Laborda, "Nuevas reglas fiscales para las comunidades autónomas [New Fiscal Rules for Autonomous Communities]"; Ruiz-Almendral, "Curbing the Deficit in Spain and Its Autonomous Communities.

18. Rodden, *Hamilton's Paradox.*

19. See Klaus Armingeon and Lucio Baccaro, "The Sorrows of Young Euro: The Sovereign Debt Crisis of Ireland and Southern Europe," in *Coping with Crisis: Government Responses to the Great Recession,* edited by Nancy Bermeo and Jonas Pontusson (New York: Russell Sage, 2012); Francisco Carballo-Cruz, "Causes and Consequences of the Spanish Economic Crisis: Why the Recovery Is Taken so Long [sic]?," *Panoeconomicus,* vol. 58, no. 3 (2011), pp. 309–28.

20. Roberto Fernández Llera and Eloy Morán, "Reacciones fiscales de las comunidades autónomas ante una crisis global [Fiscal Reactions of Autonomous Communities to the Global Crisis]," *Revista Asturiana de Economía,* vol. 42 (2008), pp. 57–80; Ruiz-Huerta, Vizán, and Benyakhlef, "Crisis Económica y Tensión Fiscal en las Comunidades Autónomas [Economic Crisis and Fiscal Stress in Autonomous Communities]."

21. Johanna M. Prieto and César Cantalapiedra, "Regional Government Debt and the Hispabonos Debate: Consideration for an Improved Regional Financing Model," *Spanish Economic and Financial Outlook,* vol. 1, no. 1 (May 2012), pp. 34–44 (www. funcas.es/Publicaciones/Detalle.aspx?IdArt=20638). For an explanation of the evolution of regional debt, see Jesús Ruiz-Huerta and Miguel A. García, "El endeudamiento de las Comunidades Autónomas: límites y problemas en el contexto de la crisis económica [The Indebtedness of Autonomous Communities: Limits and Problems in the Context of the Economic Crisis]," *Revista d'estudis autonomics i federals,* vol. 15 (April 2012), pp. 124–63.

22. Peterson and Nadler, "Freedom to Fail."

23. Elisa Chuliá, "Consolidation and Reluctant Reform of the Pension System," in *The Spanish Welfare State in European Context,* edited by Ana M. Guillén and Margarita León (Farnham, U.K.: Ashgate, 2011), pp. 285–304; Eloísa del Pino, "The Spanish Welfare State from Zapatero to Rajoy: Recalibration to Retrenchment," in *Politics and Society in Contemporary Spain: From Zapatero to Rajoy,* edited by Field and Botti.

24. Nicolas M. Sarriés, "El número de afiliados a la Seguridad Social cae a niveles de hace una década [The Number of Social Security Contributors Falls to Levels of a Decade Ago]," *20 Minutos,* October 3, 2012 (www.20minutos.es/noticia/1605961/0/ afiliados/seguridad-social/niveles-decada/).

25. Mario V. González, "El Coste de la Administración Pública en España: Una caracterización de su estructura y evolución recientes [The Cost of Public Adminstration in Spain: A Characterization of Its Structure and Recent Evolution]," Documento 03/2009, Línea Perspectivas (Spain: Strategic Research Center, EAE Business School, 2009).

26. Federico A. Castillo, "Sistema salarial, gasto público y apuntes para su reforma en el empleo público español [Wage System, Public Spending, and Reform Proposals for Spanish Public Employment]," *Presupuesto y Gasto Público,* no. 41 (2005), pp. 93–125 (www.ief.es/documentos/recursos/publicaciones/revistas/presu_gasto_publico/41-05_ FedericoACastilloBlanco.pdf).

27. For the central and regional policies to combat the crisis, see Jesús Ruiz-Huerta, Myriam Benyakhlef, and Carmen Vizán, "Las Comunidades Autónomas ante la crisis económica: impacto territorial de la recesión, políticas autonómicas de reactivación, y tensiones en las cuentas públicas [The Autonomous Communities before the Crisis: The Territorial Impact of Recession, Regional Reactivation Policies, and Tensions in Public Accounts]," in *Informe Comunidades Autónomas 2009,* edited by Joaquín Tornos (Barcelona: IDP, 2010); Ignacio Molina, Oriol Homs, and César Colino, "Spain Report," in *Sustainable Governance Indicators 2011* (Gütersloh: Bertelsmann Stiftung, 2011) (www. sgi-network.org/pdf/SGI11_Spain.pdf); Ignacio Molina, "Gobierno y desgobierno de la economía: las políticas de respuesta a la crisis [Management and Mismanagement of the Economy: Policy Responses to the Crisis]," in *España en crisis. Balance de la segunda*

legislatura de Zapatero, edited by César Colino and Ramón Cotarelo (Valencia: Tirant lo Blanch, 2012), pp. 49–73; Viver, "Impact of the Global Economic Crisis on the Political Decentralisation in Spain"; Viver, "Impact of the Economic Crisis on the Crisis of the State of the Autonomies in Spain."

28. Viver, "Impact of the Economic Crisis on the Crisis of the State of the Autonomies in Spain."

29. See Andreu Mas-Collel, *El ajuste fiscal de las comunidades autónomas visto desde dentro* [Regional Fiscal Adjustment Seen from the Inside] (Madrid: Instituto de Estudios Económicos, 2012); Cuenca, "Estabilidad Presupuestaria y Endeudamiento Autonómico en la crisis 2008-2011 [Budget Stability and Regional Debt in the 2008–2011 Crisis].

30. See López-Laborda, "Nuevas reglas fiscales para las comunidades autónomas [New Fiscal Rules for Autonomous Communities]"; Ruiz-Almendral, "Curbing the Deficit in Spain and Its Autonomous Communities."

CARLOS XABEL LASTRA-ANADÓN

10

Regional Identity and Fiscal Constraints in Spanish Federalism

"A majority of Catalans want to build a new country." With 54 percent of the popular vote going to parties that favor independence in the November 2012 elections, that assertion by Artur Mas i Gavarró, the reelected president of Catalonia, is undoubtedly true. Mas added, "The great purpose of a new country is guaranteeing the maximum civic, spiritual, and material well-being of its citizens."[1] Why has the Spanish state not been able to deliver a sense of such well-being to Catalans and other regional groups in the 36 years since the passage in 1978 of its democratic constitution—at least not to the extent that it precludes widespread support for the formation of an independent country by Catalonia?

The growing regionalist sentiment within Catalonia and other Spanish regions coincides with the increasing instability of the federal framework established by the 1978 constitution. Two major factors are at work:

— A heightened sense of regional identity clashes with the current amount and pattern of wealth redistribution by the government.

—Spain is unable to continue to pay for an acceptable pattern of regional redistribution by increasing its debt.

I argue that the amount and regional pattern of income redistribution in Spain differ from what citizens in key regions of the country prefer. The central and the regional governments have managed potential conflicts over redistribution among regions by issuing debt, which allowed for unaffordable levels of expenditures between 1990 and 2008 and muted political tensions that might otherwise have disrupted national unity. After the 2008 financial crisis, government deficits could no longer be funded and redistribution politics intensified, generating strong separatist sentiments. A system of competitive federalism that minimizes interregional redistribution may be a solution to Spain's current political crisis because each region would be responsible for its own citizens.

For that system to prevail, however, the European Union (EU) will have to exert strong influence over regional policymaking.

The Current Spanish Regional System

The 1978 constitution established the "indissoluble unity of the Spanish nation, common and indivisible fatherland [*patria*] of all Spaniards." It also created a new set of regional institutions that recognized distinct cultural identities. The government decentralization that has evolved since 1978 resembles a healthy federal system on the outside, but it suffers from a fatal flaw. While the seventeen separate regions in Spain—known as autonomous communities (ACs)—now account for up to one-half of all public spending, most depend heavily on the central government for tax revenues. Moreover, in their largest budget categories, such as health and education, decisions are heavily constrained by a national legislative framework. For instance, up to 65 percent of the contents of school curricula is dictated centrally.[2]

Centralization of Spain's government, which took place under General Francisco Franco in the aftermath of the Spanish Civil War (1936–39), was motivated in part by regionalist forces that had evolved in the buildup to internal warfare. The political bargaining that produced the democratic 1978 constitution sought to effect a peaceful transition from a heavily centralized system to one with greater scope for autonomous action by lower tiers of government. In its attempt to disassemble Franco's centralized government, the constitution divided Spain into the seventeen ACs, each with its own elected government and unicameral parliament. AC contours were broadly based on history and on the provincial system under Franco, who had appointed government officers in each of the provinces. The decentralization process that started in 1978 has resulted in a steady increase in the responsibilities of the regional governments, accompanied by the (re)creation of regional identities through promotion within the education system of regional languages, particular readings of history (such as of the conflict between Catalonia and the rest of Spain after the 1701–13 War of the Spanish Succession), and cultural traditions and through language academies, museums, and other public cultural institutions. Public regional television and radio stations, the creation of unofficial "embassies" of regional governments in national capitals across the world and regional delegations to bodies such as the EU, and a myriad of regional programs have added to the preexisting regional distinctions, which have been etched ever more deeply into Spanish political culture.

A federalist system is often cast as a bargain among sovereign states that adopt a federal arrangement in order to solve common problems.[3] In Spain, federalism evolved from quite different origins: the "Spanish fatherland" holds power by default in most policy domains, and it can delegate authority to the lower tiers of government for only the twenty-two policy areas listed in the 1978 constitution. The ACs are not deemed sovereign entities; in particular, because any change that requires a constitutional reform requires the assent of Spain's congress and senate as well as a national referendum, they cannot separate unilaterally from the federation.

In keeping with its origins in a highly centralized system, the federalist project in Spain has been one of progressive disaggregation of power. ACs steadily expanded their authority for almost 30 years, practically exhausting the range of responsibilities that they could legally hold under the constitution. Since the devolution of power was initially uneven among ACs, the system was dubbed "asymmetrical," with the self-proclaimed "historic" ACs enjoying greater levels of authority and responsibility than the rest; over time, however, levels have become similar in all ACs. Nonetheless, in certain areas, such as policing and the prison system, some ACs have powers while others do not. With regard to fiscal autonomy, limited asymmetry also remains, as two regions, the Basque Country and Navarra, enjoy nearly full fiscal authority. Table 10-1 provides details on the current distribution of responsibilities among the various levels of government in Spain.

As more responsibilities were devolved to the ACs, their expenditures grew at a rate nearly 3 percentage points higher than the central government's annual rate of increase in expenditures. Regional expenditures constitute 43 percent of total government spending, a level that is much higher than the 16 percent average for EU countries. Even in a federal country like Germany, only 37 percent of the spending is done at the regional level.[4] As can be seen in figure 10-1, government expenditures have increased more at all levels in Spain than in its EU peers.[5]

Most taxes are collected at the national level. For the ACs that operate under the "common regime," which comprises fifteen of the seventeen regions, the revenues from import taxes, social security payroll taxes, and corporate income taxes are collected and determined exclusively by the central government. However, 36 percent of the ACs' revenues are collected directly by the ACs themselves, while the remaining 64 percent come from tax sharing or equalizing grants, which are the responsibility of the central government.[6] The justification for centralized collection is that it reinforces the constitutionally enshrined solidarity principle—namely, that all regions must be able to deliver the same standard of service even though their wealth differs. Still, recent policy changes have increased the ACs' ability to collect tax revenue for their own purposes:[7]

Table 10-1. *Responsibilities by Level of Government in Spain*

Central government

Defense
International representation
Justice
National police
Economic planning and regulation
Financial system regulation
Customs
Income and wealth redistribution
Basic social security legislation and funding
Basic health care and education legislation and funding
National infrastructure: highways, railroads, and hydraulic river works across more than
    one autonomous community; public ports and airports

Autonomous communities

Education, all levels (primary, high school, and college)
Health
Agriculture
Industry, energy, and mines
Environment
Tourism and domestic trade
Social services
Protection of historical and artistic patrimony and regional language
Housing and land use regulations
Regional infrastructure: highways and railroads within the autonomous community,
    private commercial ports and airports

Local governments/municipalities

Water supply
Sewerage and garbage collection
Public lighting system
Delivery of social services
Cemeteries
Repair and maintenance of non-university school centers
Parks and public gardens
Street paving

Municipalities with more than 50,000 inhabitants

Urban transportation
Local environmental protection

Provinces

Funds destined for small municipalities for infrastructure projects and public service
    delivery. Legal assistance and managerial support to small municipalities
Delivery of services of a super-municipal nature

Source: Adapted from Julio López-Laborda, Jorge Martinez-Vazquez, and Carlos Monasterio, "The Practice of Fiscal Federalism in Spain," International Studies Program Working Paper 06-23 (Andrew Young School of Policy Studies, Georgia State University, 2006).

Figure 10-1. *Expenditure Growth in Spain and the EU Countries by Level of Government, 2002–11*

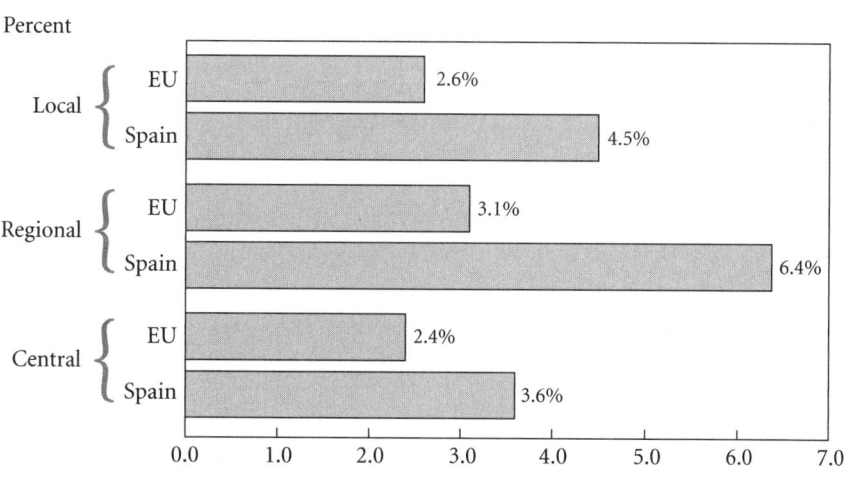

Percent

Average yearly growth in per capita expenditure

Source: Eurostat, Government Revenue, Expenditure, and Main Aggregates database (http://appsso. eurostat.ec.europa.eu/nui/show.do?dataset=gov_a_main&lang=en).

—Personal income tax: 50 percent of the revenue is collected directly and kept by the ACs, which have discretion to set a different policy for their portion, including a different tax rate.

—Sales tax (valued-added tax): 50 percent of the revenue is collected directly and kept by by the ACs, but they have no discretion to set policy.

—Revenue from smaller taxes such as the inheritance tax, the net wealth tax, the capital transfer tax, stamp duty, gambling taxes, and taxes on vehicles and gasoline have been fully assigned to regional governments.

A costing exercise is performed to determine the allocation of funds to ensure that ACs can deliver the services for which they are responsible. Wealthier ACs show a surplus in this calculation and so are net payers into the fund, which compensates less affluent ACs for shortfalls between tax revenues and required expenditures.

The Basque Country and Navarra both enjoy instead a charter regime.[8] These two regions have fiscal systems that afford them practical control of all the taxes listed above, as well as corporate income, import, and payroll taxes. The only revenue shared with the central government is a bilaterally negotiated amount that is, in theory, paid by the two ACs in return for the public goods provided by the central government. This unique system is seen to favor the two charter regions, which keep much larger portions of their revenues than the rest while still enjoying public goods provided by the national government. Public debt has provided another source of revenue for ACs. Although the central government must approve new debt, its exercise of that authority was so lax that debt issued by regional governments tripled from 1990 to 2000.[9]

The Relation between Regional Identity and Income Redistribution

Why is Spain's decentralized system in trouble? The first part of the answer has to do with the redistribution of income from richer to poorer regions in the context of an increased sense of regional identity. The second part is the financial crisis, which provided the spark that lit the kindling by closing off debt financing.

Conventional wisdom suggests that those living in wealthier regions prefer a more decentralized system of redistribution[10] because they want to collect and disburse themselves a greater share of the taxes collected within their own region. Under such an arrangement, the median voter in a wealthy region can enjoy the same level of public services at a lower tax rate than would be the case if revenues were more broadly shared. Once a decentralized system is established, however, wealthier people may move to regions where services are provided at an even lower tax rate, heightening regional inequalities.

Conventional wisdom can account for why two of the wealthiest regions, Catalonia and the Basque Country, want separation but not for why poorer ones, like Andalucía and Galicia, exhibit such a high level of regional identity and express it through ever-stronger demands for autonomy.[11] Moreover, other wealthy regions, such as Aragón and the Community of Madrid, show no signs of a strong regional identity or a desire for more autonomy. It seems that the federalism debate in Spain is not just a battle over resource redistribution. While economic issues play a definite role, other factors must be introduced to explain the instability of the type of federalism currently in place in Spain.

A Theory of Redistribution Based on Regional Identity

It is not the case, as has been argued, that "the political choice between alternative fiscal structures is largely driven by their distributive consequences," at least not alone.[12] In Spain, it does not appear that wealthier regions want more decentralization and less wealthy regions want less. In my view, the main driver of the willingness to belong to a common fiscal framework in a country like Spain is the perceived compatibility between a region's sense of identity and the regional patterns of wealth redistribution that the state enforces. In theory, if the regional flows of redistribution did not match the preferences of the citizens, one would expect political pressure for less redistribution or for a breakup or other substantial change in fiscal arrangements. For example, one might imagine that Catalans have particular preferences about the share of their income that is redistributed (through taxes) within Catalonia and the share that goes to the rest of Spain. And if the Catalans' strong regional identity influences the amount and regional flow of the redistribution that they want, their preference would be for a disproportionate amount of the redistribution (compared with needs) to go to Catalonia.

The intuitive force of the theory of preferences for redistribution may be seen in comparing the attitude of many citizens of developed countries toward the poor in other countries with their attitude toward the domestic poor. Many people feel a special affinity for citizens of their own country and would prefer that the majority of the taxes that they pay be distributed domestically and a smaller fraction be designated for poverty alleviation abroad. That holds true despite the fact that, relatively speaking, needs are much greater in the developing world than in developed countries. A similar phenomenon is at work in regions with a high level of regional identity.

If in fact there is more national redistribution than citizens' preferences warrant, there will be pressure toward a second-best solution: lower tax rates. This strategy is likely because the tax rate is more easily altered than the level of income redistribution; in practice, the former changes several times a decade in Spain and elsewhere. Altering the pattern of income redistribution is more complicated in a country like Spain because it requires constitutional reform. Put simply, if citizens disagree with the system of redistribution in place, they would rather pay less in taxes. In addition, political instability, which may manifest itself as increased separatism, is most likely to occur if the level of taxation is not altered. Citizens will seek another political structure that matches their preferences. Naturally, political pressure can also be generated if the level of regional identity changes over time and the redistribution system does not change with it.[13]

Regional Identity and Redistribution in Spain

The following observations about Spain, some of them unexpected, are consistent with the predictions of my theory:

—The level of regional identity is independent of economic status. It is not the case that richer regions have higher levels of regional identity. That is surprising, because a main component of a stronger regional identity is a desire to have more political independence, which would directly imply less cross-region redistribution from wealthier regions.

—Spain has a lower level of overall redistribution than its European peers.

—The two regions in Spain with strong regional identities and a high degree of fiscal independence have less income inequality, either through redistribution through taxes or through being more egalitarian before any redistribution takes place.

—The increase in the relevance of regional identity gives rise to instability within the federal system.

The first observation reflects the limited extent to which regional identification seems to track wealth, which is surprising. Polling data permit the construction of an index of regional identity, which reveals that regions such as Madrid, which is very wealthy, have no regional sentiment, while others such as Galicia and Andalucía, which are relatively poor, show strong signs of regional identity.[14] The relationship between regional identity and GDP per capita, portrayed in figure 10-2, indicates that for the average citizen, the level of regional identity has little to do with economic self-interest, in the sense of wanting less redistribution if they are wealthier and more redistribution if they are poorer.[15] While it is true that Catalonia and the Basque Country are both wealthy and have strong regional identities, they are only two instances. As seen in figure 10-2, panel A, only four of the nine regions for which survey data are available fall into the quadrant where one would expect to find them if there were a perfect correlation between wealth and regional identity. In fact, the correlation coefficient between wealth and regional identity is small ($\rho = 0.21$).

The evolution of wealth also seems to have little to do with the development of regional identity in Spain over the last 20 to 30 years. The index of regional identity shows that while Madrid has been reasonably steady throughout, Catalonia has gone from having a regional identity that was 38 percent higher than that of Madrid in 1988 to 48 percent higher in 2010. In the same period, the economic evolution of Catalonia has been quite different: while it started out above the Spanish average in GDP per capita (higher by 21 percentage points) and on par with Madrid (2 percentage points lower), it has now become poorer: its GDP per capita is 17 percentage points higher than the national average and 11 percentage points lower than Madrid's. Indeed, GDP growth in regions with a strong regional identity seems to be in line with or even sometimes below the Spanish average, as in the case of Catalonia, which, along with Andalucía and Galicia, had mostly weaker growth than the rest of Spain in every period. GDP growth in other regions with weak regional identities, such as Castilla y León and Asturias, was greater than the average. Thus there is no apparent relation between regional identity and economic growth.[16]

The strength of the separatist movement in the Basque Country is consistent with that finding. Operating under the charter regime, the Basque Country is already almost completely fiscally autonomous; in addition, it pays less than other regions for state services. Given that independence would have very limited distributive consequences for the Basque Country (if anything, less efficiency in services that are now centralized, such as defense), its demand for still more autonomy has to be attributed to other factors.

Figure 10-2. *Spanish Regional and National Identity*[a]

Panel A: Correlation of Identity Index with Regional GDP per Capita

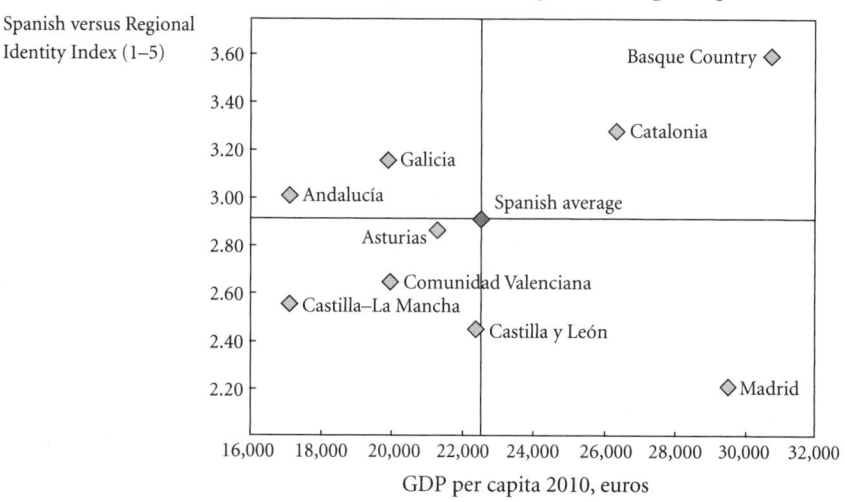

Panel B: Regional Identity Map

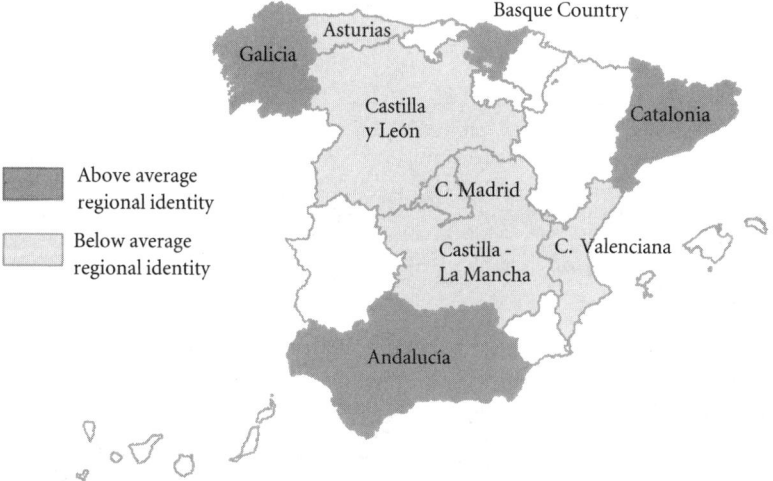

Sources: Centro de Investigaciones Sociólogicas, "Sentimiento Nacionalista [Nationalist Sentiment]," polls A202030090-A202030240 (http://datosbd.cis.es/ciswebconsultas/serieSearchLoad.htm). GDP per capita data come from Instituto Nacional de Estadística, Contabilidad Regional de España [Spanish Regional Accounts] database (www.ine.es/jaxi/menu.do?type=pcaxis&path=%2Ft35%2Fp010&file= inebase&L=0.)

a. The index is constructed on the basis of the answer to the question "To what extent do you identify with your region vis-à-vis Spain?" 1 = *I feel solely Spanish;* 5 = *I feel solely from my region.* Data are available for the nine regions shaded in the map, which comprise 81 percent of the population. Data come from latest available polls, conducted from 2010 to 2012 depending on region.

Table 10-2. *Gini Coefficient of Market and Disposable Household Income (DHI) in EU Countries*[a]

Country of EU-15	DHI Gini	Market (factor) income Gini	DHI equality ranking	Difference in Gini from factor income to DHI	Gain in equality from factor income to DHI (ranking)	Year of data
Luxembourg	0.319	0.519	1	0.201	9	2007
Denmark	0.328	0.563	2	0.235	4	2004
Sweden	0.329	0.566	3	0.236	3	2005
France	0.330	0.563	4	0.232	5	2000
Netherlands	0.331	0.570	5	0.238	2	2007
Austria	0.333	0.549	6	0.216	8	2007
Finland	0.354	0.580	7	0.226	7	2004
Spain	**0.357**	**0.516**	**8**	**0.159**	**14**	**2007**
Germany	0.358	0.597	9	0.238	1	2007
Italy	0.367	0.561	10	0.195	13	2007
Greece	0.372	0.571	11	0.199	11	2007
Ireland	0.387	0.586	12	0.200	10	2008
Belgium	0.402	0.629	13	0.227	6	2004
United Kingdom	0.415	0.613	14	0.198	12	2004

Source: Luxembourg Income Study data at the household level (www.lisdatacenter.org/data-access/). Data taken from period before 2009 to avoid confounding by financial crisis.

a. Disposable household income: total monetary and non-monetary current income net of income taxes and social security contributions; factor income: total current monetary and non-monetary income from labor and capital. Gini coefficients are a measure of income inequality ranging from 0 (complete equality) to 1 (complete inequality). Data are not available for Portugal.

The second observation is that a country with Spain's federal setup can be expected to have less redistribution than would be predicted for either a centralized state (with no sense of regional identity) or one with a more developed type of federalism in which each region does most of the redistribution within its boundaries. Table 10-2 shows that Spain's tax system produces less reduction in inequality than the systems of all other EU countries.[17] Spain's expenditure on public social services is just 21 percent of GDP, or 2 percentage points lower than that of the average EU country. That rate is higher than the rate of only the two Anglo-Saxon countries (United Kingdom and the Republic of Ireland) and two relatively small countries (Luxembourg and the Netherlands), and it is 9 percentage points lower than the rate of France and of Sweden.[18] Spain's spending on public social services is also lower than in other Southern

European countries such as Italy, Portugal, and Greece and other EU countries in the bottom half in terms of income.[19]

The third observation is that in Spain more regional independence is associated with more equality. Both of the two wealthy regions that enjoy the charter regime, the Basque Country and Navarra, have strong historic roots and a high level of regional identity and are largely fiscally independent from the rest of Spain. In both regions, the level of income inequality after transfers is low. Navarra is ranked as the second-most egalitarian of the seventeen ACs in Spain while the Basque Country is ranked fifth. They also have among the very lowest levels of income inequality in the EU. In the Basque Country, that is the result of high levels of redistribution; in Navarra, there is some redistribution, but even before transfers, it is already one of the most egalitarian societies in terms of market income, perhaps because there is less disparity in workers' skills or employers are more egalitarian-minded.

The theory would predict that the greater autonomy enjoyed by these regions would be associated with a higher level of redistribution than elsewhere in Spain, enough to reach high levels of equality. The reality, although consistent with the theory, is not as compelling as one might hope, given that these two regions are among the wealthiest regions in Spain and thus, within the European context, more likely to be egalitarian.

The fourth observation is that as levels of regional identity have risen, the taxation level has increasingly been deemed unacceptable and thus been subject to downward pressure. In the case of Spain, most of the relevant regulations were set in the 1978 constitution or subsequent laws, such as the 1980 Organic Law of Autonomous Community Finances. Regional identity has been on the upswing since that time. In 2011, six of the seventeen governing parties in the ACs were regionalist or separatist parties, more than at any point since 1978. These parties typically vow to reform the constitution to establish a new fiscal arrangement. Outright separatist governments have been elected in two regions (Catalonia and the Basque Country). My theory predicts downward pressure on the tax level from the increase in regional identity. I suggest that the current political turmoil surrounding Spain's system of decentralization, including the separatist movements, is largely an expression of discontent with current fiscal arrangements.

The Dependence of the Spanish Regional System on Access to Sovereign Financing

The mismatch between redistribution levels across regions and the preferences of citizens cannot fully explain the current political crisis in Spain. The crisis did not occur until 2012, and it could not have happened before because expenditure levels in the regions had not yet diminished.

The System before 2008

Until the closure of international capital markets, the financing of expenditure with debt concealed the pattern of redistribution. Only in the aftermath of the 2008 crisis was the effect of redistribution at the AC level seen for the first time. The Spanish regional framework does not allow for ACs to increase their expenditures according to the taxes collected within the region because part of those taxes is destined for redistribution. Since the ACs' budget must be balanced overall, redistribution among regions will cause some regions to win and others to lose. This pattern was hidden while a decade of strong growth and increasing use of debt financing brought in temporary revenues.

Transfers from the ACs to the state were artificially balanced. Wealthier regions received from the state nearly as much as they collected; poorer regions were net beneficiaries as well. The arrangement was maintained through significant deficits, financed with debt at both the regional and the national level.[20] Indeed, the debt of ACs grew at an annual rate of 15 percent from 1990 to 2008 and at a rate of 25 percent from 2008 to 2011.[21] Although the EU Maastricht Treaty, in place since 1993, set the maximum debt at 60 percent of GDP for public administrations, total debt volume of Spanish public administrations rose from 44 percent to 86 percent of GDP from 1990 to 2012. All of the increase before 2008 reflected debt issued and guaranteed by ACs, which rose, on average, from 2 percent of GDP in 1990 to 7 percent in 2008 and 16 percent in 2012. This evolution has been uneven across ACs, with no clear relation between the level of regional identity and debt level. In Catalonia and Comunidad Valenciana, debt reached 23 to 25 percent of GDP in 2012.[22]

The expansion of debt was fueled by a benign economic climate that favored leveraging at every level of government and by the central government's unwillingness to impose fiscal discipline. That, in turn, was likely related to the central government's dependence on the political support of regionalist parties, which were necessary to sustain minority governments. In the last six national elections (since 1993), regionalist parties have never had more than 11 percent of the popular vote. Whichever of the two large national parties garnered the most votes, however, sought their support in pursuit of a parliamentary majority, succeeding in four of the six instances.[23] The system of representation in the national parliament favors party lists that are large in each constituency (typically provinces). Large regional parties with strong support in one or a few provinces are thus overrepresented in parliament relative to their popular support.[24] Minority national parties have less parliamentary representation than strong regionalist

Figure 10-3. *Representation of National Minority Parties and Regionalist Parties since the First Democratic Elections*[a]

Percent of total deputies in national parliament[b]

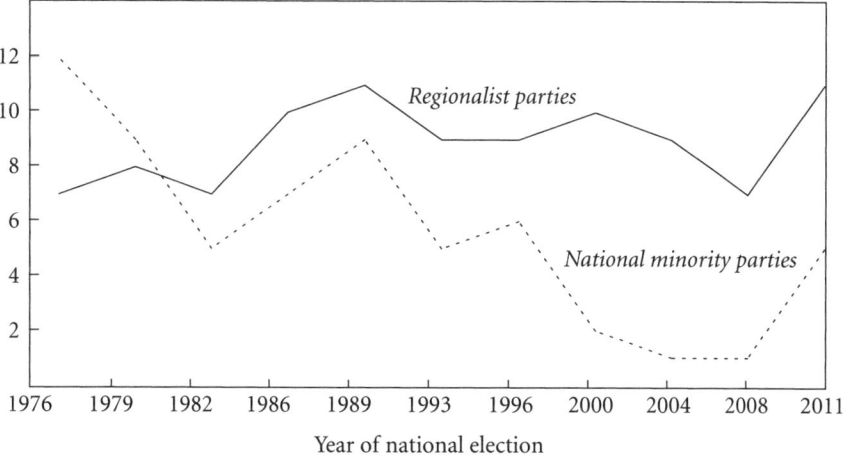

Year of national election

Source: Author's calculations, based on official election results (www.elecciones.mir.es).

a. National minority parties include all national parties except Partido Popular (PP) and Partido Socialista Obrero Español (PSOE).

b. 100 percent = 350 deputies.

parties. For example, support for Izquierda Unida, traditionally the national (left-wing) third party, is scattered around Spain rather than focused in one particular region; in the 2008 elections, it won 3.9 percent of the votes nationwide and took two deputies. In contrast, Convergència i Unió (CiU), the leading party in Catalonia, took ten deputies with just 3.0 percent of the national vote.

Representation in parliament of minority national parties has been declining since 1978 while that of regionalist parties has been rising. This is no doubt in part because of the perception that voting for one of the minority national parties is not an efficient use of one's vote, as it takes them many more votes to get a national deputy. As seen in figure 10-3, while minority national parties obtained 12 percent of the national parliament deputies in the inaugural 1977 elections, they took a mere 1 percent in 2008. Regionalist parties thus hold the key to government in Spain when one of the largest parties does not enjoy an outright majority. Typically the regionalist parties also govern their home regions, as does CiU, and the central government must authorize them to issue debt. However, the central government would be reluctant to exercise its duty to control regional finances and thereby risk alienating the very parties whose support it needs. Even when one of the two largest parties does win an outright

Figure 10-4. *Government Consumption, Debt, and Tax Collections in Spain,*
1990–2009[a]

Index

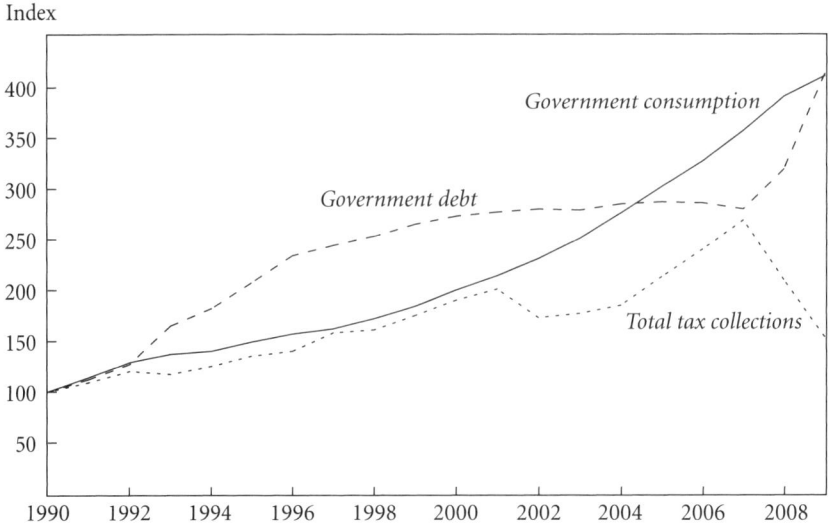

Sources: Debt: Bank of Spain, *Boletín Estadístico,* chart 11.7 (www.bde.es/webbde/es/estadis/infoest/
bolest11.html); government consumption and taxes: Instituto Nacional de Estadística, "Cuentas
Nacionales de España, Información Tributaria [Spanish National Accounts, Tax Information]" (www.
ine.es/jaxi/menu.do?type=pcaxis&path=%2Ft35%2Fp008&file=inebase&L=0).
    a. Index of nominal value in euros, set at 100 in 1990.

majority, party leaders are concerned about alienating partners that they will
need in the future. Only a major crisis could compel the central government to
risk disputes with its coalition partners over the finances of the regions that the
central government governs.

The Global Debt Crisis

The ACs' ability to finance significant spending through debt changed in 2011.
With concerns looming over Spain's ability to repay its debt, the yield on the
Spanish ten-year state bond (*bono del estado*) reached 7.7 percent in the secondary market, 6.5 percentage points above the German bond.[25] The debt issued
by ACs reached an 11-percentage-point risk premium, and indeed access was
closed to sovereign debt markets for all ACs by July 2012.[26]
    Figure 10-4 summarizes the evolution of the expenditures, tax collections,
and debt burden of the Spanish government (central, regional, and local).
Consistent with the argument above, accumulated government consumption
growth was higher than tax revenue every year since 1990. In fact, government

consumption grew exponentially, at an average rate of 8 percent every year from 1990 to 2009. Given that Spain was already incurring a yearly deficit at the start of the period, the need for debt financing grew very fast: debt levels doubled between 1990 and 1995 and nearly tripled between 1990 and 2000.[27] While consumption levels continued to grow exponentially, debt levels stabilized until the current crisis. From 2007 to 2009, tax collections fell by 43 percent, while debt grew by 48 percent.

Faced with a financial crisis, the central government took two extraordinary measures. First, for the first time, it attempted to enforce fiscal discipline at the AC level by imposing deficit and debt ceilings. The Law of Budget Stability and Financial Sustainability, which enshrines in Spanish law the Eurozone's Growth and Stability Pact, strengthened in 2011, sets a nationwide maximum of 3 percent for the budget deficit and a 60 percent debt-to-GDP ratio. For the ACs that means a maximum deficit of 1.5 percent and a 15 percent debt-to-GDP ratio.[28] The law develops a model for central government oversight of AC finances, which includes the possibility of a takeover of an AC government by the central government.[29] For the first time, Spain's finance minister requested that the ACs compile a financial-economic rebalancing plan for meeting deficit and debt targets, which had to be approved by May 2012.

The second measure was the explicit backing of AC-issued debt by the central government. Before that, ACs required authorization to issue debt, which "could well be seen as a *tacit* central government guarantee" but was not an unambiguous one.[30] The Fund for Autonomous Community Liquidity was established, with €18,000 million that ACs could tap in order to fulfill their debt obligations.[31] Nine of the seventeen ACs had requested rescue funds by December 2012.

The Situation in 2013

Today the Spanish system is no longer sustainable. A pattern of wealth redistribution commensurate with a more centralized system has clashed with a vision of competitive federalism in which regions have freedom to spend. Spain tried to have it all: moderate levels of taxation befitting a collection of self-interested regions; some redistribution from wealthier to poorer regions; expenditures at the regional level that exceeded income after redistribution; favorable borrowing terms for the ACs through an implicit guarantee of their debts by the state; and no oversight of AC deficits. With the global debt crisis in 2008 economic growth stopped and social policy measures automatically came into play, generating new expenditures as the tax base contracted. The decentralized system designed in 1978 had become untenable. Unfortunately, the solutions that have been proposed do little to resolve the problem.

Current Proposals

A casual observer could identify two themes in Spanish politics today: severe fiscal austerity and a great deal of political unrest coming from separatist forces. Both are results of the incipient development of the two alternatives that have been offered to solve the current crisis.

The first alternative has been a return to centralized government: centrally enforced discipline in spending and deficit reduction and more discriminating use of the central government's authorization of AC debt. Those actions amount to an enforced cap on the indebtedness and deficits of the ACs and much more strenuous control of spending. Through the rescue facility, the central government has also turned into the main liquidity provider for the ACs. This new setup takes Spain back to the system of the early 1980s and before. Regardless of its economic soundness, it is politically infeasible given the degree of autonomy that the ACs have attained since then, as demanded by their citizens. Very quickly, regional governments have accused the central government of "disloyalty," and Catalonia, Andalucía, Asturias, and Canarias all proceeded to boycott the central government's financial oversight meetings or oppose their deficit ceilings.[32]

The alternative approach, which has been put forward unilaterally in Catalonia but could easily be followed by other regions, is independence. In this scenario, Catalans would hold a referendum to decide whether they want Catalonia to be an independent entity within the EU. According to CiU's 2012 manifesto, "the answer of the central government [to Catalonia's political evolution over the last 20 years] has involved insufficient financing, constant intervention in Catalonia's competencies, an institutional disloyalty that has been accentuated in times of crisis, and a lack of respect for symbols of our identity." The objective is clear: "We want a social majority [not an absolute 51 percent but a significant majority] that would allow us to have our own state within the European framework."[33] Catalonia would seek the following:

—fiscal autonomy: no redistribution of Catalan taxes elsewhere in Spain and no oversight of Catalan finances

—the ability to access international markets in terms that are more favorable than current ones

—full expression of Catalan identity.

However, it is unlikely that joining the European Union as an independent state would result in financial autonomy for Catalonia or give it an especially favorable position for accessing international markets.[34] "Reasonably priced" access to international markets would seem to require a change in policy so that the rest of the EU countries guaranteed debt issued by an independent

Catalonia,[35] and that would be unlikely to happen. Germany, which has resisted the issuing of eurobonds and European Central Bank repurchases of Spanish debt, would have to agree to be a guarantor of Catalan debt but would not be able to exert oversight over Catalan accounts. Also, countries like Germany could be put in the unusual position of guaranteeing Catalan debt while Catalonia declined to share its considerable wealth with other countries and regions throughout Europe. The most powerful countries in Europe would be unlikely to support a middle-income nation such as an independent Catalonia without requiring it to support low-income regions in Eastern Europe in the form of transfers. It is more likely that if Spanish regions and perhaps others became independent members of the EU and fiscal integration and oversight within the EU became tighter, those changes would engender integration of the different member states' social policies, with all countries giving something (such as transfers) in return for something else (such as market access at reasonable prices). At an average income of €26,000 per capita in 2010, Catalonia is 60 percent richer than Extremadura, Spain's poorest region, and 162 percent richer than Bulgaria or Romania. It would be the ninth-richest country in the European Union (Spain is only the fourteenth richest).[36] Integration of social policies has always lagged market integration, and there could be resistance on the part of some countries to further such integration on account of inequalities in wealth and labor market risk. But with an increasing number of smaller and less wealthy countries, the process of fiscal integration would likely speed social integration along.[37] Both types of integration would be costly for wealthier states, although the costs would be incurred in different ways, depending on the political arrangement adopted: the costs would be direct in the case of social integration through redistribution and indirect in the case of fiscal integration. In the latter case, the backing of debt would entail a higher risk of default and thus higher costs of financing in international markets.

A Way Forward

An alternative solution to this political crisis would be a settlement akin to the competitive federalism that Nadler and Peterson identify in the United States (see chapter 2 in this volume), wherein the states (or regions) are granted wide discretion by the central government while "lower tiers of government are held accountable to the marketplace—most specifically, to the market for government bonds."[38] While the United States has come to this model from a rather different historical background, which if anything has involved increased centralization of expenditures, the Spanish model (much younger) has worked in the opposite direction.[39] Nevertheless, it is perhaps time to defend a similar model for both nations. In fact, the model already exists in the relationship of the Spanish government with the Basque Country and Navarra, the charter regions. They have maintained low debt levels and therefore still enjoy access to capital markets.

Nadler and Peterson argue that in the United States, "when sovereignty is divided, lower-tier governments are tempted to run debts that place them at grave risk of default in times of financial crisis." A similar lack of responsibility has been facilitated in Spain by a political center that relied on regionalist support. A truly competitive federalism with greater devolution of taxation powers to the ACs and the explicit assignment to them of responsibility for their fiscal stability seems appropriate. Within the new fiscal framework, they could expect no debt guarantee from the central government. Two issues would have to be resolved: how to ensure some degree of national solidarity (in accordance with the preferences that Spanish citizens are believed to have) and how such fiscally autonomous entities would operate within the European Union framework and in particular within the increasingly fiscally centralized Eurozone.[40]

Given the solidarity principle, the new framework would have to resolve current tensions regarding the redistribution of wealth. The goal would be something akin to the system of the Basque Country and Navarra, which collect most of their taxes and then provide some funds to support common national services and to be redistributed to the rest of Spain. Those funds are typically less than are collected from other regions. One study found that the Basque Country and Navarra, which had the second- and third-largest amounts of per capita wealth respectively, contributed the fifth- and eighth-largest amounts per capita to redistribution.[41] A system similar to the charter regime extended to the entire country would seem to be a reasonable way forward, with an important caveat: for the new system to become sustainable, it would have to be coupled with a substantial reduction in expenditures at the central level that reflected the central government's diminished responsibilities. Such a reduction has not yet been undertaken.

With respect to the status of this potential system of competitive federalism within the EU, the European Council could exercise oversight of the ACs' finances directly, as it does for EU members at the national level. That would likely be a more credible and acceptable type of accountability for the ACs than oversight by Spain's central government, whose authority is crippled by its need for the political support of regionalist parties. And it would be more acceptable to regionalist parties as it would not run counter to the perceived progress in achieving greater autonomy from Spain. Control would rest in a "third party," and issues of European and national identity would not come into the picture. This new system would be novel and potentially politically unpalatable to the Spanish government, as it does entail a high degree of fiscal independence of the ACs. It would also be unique within the European framework, and some countries might see it as encouraging their own separatist movements. It would likely require an arrangement involving a form of EU-based technocratic oversight rather than the political oversight now in place.[42] That would ensure that it is not the other Eurozone countries that are evaluating Spanish regions as peers but a new EU entity that is evaluating all autonomous spending entities in the Eurozone.

While Europe has to be an integral part of the solution to the political crisis in Spain, it is unlikely that outright independence would prove a desirable and acceptable way of securing a settlement. Similarly, the time for a centralized Spanish state has passed. A better solution would be a new constitutional arrangement that reflects changing regional identities and thus the relation that many Spanish citizens want to have with the rest of Spain. Competitive federalism similar to what was once enjoyed by the United States, with adequate oversight from the European Union, may be the best, if an imperfect, way forward for Spain.

Notes

1. "Institutional Message of the President of the Generalitat, on Occasion of the New Year," December 30, 2012 (http://estaticos.elperiodico.com/resources/pdf/2/8/1356884574982.pdf).

2. As contained in the current Ley Orgánica de Educación [Organic Law of Education] (Law 3/2006, May 3, 2006) and in the draft of Ley Orgánica de Mejora de Calidad Educativa (www.mecd.gob.es/) [Organic Law for Improvement in Education].

3. Jonathan Rodden, *Hamilton's Paradox: The Promise and Peril of Fiscal Federalism* (Cambridge University Press, 2006).

4. Eurostat, Government Expenditure in Europe database (http://epp.eurostat.ec.europa.eu/portal/page/portal/eurostat/home/).

5. Throughout this chapter, unless otherwise noted, I use "EU" as shorthand for the so-called EU-15, which includes the members who joined the EU up to 2004: Austria, Belgium, Denmark, Finland, France, Germany, Greece, Ireland, Italy, Luxembourg, Netherlands, Portugal, Spain, Sweden, and the United Kingdom.

6. Reflecting the fact that 82 percent of the Spanish tax revenues handled by the Central Tax Agency consist of personal income tax (42 percent), sales tax (31 percent), and corporate income tax (10 percent). That means that ACs have full control of 36 percent of those taxes. For more details, see Servicio de Estudios del REAF-CGCEE, *Panorama de la Fiscalidad Autónomica y Foral 2012,* Madrid (2012).

7. Ley Orgánica de Financiación de las Comunidades Autónomas (Law 3/2009, December 18, 2009) [Organic Law on Financing of Autonomous Communities].

8. The charter regimes were a reward for the support given by those regions to the Bourbon dynasty during the 1701–13 War of the Spanish Succession.

9. The account of AC finances has been summarized and updated from Julio López-Laborda, Jorge Martinez-Vazquez, and Carlos Monasterio, "The Practice of Fiscal

Federalism in Spain," International Studies Program Working Paper 06-23 (Andrew Young School of Policy Studies, Georgia State University, 2006).

10. See, for instance, Patrick Bolton and Gérard Roland, "The Breakup of Nations: A Political Economy Analysis," *Quarterly Journal of Economics,* vol. 112, no. 4 (1997).

11. It can be argued that a similar phenomenon is observed in other regions, such as Scotland, Corsica, Flemish Belgium, and others throughout the EU.

12. The view that a large part of the variation in the taste for political decentralization reflects the regional distribution of income is developed in Pablo Beramendi, "Inequality and the Territorial Fragmentation of Solidarity," *International Organization,* vol. 61 (2007); the quote comes from page 783.

13. We can easily formalize this argument by positing that the generic utility function of a representative individual i in a region c within a nation-state s takes the form

$$U_i = \theta_i V[(1-t)y_i] + \theta_c V(\gamma_c t y_i) + \theta_s V[(1-\gamma_c)ty_i].$$

Here V is a quasi-concave continuous function and y_i is the individual's income level. The remaining parameters are as follows:

θ_i weighs the impact of i's wealth on his utility (assumed to be similar throughout the region).

θ_c weighs the impact of welfare in region c on i's utility.

θ_s weighs the impact of welfare in the rest of the country s on i's utility.

γ_c is the fraction of taxes staying in the region c.

Taking first-order conditions gives the optimal level of taxation t, which changes in the manner described in the text, for different values of θ_c and θ_s and as they shift (with $\gamma_c < 0.5$).

14. Spanish versus Regional Identity Index (1–5), constructed on the basis of the respondent's answer to the question "To what extent do you identify with your region vis-à-vis Spain?" The numerical index is the population average constructed from 1 = *I feel solely Spanish* and 5= *I feel solely from my region.* The average for Spain was 2.92. Data are available from Centro de Investigaciones Sociólogicas, Pols A202030090-A202030240, 2010 (http://datosbd.cis.es/ciswebconsultas/serieSearchLoad.htm).

15. That is, if we assume, as appears plausible, that regional identity level is positively correlated with desire for increased decentralization.

16. Income data are based on author's calculations using 2010 data from Instituto Nacional de Estadística, Contabilidad Regional de España [Spanish Regional Accounts] database (www.ine.es/jaxi/menu.do?type=pcaxis&path=%2Ft35%2Fp010&file=inebas e&L=0). Regional identity data are as described in note 14 above.

17. In the Luxembourg Income Study, factor income is all income from labor and capital while disposable household income includes transfers and is net of taxes. Most of the difference will therefore be related to the public social expenditure programs, similar to what the OECD calls social expenditure.

18. Social expenditure data taken from OECD's Social Expenditure Database (www. oecd.org/els/social/expenditure)

19. In terms of purchasing power parity–adjusted GDP per capita within the EU.

20. This is the argument that the government of Catalonia has used to advance the view that the fact that the balance between the taxes collected in Catalonia and government transfers into Catalonia is close to zero is too simplistic a portrait of the fiscal position of Catalonia as part of Spain. They argue that this balancing is financed with central government debt, which means that Catalonia, if one takes into account its share of Spanish debt based on its GDP, is fiscally worse off than it would be as an independent country. If it were independent, less debt would have been needed to finance its expenditure levels. See, for instance, chapter 6 of Generalitat de Catalunya, *Resultados de la balanza fiscal de Cataluña con el sector público central 2006–2009* [Results from Catalonia's Fiscal Balance with the Central Public Sector 2006–2009] (Barcelona: Generalitat de Catalunya 2012).

21. Bank of Spain, *Boletín Estadístico 2012* [Statistical Bulletin], chart 13.9 (www.bde.es/webbde/es/estadis/infoest/bolest.html).

22. Ibid., charts 13.9, 13.10, 12.6, and 14.8.

23. Author's calculations based on official election results (www.elecciones.mir.es).

24. Constituencies coincide for the most part with provinces (one hierarchical level down from ACs). In turn, voting patterns of provinces and ACs are largely similar—that is, in those ACs where regional parties have large representation, those parties have it in their provinces as well.

25. On July 24, 2012, according to Bloomberg (www.bloomberg.com/quote/GSPG 10YR:IND).

26. Matteo Cominetta, "Can Catalonia Leave? Hardly," UBS Investment Research Note (2012).

27. The yearly deficit was €14.2 billion in 1995, the first year in the period for which data are available. Bank of Spain, *Boletín Estadístico,* chart 11.1.

28. The Growth and Stability Pact of 2011 gives more power to the Euro Council to ensure that Euro members' deficits and debt are contained and to oversee their budget processes. This pact was meant to be more binding than previous agreements with a similar spirit, as noncompliance would lead to the implementation of "automatic consequences." European Council, Statement by the Euro Area Heads of State or Government, 2011 (http://consilium.europa.eu/uedocs/cms_data/docs/pressdata/en/ec/126658.pdf).

29. Spanish Organic Law 2/2012 (April 27, 2012).

30. Isabelle Joumard and Claude Giorno, "Getting the Most Out of Public Sector Decentralisation in Spain." OECD Economics Department Working Paper 436 (2005) (http://search.oecd.org/officialdocuments/displaydocumentpdf/?doclanguage=en&cote =ECO/WKP(2005)23).

31. Quoted from Radio Televisión Española, the national public radio and television organization (www.rtve.es/noticias/20121211/cuatro-comunidades-comprometen-58-18000-millones-del-fondo-liquidez-autonomica/572719.shtml).

32. The quote is from Artur Mas, president of Catalonia, in "Mas afea la 'deslealtad' de Rajoy con el déficit y el PPC pide respeto al pacto tácito [Mas Censures the 'Disloyalty' of Rajoy on the Deficit and the Popular Party of Catalonia Demands Respect for the Tacit Pact]," *La Vanguardia,* July 18, 2012 (www.lavanguardia.com/politica/20120718/54326364424/mas-afea-deslealtad-rajoy-ppc-respecto-pacto-tacito.html).

33. Quoted from Convergència i Unió's electoral manifesto: "Programa Electoral 2012" (www.ciu.cat/media/76990.pdf).

34. There are, in addition, two important considerations outside the scope of this study: first, it is unclear whether Catalonia can declare independence unilaterally, as to do so would require a change to the constitution. Second, Catalonia would likely have to reapply for membership in the European Union, which would have to be granted unanimously by its members.

35. Full control of tax collections is unlikely to be enough, as is sometimes claimed, for the same reasons that it was not enough throughout 2012 for the Spanish central government to have that control.

36. Author's calculations based on Eurostat, National Accounts database (http://epp.eurostat.ec.europa.eu/portal/page/portal/national_accounts/data/database) and Instituto Nacional de Estadística, Contabilidad Regional de España [Spanish Regional Accounts] database (www.ine.es/jaxi/menu.do?type=pcaxis&path=%2Ft35%2Fp010&file=inebase&L=0.

37. See Beramendi, "Inequality and the Territorial Fragmentation of Solidarity" for an argument along these lines.

38. See chapter 2 of this volume.

39. Ibid.

40. Following renewal of the Growth and Stability Pact of 2011. See note 28.

41. Instituto de Estudios Fiscales, "Las Balanzas Fiscales de las CC.AA. españolas con las AA. Públicas Centrales 2005 [The Fiscal Balances of the Spanish ACs with the Central Public Administrations 2005]" (Madrid: Ministerio de Economía y Hacienda, 2008)

42. An example, perhaps, would be a system wherein a committee of the EU Commission assesses members' budgets and makes binding decisions, with no veto power by the European Council.

RICHARD SIMEON, JAMES PEARCE, *and* AMY NUGENT

11

The Resilience of Canadian Federalism

This volume explores the idea that federal or decentralized systems of government may pose special difficulties for countries experiencing a fiscal crisis of the sort that has disrupted North America and Europe in recent years. On the one hand, autonomous subnational units—states and provinces—may use their powers to tax and spend in ways that are fiscally undisciplined and even irresponsible, exacerbating the crisis at the national and the international level. On the other hand, in responding to a crisis central governments may employ controls, regulations, and reductions in intergovernmental transfers that seriously limit the ability of subnational governments to make choices and manage their own affairs. The result may be a heightened level of conflict between central and state governments and increased tension between the regions that fare reasonably well and those that experience the greatest economic stress.

This chapter explores the case of Canada. It challenges the idea that high levels of fiscal decentralization necessarily lead to fiscal irresponsibility or incapacity or to unmanageable conflict. That is not to say that there has not been tension or disagreement between the federal and provincial governments in Canada but that it has been limited and has not had serious ramifications in wider markets.

That may come as a surprise. Canada is among the most decentralized federations in the world.[1] Canadian provinces have very broad fiscal autonomy to impose almost any form of tax—income, consumption, corporate, and so forth. Provinces have unlimited power to borrow, in both domestic and international markets. There are no provisions for federal monitoring, regulation, or control of provincial taxing, spending, and borrowing. Intergovernmental transfers are central to Canadian federalism, but relative to those of other federations, the amounts are small and come with few conditions attached.[2]

So it could be argued that it might be especially difficult to manage and coordinate the actions and policies of Canadian governments in the face of the international fiscal crisis, but generally that has not been the case. Canadian federalism responded to the crisis in a broadly coordinated way. Federal and provincial policies were well linked, and there was relatively little tension between the federal and provincial governments. The post-recovery period from 2011 onward has seen somewhat greater interregional tension, basically between the oil- and gas-producing provinces (Alberta, Saskatchewan, and Newfoundland and Labrador) and other provinces, notably Ontario and Quebec, whose economies are much more rooted in traditional manufacturing. Balancing the differing economic challenges of the provinces is difficult, with increasing economic disparities (once wealthy Ontario is now an equalization recipient) adding further strain. But those disparities are not a creature of the economic crisis—they long predated it—nor are they a cause of it. All of this presents a puzzle. Canada—highly decentralized, regionally and linguistically divided—seems to have done relatively well. Why?

In an effort to answer that question, we first provide a brief overview of the structural, political, and institutional forces that have shaped Canadian federalism and its political culture. We then map the contours of fiscal federalism in Canada, in terms of both formal powers and changes in Canadian governments' relative shares of tax revenues, expenditures, and debts.

We assume that the legacies of the past cast a strong shadow over current policy and policymaking. Accordingly, we briefly explore some previous episodes of fiscal crisis in Canada during which the ability of governments to respond would have been similarly challenged. In the 1930s, the Great Depression brought several provinces close to bankruptcy. It also led to a set of fundamental policy changes that laid the foundation for much of the Canadian welfare state and for the Equalization Program, which is one of the most fundamental features of the Canadian federal bargain. The energy crises of the early 1970s and the early 1980s dramatically shifted the Canadian political economy toward western Canada, triggering a regional and intergovernmental battle over control of energy policy and revenues—exemplified by the National Energy Program—that reverberates to this day. Finally, draconian federal spending cuts in the 1990s, including substantial reductions in federal transfers to the provinces, generated much protest but paradoxically laid the foundation for a more ideologically and fiscally coordinated approach when the current global crisis developed.[3]

Overall, the lessons learned and policies adopted in these earlier periods set the stage for intergovernmental relations in the current crisis. We briefly discuss some basic features of federalism in Canada before presenting its fiscal framework. We then tell the story in more detail, from the 1990s to the 2008 financial crisis and the subsequent recession. What policies did the federal and provincial governments undertake, and how did they interact? What explains the patterns in intergovernmental relations? And what might be the lasting effects on Canadian federalism?

The Structure of Canadian Federalism

First, Canada is an extraordinarily robust *federal society*. It is a multinational society, characterized by the presence of anglophone Canada, the majority, which is spread across the northern half of the North American continent, and by that of francophone Canada, which constitutes about a quarter of the Canadian population and is concentrated mainly in Quebec. Ever since the British conquest of the French in the eighteenth century, French-speaking Canadians have been deeply committed to retaining their language, identity, and, until the 1960s, their religion.

As a highly conservative Catholic society in the early decades of the Canadian federation, Quebec focused chiefly on resisting the growth of federal authority and federal intrusions into areas of provincial jurisdiction. In the 1960s, however, Quebec underwent a dramatic period of growth and modernization known as the Quiet Revolution.[4] Quebec embraced secularism, the modern welfare state, and a social democratic approach to government. But it was committed to modernization on its own terms, to being *maîtres chez nous* (masters of our own house). Now the goal was not simply resistance to federal expansion but also greater policy and fiscal autonomy for the province. It was accompanied by a call for constitutional recognition of Quebec as a "distinct society" with a mission to protect and promote the francophone community. Along with calls for a reformed decentralized or asymmetrical federalism, a significant secessionist movement also developed. A sovereignist government was first elected in 1976, controlled by the Parti Québécois, which since then has alternated in power with the federalist Parti Liberal. The Parti Québécois has held two referendums aimed at Quebec independence in conjunction with an ill-defined "association" or "partnership" with the rest of Canada.

The relevance of this story for our purposes is that since the outset, Quebec has been the principal driver of Canada's high degree of decentralization. Centralization was a recipe for disintegration of the federation. But Canada also includes nine other provinces and three territories—"from sea, to sea, to sea"—that have strong identities and interests of their own.[5] Canada's constituent parts vary with respect to

—*Population:* Ontario has approximately 13.5 million inhabitants, constituting 38 percent of the population; Quebec has approximately 8 million (24 percent). British Columbia (BC) and Alberta have rapidly growing populations

(4.6 and 3.8 million, respectively), while tiny Prince Edward Island has only 146,000 residents—less than 1 percent of the total population.[6]

—*History, culture, and traditions:* Canada is becoming increasingly divided between highly urban and multicultural societies in Ontario, BC, Alberta, and Quebec and more homogeneous, aging rural societies in nonurban areas (with Atlantic Canada having a 50-50 urban-rural split).

—*Economic strength:* Regional disparities in per capita income, GDP per capita, and employment rates are large and persistent, mitigated only in part by growing interprovincial mobility. For example, GDP per capita in oil-rich Alberta was approximately C$49,000 (Canadian currency) in 2009. GDP per capita in Ontario, once the wealthiest province, was approximately C$39,000, while it hovered just above C$30,000 in most of Atlantic Canada.[7]

—*Economic structures:* Broadly speaking (though it is easy to conjure oversimplified stereotypes), the Atlantic Provinces have resource-based (fishing and forestry) economies. The region has lagged economically, but recent development of offshore oil and natural gas has contributed to significant economic growth. Ontario and Quebec—Canada's economic heartland—are the centers of manufacturing, finance, and transportation. Public policy in the nineteenth century facilitated their development as such: in 1879, John A. Macdonald's National Policy protected industries in central Canada while leveraging resource-producing western Canada as a market for tariff-protected industries in central Canada. That provoked a long-standing grievance in Canadian federalism.

The Prairies—Manitoba, Saskatchewan, and Alberta—were a classic agricultural hinterland until the discovery of oil, natural gas, potash, and other resources began to transform the region into Canada's economic powerhouse. That initiated what many consider a fundamental power shift from central to western Canada. In addition, after an attempt in the 1980s by the federal government to assert control over the energy industry by setting a national price for oil and natural gas, the western provinces succeeded in winning further constitutional protections for natural resource management across provinces. The passage of the North American Free Trade Agreement (NAFTA), in force since 1994, put the last nails into the coffin of the nineteenth-century National Policy.

Again this story has important implications for fiscal federalism. First, it is clear that the economic interests of central and western Canada often differ. The center is (like the states of the U.S. Midwest) committed to preserving its manufacturing economy, which, among other things, requires a relatively low-valued Canadian dollar. Massive increases in commodity prices, of course, drive up the value of the dollar, creating a regionally structured, Canadian version of the "Dutch disease."

Second, large disparities in wealth and income exist across provinces, raising fundamental questions of values: To what extent are such disparities tolerable? To what extent should there be equality and revenue sharing across provinces? They also raise the question of economic efficiency: To what extent is interprovincial redistribution consistent with the most effective deployment of resources? The recent economic challenges have heightened the efficiency debate, but the idea of Canada as a "sharing community" is deeply entrenched and has strong support in both richer and poorer regions. A constitutional amendment in 1982 committed Canada to the idea of equalization, stating that

> Parliament and the Government of Canada are committed to the principle of making equalization payments to ensure that provincial governments have sufficient revenues to provide reasonably comparable levels of public service at reasonably comparable levels of taxation.[8]

As the economy changes, that principle is becoming more difficult to maintain.

Thus the dynamics of fiscal federalism in Canada are driven by the larger political economy in which they are embedded. But the institutional structure of Canadian federalism also exerts a large influence. Canada's is a parliamentary system, based on the British Westminster model. Two factors crucial for Canadian federalism flow from that structure. First, as it has evolved, parliamentary government has become executive-centered government. Power is concentrated in the hands of the executive, especially the prime minister and the provincial premiers—"First Ministers," in Canadian parlance.[9] The second, directly related, factor is party discipline. Members speak and vote according to instructions from elected executives. They have little freedom to speak for and represent the interests of their province or region, although they often advocate for their local constituents in the privacy of the party caucus.

This discipline is reinforced by two other factors. The Senate, often seen in federations as the institution designed to bring regional interests to bear on central decisionmaking, is appointed by the prime minister and fails to play a significant role in Canadian federalism. Second, in a highly regionalized country, the first-past-the-post electoral system tends to greatly favor regionally concentrated minority parties (such as, for many years, the Bloc Québécois in Quebec) and to disadvantage minority parties that have scattered support across the country. Canada has an increasingly regionalized party system in which no national party is able to gain sweeping electoral success across all regions.[10]

The result is that the federal parliament is relatively ineffective at representing and accommodating regional interests. Often, large sections of the country (such as Quebec today and western Canada in the 1960s and 1970s) find that they have little voice in the governing party or executive. One consequence is that citizens turn to powerful provincial premiers to advocate their positions in intergovernmental negotiations. The result is that premiers not only manage their own affairs but often take on the role of a national actor defending regional interests.

Canadian federalism thus becomes what is described as "executive federalism," or "federal-provincial diplomacy," wherein politically autonomous governments engage in bargaining relationships with outside legislatures.[11] In the post–World War II period Ottawa tended to dominate those relationships. Today they are much more relationships of equals.

Interpretations of the basic nature of Canadian federalism have varied over time. The 1867 constitution had many centralist elements, and its chief anglophone founder, John A. Macdonald, confidently expected that Canada would soon become a unitary state with a dominant center. But for Quebec leaders, Canada was a compact between two nations; strong centralization was simply not acceptable. In the early years of the federation, Ottawa used its powers over the provinces freely, but by the 1930s the growth of provincial influence and a series of court decisions had eroded federal dominance. Centralizing federal powers in the constitution, such as the ability to disallow provincial legislation, fell into disuse and are now generally considered constitutional dead letters whose use by Ottawa against either Quebec or western Canada would provoke political crisis.

In the 1930s the Great Depression and the subsequent war effort saw a reassertion of federal power. Ottawa, over the strenuous objections of Quebec but with broad support across the rest of the country, was the principal architect of the postwar Canadian welfare state. Responsibility for old age pensions and for unemployment insurance was transferred by constitutional amendment to Ottawa, but most policy was developed and delivered, usually with federal transfer support, by the provinces. Accordingly, the provinces' share of total public sector spending and employment steadily increased. There was no sweeping assertion of federal power on the model of the American New Deal.

By the 1960s and 1970s, the federation faced a number of challenges. The welfare state was now largely complete. With the energy crises of the 1970s, the long postwar boom was replaced by economic uncertainty and volatility. The country was consumed with conflict over the constitution and national unity. Provincial competence and assertiveness was growing. Globalization and free trade challenged the historic economic model.

The institutions of intergovernmental relations took on added importance as "collaborative federalism" took hold.[12] National policy in areas such as health care and the environment became increasingly negotiated by governments acting as equals and was expressed in a series of intergovernmental agreements or accords that set out broad common objectives and financial arrangements.

The agreements had no legal force or status and few if any conditions attached. Implementation was up to provincial governments and legislatures. Governments were to report on their progress to their voters, but they were not to be accountable to Ottawa. Quebec frequently opted out of some or all provisions but retained its share of funding.

The peak institution for this executive-dominated "collaborative federalism" is the First Ministers' Conference, now termed First Ministers' Meetings, or FMMs. Again, meetings are informal, with no set schedule and no votes. Below the FMMs are a number of ministerial councils in specific policy areas that often are chaired or co-chaired by provincial ministers; these councils can be useful arenas for information exchange and mutual learning. A relatively recent addition to this machinery is the Council of the Federation, a body constituted by the provincial premiers, with no federal participation. It serves as a forum for relationship building, managing interprovincial conflict, sharing ideas in major policy areas, and coordinating political strategies vis à vis the federal government.

Despite some successes, by the first decade of the 2000s there was increasing dissatisfaction with the collaborative model. Too often it seemed less like an arena for achieving consensus, cooperation, and compromise than for engaging in turf wars, hogging credit, avoiding blame, and arguing over dollars and cents rather than substantive policy issues. There also was criticism of the closed-door nature of intergovernmental relations and the lack of clear accountability, which were seen as evidence of a "democratic deficit."

Recent Parti Liberal prime ministers (Jean Chrétien and Paul Martin) continued to believe in a strong role for the federal government, especially in social policy. (Federal transfer payments and funding during the mid-1990s, however, did not necessarily reflect that belief). The election of a Conservative Party government led by Stephen Harper in 2006 signaled change. Harper pledged to respect provincial jurisdiction with his concept of "open federalism."[13] In contrast to the interdependence, overlapping, and shared jurisdiction that had characterized intergovernmental relations in the past, Harper proposed a more classical model of federalism, based on what Canadians call "watertight compartments," set out in sections 91 and 92 of the constitution. In this model there are clear lists of federal and provincial responsibilities and each order of government sticks to its assigned roles and responsibilities, acting independently. The solution to the inadequacies of intergovernmental relations is simply to have less of them.

Harper has followed through on open federalism. FMMs are no longer a regular forum in the federation. Harper deals with provinces one on one.[14] In health care, for example, a shared area of great importance, Harper recently announced that there would be no negotiations with the provinces on the new Health Accord, just a federal allocation of funds, with no further federal engagement with provinces in the design of the transfer. Whether this model can be sustained, given the need for close cooperation in areas like energy and aboriginal policies, remains an open question.

Provinces as Fiscal Actors

By almost any measure, Canada is perhaps the most fiscally decentralized modern federation, with the possible exception of Switzerland. It was not always so. The 1867 British North America Act gave both levels of government broad powers to raise revenues but gave exclusive power over tariffs, then the central revenue source, to the federal government. The early years of the federation were characterized by constant provincial demands for federal financial assistance from Ottawa. The development of modern taxation systems, including income and sales taxes, opened the door to broader revenue raising by the provinces themselves, but Ottawa remained dominant. Indeed, during and immediately after World War II, provinces "rented" their tax powers to Ottawa in return for unconditional fiscal transfers. But that too changed as provinces, led by Quebec, demanded both a greater share of tax revenues and greater autonomy in setting their own tax rates. Thus began a period of rapid decentralization.[15]

The building of the welfare state took two forms and took place in two phases. First, in response to the Great Depression, a few central responsibilities, notably old age pensions and unemployment insurance, were constitutionally transferred to the federal government. Other social programs, such as social assistance (welfare), remained under provincial control, but using its power to spend, the federal government influenced provincial programs in areas of welfare and later health care through "conditional grants" to help cover provincial costs (generally 50 percent).

Quebec had always argued that for the federal government to use its spending power to shape provincial policies was unacceptable. Anglophone scholars tended to see the spending power as an essential device for building national programs. The growth of Quebec nationalism, the assertiveness and the growing confidence of the other provinces, and the critical withdrawal of federal support for 50-50 cost sharing changed that perception. Increasingly the federal spending power was seen as illegitimate, as encouraging "intrusions" into areas of provincial jurisdiction. Conditions were now to be negotiated, not imposed.

As a result, the federal government has become a much smaller player in provincial policies. Federal transfers were significantly reduced in the mid to late 1990s, only to rise slowly throughout the 2000s, and conditional transfers have almost disappeared, with the exception of transfers for health care, to which a broad set of conditions (seldom enforced) apply, and now transfers for infrastructure projects, which are cost-matched on the basis of merit. The current federal government has strongly reinforced this trend. Each government is to be responsible for matters under its own jurisdiction; therefore, in most situations, collective intergovernmental decisionmaking is unnecessary.

The result would seem to be greater provincial fiscal autonomy and fewer federal policy levers, but that is not entirely true. In a globalized fiscal crisis such as the current one, the federal government retains policy levers and tools not available to provinces. The federal department of finance is strong and capable, and Canada's central bank is one of the most respected in the world. Ottawa has full control of monetary policy and banking and speaks for Canada in international forums such as the G-8 and the G-20. Provinces are strongly motivated to defer to Ottawa in those forums.

Moreover, there is much coordination and cooperation in the fiscal field. A joint body, the Canada Revenue Agency, administers the tax system—with the exception of Quebec's system (and Ontario's for corporate taxes)—although there is wide variation in provincial tax rates and exemptions. Federal and provincial sales taxes, once separate, have now been "harmonized" in most provinces. The federal and the Quebec government have separate contributory pension schemes, but their investment policies are closely coordinated. While they do not always agree, relations between the federal finance department and provincial treasuries are close, largely out of necessary deference to the weight of the federal finance minister's suasion and authority. And while regional differences are often intense, on the macro policy level both federal and provincial governments have in recent years broadly accepted a neoliberal vision of public policy, thus muting conflict and ensuring fiscal rectitude at both levels.

Arguably, the global fiscal crisis has muted two important recent fiscal conflicts. Quebec has argued strongly that there is a fundamental mismatch between provincially raised revenues and the spending requirements of the provinces—the so-called "fiscal imbalance."[16] The federal government's relatively greater fiscal capacity is seen as just another opportunity for federal meddling in provincial affairs. Quebec's preferred solution is a broad shift of "tax points" (that is, a reduction of federal tax rates offset by increases in corresponding provincial tax rates) from Ottawa to the provinces. However, after Ottawa bailed out the auto industry and adopted other stimulus measures, its deficits rose, so the provincial argument lost much of its force. Similarly, Ontario has argued that it has been short-changed by federal transfer programs, receiving less than its population or economic condition warrants. The province has a strong case, especially as it is faced with the challenges of deindustrialization. Ontario premiers of all political parties have argued for a "fair share" of federal spending.[17] They have met with some success: programs that had a regional bias built in to help poorer provinces are now funded on an equal per capita basis. But the federal employment insurance program continues to provide less support to unemployed workers in Ontario than to workers in traditional slow-growth areas. Again, however, federal efforts, including auto sector bailouts, per capita transfers in health care, and the harmonized sales tax, decreased Ontario's appetite and leverage to address other grievances.

Perhaps the most distinctive element of fiscal federalism in Canada is its fiscal equalization program.[18] Disparities in income and public revenues among the Canadian provinces are large and persistent. As provincial fiscal autonomy grew in the postwar period, those disparities became more problematic because they led to major differences in the capacity of different provinces to provide comparable levels of service to their citizens. Hence, the Canadian equalization program was designed to ensure that each province, rich or poor, would be able to provide similar programs at a similar cost to taxpayers. The system, which evolved over many years, was enshrined in the Constitution Act of 1982.

The program's design was interesting. The obligation to make equalization payments fell on the federal government, not wealthy provinces. Yet the policies and to some extent circumstances—fiscal capacity and local economic conditions, for example—that would give rise to such an obligation rested largely on decisions of provincial governments, over which Ottawa had little control. As economic conditions changed there was much debate about how the payments would be calculated and about the level to which the revenues of poorer provinces would be raised. To the level of the top province? To the national average? To some other standard? Would natural resource revenues be counted or not? Sharp debates on those questions, especially in Newfoundland and Labrador and Saskatchewan, led to overtly political accommodations, leading some to worry that the fundamental principles underlying the equalization program were being eroded and thereby would perhaps lead to loss of legitimacy and public support.

But those issues were relatively minor until two developments took place. First and most important, the boom in oil and gas revenues pushed Alberta's per capita income to unprecedented levels. Alberta expects C$350 billion in royalties from oil sands production over the next 25 years.[19] Alberta's 2009 GDP per capita was the highest among the provinces—19.7 percent higher than that of second-place Ontario. But it would be Ottawa that would be responsible for compensating the provinces that did not benefit from the boom. How, with a constitutional injunction denying Ottawa access to oil and gas royalty revenues, could Ottawa balance those disparities? Were disparities in fiscal capacity across provinces bound to grow? Second, economic changes, including the decline of Ontario's manufacturing industry, meant that the largest, historically most wealthy province was now itself eligible for equalization. How could equalization be sustained?

Moreover, the fiscal crisis and the resulting neoliberal emphasis on promoting efficiency have led to increasing debate about the very foundations of equalization in Canada, with many wondering whether the idea of Canada as a "sharing community" or, as a former premier of Saskatchewan put it, "a giant mutual insurance company" is now unsustainable. But vital as they are to the state of the federation, these debates are not a product of the global crisis or a barrier to responding to it.

Despite these broadly positive assessments of Canadian federalism, the country was not immune from what was going on in the rest of the world, and its consequences certainly reverberated across all governments.

The Shape of the Crisis

Much has been written about Canada's relative economic stability during the 2008 global financial crisis and the recession that followed. Canada's stability stood out against the chaos in U.S. banking, which plunged the U.S. economy headlong into recession, and, soon after that, the crisis in Europe. In the end, Canadian banks—due, in part, to stringent Canadian banking regulations—were less exposed to the toxic mortgage-backed securities that kicked off the global crisis. As a result, the Canadian economy needed only to brace itself against the contagion effects of financial interdependence, and it was able to avoid many of problems of its southern neighbor. In a 2009 special report, TD Economics notes that "in contrast to the U.S., Canada's financial system weathered the global financial storm reasonably well and the economy was ultimately driven into recession by the external shock of a global downturn."[20]

But, however gently Canada entered the global recession, the country still experienced its first significant economic crisis in almost two decades. It is important to consider the real dollars-and-cents impact of the financial crisis on the Canadian economy. When subjected to greater scrutiny, what does the "relative success" of the country's financial situation look like? How does this experience compare with Canada's previous experiences with recession during the global downturns of the early 1980s and 1990s? Were there regional differences—for governments and for individuals—in how the crisis and recession were experienced? It is also important to consider public finances in the years leading up to the crisis. Were Canadian governments well placed to deal with the 2008 crisis? Did their fiscal position protect them from undergoing a more exaggerated economic decline?

A closer look at key economic indicators reveals that, yes, the Canadian economy fared better than its international counterparts but that even so the global economic downturn did not leave the country unscathed. As estimated by the Centre for the Study of Living Standards (CSLS), the crisis and recession will ultimately result in a shortfall of C$12,000 (2007 Canadian dollars) per capita. "In other words, given no economic crisis, GDP per capita in Canada would have likely been $1,736 higher on average each year over the 2008–2014 period."[21]

Canada has experienced three recessionary periods since the early 1980s, in 1982–83, 1991–93, and 2008–09. The 1980s recession was the most severe, with national GDP falling almost 5 percent, and the first quarter of 2009 marked the steepest single-quarter decline, at 1.85 percent. In aggregate terms, the most recent recession was the least severe of the three, with a decline of 3.4 percent in GDP.[22] The Canadian economy also snapped out of the most recent recession much more quickly than it did in either the 1980s or 1990s. Statistics Canada notes that "the recovery in 2009–2010 was almost over in the same amount of time as it took for the recession to hit bottom in 1982 and well before the trough in 1992."[23]

Another sign of the more moderate decline experienced during 2008–09 is the scale of the recession in Canada compared with that in the United States. In 2008–09, when Canada's peak-to-trough downturn was 3.397 percent of GDP, that of the United States was 4.1 percent.[24] The two previous recessions had hit the Canadian economy harder than the U.S. economy. During the 1982–83 recession, when the peak-to-trough decline in Canadian real GDP was 4.9 percent, the decline was 2.7 percent in the United States. During the 1990s recession, when the decline in Canada was 3.4 percent, the decline south of the border was only 1.4 percent. Clearly, when the United States sneezed, Canada caught a cold, but that certainly is not the case now.[25]

A comparison of Canadian and U.S. employment figures for 2008–09 tells a similar story. Beginning in August 2008, the U.S. unemployment rate inched above the Canadian rate, 6.2 and 6.1 percent respectively. It has remained higher ever since, even widening during recovery.[26] However, the industry composition of unemployment is significantly different. While Canadian job losses were experienced primarily in the manufacturing sector (over 50 percent), in the United States the financial and business sector was responsible for 25 percent of job losses (that sector grew in Canada over the same period).[27] That comparison shows the differences in how each country experienced the crisis. The crisis in the United States hit the financial industry hard, while the fallout in Canada was experienced primarily in goods-producing sectors that are especially sensitive to market downturns. As a result, nationwide macroeconomic data capture only part of the story.

The effects of the economic crisis in Canada differed from province to province and region to region. The fall in provincial GDP, perhaps surprisingly, was most severe in the oil-rich provinces—Newfoundland and Labrador, Saskatchewan, and Alberta—and in Ontario, Canada's manufacturing heartland. In almost all cases, however, provincial GDP recovered entirely within two years of the crisis. The major source of the GDP downturn was in Canada's goods-producing industries, which accounted for 30 percent of real GDP when the crisis hit and 72 percent of the decline in GDP between the third quarter of 2008 and the first quarter of 2009—the most severe quarterly drop of the last three recessions.[28]

The manufacturing sector alone contributed more than 55 percent of the downturn. A significant factor in Ontario's struggle, not surprisingly, was automotive manufacturing. "Automotive products were down 19 percent, accounting for nearly half of the quarterly decline in total exports" in the fourth quarter of 2008.[29] Meanwhile, the mining and oil and gas industries suffered significant losses, but they accounted for just over 7 percent of the total.[30] That 7 percent, however, was largely responsible for the sizable GDP decline in Alberta, Saskatchewan, and Newfoundland and Labrador. The drop in commodity prices—exacerbated by the slowdown of the U.S. economy—reversed the long trend of growth in Canada's resource-rich provinces for a brief period.

Although GDP rebounded, there have been significant economic implications for some regions. Most notable, job losses sustained by a few industries have led to an uneven distribution of unemployment. In less than a year (October 2008 to April 2009), more than 320,000 jobs were lost in the goods-producing sector, especially in manufacturing.[31] It is important, however, to note that Canadian manufacturing employment had been shrinking for quite some time prior to the recent crisis. The global crisis merely exacerbated an alarming downturn, begun in 2004, that witnessed the loss of more than 550,000 jobs in just five years, mostly in Ontario.

Despite significant spikes in unemployment in both British Columbia and Alberta, during the recession overall rates were higher in Atlantic and central Canada and lower in western Canada. Ontario, Newfoundland and Labrador, and Nova Scotia were the only three provinces whose unemployment rates were above the national average in every quarter over the two-year period of recession. Western Canada, by contrast, remained below the Canadian average for the duration of the recession.

Beyond the domestic picture, how did the fiscal health of Canadian governments compare with that of other G-7 nations in the years leading up to the financial crisis? In 2007–08, both the federal government and the provinces and territories continued the trend of building government surpluses.

With C\$9.6 billion in 2007–08, the federal government posted its eleventh straight surplus. In the same year, the provinces and territories had a combined C\$11.2 billion surplus, their seventh in nine years. Canadian governments also were on track to post surpluses in 2008–09 (C\$0.8 billion for the federal government and C\$5.8 billion for the provinces and territories) despite the onset of recession.[32] As a result, debt-to-GDP ratios also were falling significantly.

Canada's total government financial balance was considerably above the G-7 average. Provincial and territorial surpluses represented a significant contribution to the country's overall fiscal performance, having outpaced federal surpluses for five consecutive years before 2008–09. This evidence suggests that the relative fiscal independence of Canada's subnational governments was, indeed, a boon to the Canadian economy, not a problem as in other federations.

Those surpluses allowed both orders of government to reduce their debt-to-GDP ratios at a much faster pace than the rest of the G-7 countries were able to do. The aggregate provincial-territorial debt-to-GDP ratio fell steadily from its peak of 29.2 percent in 1999–2000 to 17.4 percent in 2008–09, while the federal ratio fell from 68.4 percent in 1995–96 to 28.5 percent in 2008–09. That put total Canadian government net debt as a percentage of GDP at 22.3 percent, less than half the G-7 average.[33] Those data tell us that the fiscal health of both the federal and provincial and territorial governments leading up to the 2008 crisis was strong. Canadian governments were very well positioned to absorb the economic shocks that were to come.

Federal and Provincial Fiscal Indicators

Neither spending nor borrowing by the federal or provincial governments was out of control during the crisis. Despite the large disparities across provinces in income, employment, and so forth, the costs of borrowing for provinces were remarkably similar across the country. A recent analysis of returns on Canadian government bonds during 2008–09 revealed remarkable homogeneity of federal and provincial bond returns, quite unlike in the U.S. bond market. The study found that, as assessed by the major credit rating agencies, "markets for provincial bonds are highly correlated amongst one another," despite the differences in creditworthiness between provinces.[34] The study reported:

> This homogeneity of federal and provincial bond returns, in the face of significant variability of credit ratings, suggests that market participants systematically underplay agencies' risk assessments and/or the risk factors that drive these agencies' assessments. A plausible explanation for this behavior might be ascribed to the market's expectations of an

implicit federal guarantee for provincial debt. In fact, granted that market agents perceive that the federal government would step in as last-resort guarantor for provinces in financial distress, default risk becomes negligible for provincial bonds. Consequently, return spreads between federal and provincial bonds should be small, as is in fact documented by our empirical analysis.[35]

Thus credit markets are not behaving as though provinces can default. The implicit assumption that the federal government will intervene to bail out fiscally bereft subnationals has also been noted by economists Richard Bird and Almos-Tassonyi, who observed that two provinces—Alberta and Saskatchewan—faced default in the mid-1930s. Ottawa allowed Alberta to default (although it bailed out Saskatchewan) but eventually came through in 1945 in an effort to protect the country's creditworthiness. The federal government's Stabilization Agreement, which is part of the equalization system, guarantees stabilization payments to provinces whose revenues (from formula-defined revenue sources) decline in any given year. The authors contend that this agreement signals "an underlying federal guarantee of provincial debt-servicing capacity"even though it is not explicitly enshrined in law.[36]

This convention could be especially relevant as some provinces flirt with high debt-to-GDP ratios. There is considerable variation in the level of indebtedness among provinces. As of 2011, Quebec had a debt-to-GDP ratio of nearly 50 percent, while Ontario's was 35 percent and Alberta was in the black. However, it is important to remember the disproportionate impact of the crisis on central Canadian manufacturing. Meanwhile, the federal government's debt-to-GDP ratio in 2011 was 38 percent.[37]

In addition to high debt-to-GDP ratios, another area of potential fiscal stress is the funding of public sector pensions. There is growing consensus that the Canada Pension Plan (CPP) and public sector pensions across the country will face a funding shortfall. In December 2010, Canada's chief actuary reported the CPP's unfunded liabilities at C$748 billion—85.5 percent of the total actuarial liability.[38] The CD Howe Institute estimated in 2009 that the value of the federal government's obligations for its deferred compensation arrangements (as part of defined benefit plans) was C$197.7 billion. That estimate was C$58 billion higher than the amount reported in the federal government's Public Accounts.[39] The Canadian Federation of Independent Business (CFIB), using Public Accounts data from 2010–11, cites federal and provincial public sector unfunded pension liabilities at C$186 billion. The federal portion of that total is approximately C$146 billion, and the provincial portion is approximately C$40 billion.[40]

Moreover, the CFIB notes that those figures represent only the unfunded liabilities of federal, provincial, and territorial governments, leaving out the other public sector pension plans for school, hospital, and municipal employees. Both CD Howe and the CFIB argue that in addition to the fact that pension obligations are ignored in Public Accounts, public reporting overstates future rates of return on plan assets by the use of unrealistically high interest rates—as high as 7.63 percent by Prince Edward Island.[41] They contend that as a result, "the unfunded shortfall of public plans may well exceed $300 billion, which is equivalent to $100,000 per government employee, or $9,000 for every man, woman, and child in this country."[42]

These issues, which long predate the current global crisis, are major challenges for all Canadian governments. But for the purposes of this chapter, it is important to note that the provinces have not faced problems greater than those of the federal government. The federal government has acted to mitigate its situation—for example, by delaying the age of eligibility for old age pensions. Provinces have acted similarly, placing strict limits on wages and benefits. Since public sector workers at both levels are virtually 100 percent unionized, doing so has required difficult negotiations.

Governments Respond

The federal government's first response to the global economic crisis—the fall 2008 Economic and Fiscal Statement—was a political disaster that nearly led to a constitutional crisis. The prorogation of Parliament to avert the forming of a new coalition government by the opposition parties—the subject of volumes—is not the focus here.[43] It is nonetheless important to note that prorogation, coinciding with the beginning of the economic downturn, distracted the country from policy questions and federal-provincial conflict and instead focused its energies on federal party politics.

With the gears of Parliament haltingly slow, two extra-parliamentary factors continued to shape the nature of Canada's response to recovery: intergovernmental affairs and the international political economy. Intergovernmental meetings—at the level of First Ministers, ministers, and officials—which numbered in the thousands, focused predominantly on economic recovery.[44] Canada's position going into key international meetings and the results of the same meetings were an agenda topic for FMMs. The International Monetary Fund (IMF) urged governments to spend at least 2 percent of GDP on economic stimulus measures. Canada's commitment to meeting the IMF's target—as with those of most of the countries covered in this volume—began quite broadly in 2008 and became more defined through 2009. It included commitments to stabilize and strengthen the financial system; to provide access to credit for banking and other key sectors; and to increase spending to stimulate demand.

Federal finance minister Jim Flaherty was asked in early 2009 whether he could rely on the provinces and territories to implement the identified measures. Yes, he said: "We met with the provincial finance ministers. . . . We met with them again. . . . In fact, we agreed in writing that we would all work to provide this sort of stimulus for the Canadian economy, and so did the first ministers when they met in the middle of January in Ottawa."[45] Since the election of the current government in 2006, despite consistent calls by provincial premiers for regular FMMs, only five meetings of First Ministers have taken place. Four were held during the heart of the recession, and all of them were focused on the economy and characterized by a sense of responsibility for undertaking a national or coordinated effort to tackle the problems.

The federal budget of January 2009 was carefully designed to bolster relationships with the provinces and fulfill Canada's international commitments as well as to respond to political events in the House of Commons. It introduced a two-year stimulus package, the Economic Action Plan, following two FMMs and two G-20 leaders' summits (in the three months preceding January 2009). The IMF assessed the package as follows:

> All told, and taking into account supplementary provincial actions announced following the federal budget, the measures total around 2 percent of GDP per year in 2009 and in 2010, making them among the largest across G-20 countries.[46]

Whether Canada's stimulus was a low 1.1 percent of GDP or a high 4 percent, the main components of the stimulus are well documented.[47] In 2009–10 provincial and territorial contributions to the stimulus measures came largely through cost matching in infrastructure—approximately C$8 billion in federal funds and C$6 billion in provincial-territorial funds for an estimated 7,000 projects.[48] The Infrastructure Stimulus Fund was the largest (C$4 billion). Merit-based new projects that were shovel-ready and able to be completed by March 31, 2011, were eligible (the date was later extended on provincial request to October 31, 2011), and funding was cost-matched, 50-50, although the federal contribution was 33 percent when municipalities were also partners. Maximum funding was capped on an equal per capita basis.[49] Federal money was on the table with explicit "use it or lose it" terms.

Infrastructure stimulus was the federal government's flagship effort because it reflected Canada's international commitment to provide a targeted, timely, and temporary stimulus; because it would help stimulate jobs in a sector hit by the recession; and—it must be said—because it was politically attractive. Who can quantify the value of Government of Canada signage on hockey arenas across the country?

Infrastructure spending would have been attractive to the federal government also because the funding criteria were similar to those for an existing infrastructure program (2007 Building Canada Plan) and it was not politically charged territory—like health, for example. But why were the provinces eager participants in the program?

Except for rare exceptions (for example, funding for Quebec and for universities), the 50-50 cost match has always proven attractive to provinces. But the usual complaints—regarding one-time federal spending leading to long-term operational costs for provinces; federal conditions for funding in areas of provincial jurisdiction; accountability requirements; and signage and communications issues—were muted.

Conclusion

The Canadian federal system has managed recent fiscal crises with considerable success. Collectively, government deficits remained under control and debt-to-GDP ratios remained low. Public finances were challenged—for example, by the burden of public sector pensions on government budgets—but there has been little sense of crisis.

The policy responses of both orders of government were broadly cooperative and consistent; there was no pulling in different directions. There were no provincial claims for a federal financial rescue, no fears of provincial or municipal bankruptcy. Did the crisis lead to a reassertion of federal control of provinces and cities? No. Did it result in fears that subnational governments might threaten to go their own way, pursuing radically different policies and mobilizing to attack the center? No.

This favorable assessment may come as a surprise. Canada is, after all, a deeply divided society in both linguistic and regional terms, and one might have expected the crisis to exacerbate its underlying tensions. Canada is also one of the world's most decentralized federations. The long-term trend has been to diminish federal control of taxing, spending, and borrowing and to increase the fiscal clout of the provinces. The federal government has very few levers with which to control provincial actions. It might have been expected, therefore, that provinces would pursue policies in response to the crisis that would differ from those of the federal government and that the federal government would have little ability to restrain. But that has not been the case.

Why? There is no single explanation. One might be plain economic luck: Canada's resource-based economy was well placed to minimize the effects of the crisis. But political and institutional factors also played a very important role. First, Canada is one of the world's oldest federations (after the United States and Switzerland) and thus has had very long experience in managing the intergovernmental relationship. From very early in the country's history a norm of compromise across even deep differences was developed.[50] Second, despite the influences of language and region, Canadian governments have shared broadly similar ideological predispositions about the role of government, so it was not hard to agree on a common response to the crisis. But perhaps most important is institutional strength and capacity. As discussed, Canadian governments at both levels are characterized by strong executives, relatively little "hamstrung" by legislatures and interest groups. Therefore their political, bureaucratic, and fiscal capacity to develop and implement policies is strong. In addition, while intergovernmental relations are often adversarial and fractious, there is a strong tradition of fiscal coordination between federal and provincial treasuries. Cooperation is not the result of federal coercion but of shared values.

These conclusions seem at odds with much of the analysis of and commentary on Canadian federalism, which have tended to emphasize the conflicted, adversarial nature of the system; to criticize how much intergovernmental relations are characterized by turf protecting, blame shifting, and credit claiming; to insist that good policy is too often subordinated to fiscal issues; to worry about the absence of formal rules and institutions to govern the intergovernmental relationship. In the daily hurly-burly of intergovernmental relations, all of that is largely true. But on the large issues of fiscal crisis that are the focus of this book, the federal system has not been a barrier to and may even have facilitated implementation of an effective response.

Notes

1. Richard Simeon and Ian Robinson, *State, Society, and the Development of Canadian Federalism* (University of Toronto Press, 1990).

2. Douglas M. Brown, "Fiscal Federalism: Searching for a Balance," in *Canadian Federalism: Performance, Effectiveness, and Legitimacy,* edited by Herman Bakvis and Grace Skogstad(Oxford University Press, 2008), pp. 62–87.

3. Timothy Lewis, *In The Long Run We're All Dead: The Canadian Turn to Fiscal Restraint* (University of British Columbia Press, 2003).

4. Alain G. Gagnon, *Quebec: State and Society* (Toronto: Methuen, 1984); Kenneth McRoberts and Dale Posgate, *Quebec: Social Change and Political Crisis* (Toronto: McClelland and Stewart, 1980).

5. The ten provinces are Alberta, British Columbia, Manitoba, New Brunswick, Newfoundland and Labrador, Nova Scotia, Ontario, Prince Edward Island, Quebec, and Saskatchewan. The three territories are Northwest Territories, Nunavut, and Yukon.

6. Statistics Canada, "Estimates of Population, by Age Group and Sex for July 1, Canada, Provinces, and Territories," CANSIM Table: 051-0001 (www5.statcan.gc.ca/cansim/a26?lang=eng&retrLang=eng&id=0510001&pattern=051&tabMode=dataTable &srchLan=-1&p1=1&p2=-1).

7. BC Statistics, "Real GDP Per Capita" (Victoria: Government of British Columbia, 2013) (www.bcstats.gov.bc.ca/StatisticsBySubject/Economy/OtherEconomicStatistics/ ProvincialComparisons.aspx).

8. Government of Canada, Constitution Act, 1982, S.36(2).

9. Donald Savoie, *Governing from the Centre: The Concentration of Power in Canadian Politics* (University of Toronto Press, 1999); Jeffrey Simpson, *The Friendly Dictatorship* (Toronto: McClelland and Stewart, 2001); Graham White, "The Centre of the Democratic Deficit: Power and Influence in Canadian Political Executives," in *Imperfect Democracies: The Democratic Deficit in Canada and the United States,* edited by Patti Tamara Lenard and Richard Simeon (University of British Columbia Press, 2012), pp. 226–47.

10. Herman Bakvis and A. Brian Tanguay, "Federalism, Political Parties, and the Burden of National Unity: Still Making Federalism Do the Heavy Lifting?," in *Canadian Federalism,* edited by Bakvis and Skogstad, pp. 96–115.

11. D. V. Smiley, *Constitutional Adaptation and Canadian Federalism since 1945: Volume 4 of Documents* (Ottawa: Royal Commission on Bilingualism and Biculturalism, 1970); Richard Simeon, *Federal-Provincial Diplomacy: The Making of Recent Policy in Canada* (University of Toronto Press, 2006).

12. David Cameron and Richard Simeon, "Intergovernmental Relations in Canada: The Emergence of Collaborative Federalism," *Publius: The Journal of Federalism,* vol. 32 (Spring 2002), pp. 49–72.

13. Keith Banting, *Open Federalism: Interpretations, Significance* (Kingston, Canada: Institute of Intergovernmental Relations, Queen's University, 2007).

14. "PMO Says Harper Will Not Attend First Ministers' Meeting: Spokesman Says Prime Minister Has Met with Premiers Individually 74 Times since 2010," Canadian Press, August 1, 2012 (www.cbc.ca/m/touch/politics/story/2012/08/01/pol-harper-first-ministers-conference.html).

15. Ronald L. Watts, *The Spending Power in Federal Systems: A Comparative Study* (Kingston: Institute of Intergovernmental Relations, Queen's University, 1999); Harvey Lazar, *Canadian Fiscal Arrangements: What Works, What Might Work Better* (McGill–Queen's University Press, 2005); Douglas M. Brown, "Fiscal Federalism: Searching for Balance," in *Canadian Federalism,* edited by Bakvis and Skogstad, pp. 63–88.

16. Finances Québec, "Correcting the Fiscal Imbalance," Budget Background Paper 2004-05 (Quebec City: Government of Quebec); Council of the Federation Advisory Panel on Fiscal Imbalance, "Reconciling the Irreconcilable: Addressing Canada's Fiscal Imbalance"(Ottawa: Council of the Federation, 2006).

17. Joshua Hjartarson, Matthew Mendelsohn, and James Pearce, "A Report Card on Canada's Fiscal Arrangements" (Toronto: Mowat Centre, 2010).

18. John R. Allan, Thomas J. Courchene, and Christian Leuprecht, *Canada: The State of the Federation 2006–07: Transitions: Fiscal and Political Federalism in an Era of Change* (McGill–Queen's University Press, 2009.

19. Government of Alberta, "Alberta's Oil Sands," 2013 (http://oilsands.alberta.ca/economicinvestment.html).

20. TD Economics, "Special Report: How Will the Great Recession and Its Recovery Compare to the Past?" (Toronto: November 6, 2009), p. 5 (www.tdbank.com/investments/exc/pdfs/ff1109_recoveries.pdf).

21. Jean-François Arsenault and Andrew Sharpe, "The Economic Crisis through the Lens of Economic Well-Being" (Ottawa: Centre for the Study of Living Standards, 2009), p.16.

22. Statistics Canada, "Gross Domestic Product (GDP), Expenditure-Based," CANSIM Table: 380-0002 (www5.statcan.gc.ca/cansim/a26?lang=eng&retrLang=eng&id=3800002&pattern=380&tabMode=dataTable&srchLan=-1&p1=1&p2=-1).

23. Statistics Canada, "The Daily: Comparing the 2008–2010 Recession and Recovery with Previous Cycles," January 13, 2011 (www.statcan.gc.ca/daily-quotidien/110113/dq110113b-eng.htm).

24. Government of Alberta Finance and Enterprise, "Economic Spotlight: A Comparison of the U.S. and Canadian Economic Recoveries," October 21, 2010 (www.finance.alberta.ca/aboutalberta/spotlights/2010-1021-comparision-us-canadian-economic-recoveries.pdf).

25. TD Economics, "Special Report."

26. CBC News, "Chart: Unemployment Rates in Canada and the U.S.," November 4, 2011 (www.cbc.ca/news/interactives/us-unemployment/).

27. Arsenault and Sharpe, "The Economic Crisis through the Lens of Economic Well-Being," p. 16.

28. Ibid., p. 9.

29. Statistics Canada, "The Daily: Canadian Economic Accounts," March 2, 2009 (www.statcan.gc.ca/daily-quotidien/090302/dq090302a-eng.htm).

30. Arsenault and Sharpe, "The Economic Crisis through the Lens of Economic Well-Being," p. 9.

31. Sébastien LaRochelle-Cote and Jason Gilmore, "Canada's Employment Downturn," Statistics Canada Catalogue no. 75-001-X (Ottawa: Statistics Canada, 2009), p. 6.

32. Finance Canada, "Economic and Fiscal Statement: Protecting Canada's Future," November 27, 2008, p.109 (www.fin.gc.ca/ec2008/pdf/EconomicStatement2008_Eng.pdf).

33. Ibid., p.118.

34. Valentina Galvani and Aslan Behnamian, "A Comparative Analysis of the Returns on Federal and Provincial Bonds," Working Paper 2009-7, University of Alberta Department of Economics, 2009 (www.researchgate.net/profile/Aslan_Behnamian/publications/).

35. Ibid., p. 19.

36. Richard Bird and Almos Tassonyi, "Constraining Subnational Fiscal Behavior in Canada : Different Approaches, Similar Results?," in *Fiscal Decentralization and the Challenge of Hard Budget Constraints,* edited by Jonathan A. Rodden, Gunnar S. Eskeland, and Jennie Litvack (MIT Press, 2003), pp. 85–132, pp.15–16, 55.

37. Institut de la Statistique Québec, "Interprovincial Comparisons," chapter 13, section 12, February 11, 2013 (www.stat.gouv.qc.ca/donstat/econm_finnc/conjn_econm/TSC/index_an.htm).

38. Office of the Superintendent of Financial Institutions Canada, "Actuarial Report on the Canada Pension Plan," (Ottawa: 2010), p. 70.

39. André Laurin and William B. P. Robson, "Supersized Superannuation: The Startling Fair-Value Cost of Federal Government Pensions" (Toronto: CD Howe Institute, 2009).

40. Ted Mallett, "Canada's Hidden Unfunded Public Sector Pension Liabilities" (Toronto: Canadian Federation of Independent Business, 2012).

41. Laurin and Robson, "Supersized Superannuation"; Mallett, "Canada's Hidden Unfunded Public Sector Pension Liabilities," p. 3.

42. Mallett, "Canada's Hidden Unfunded Public Sector Pension Liabilities," p. 1.

43. Peter H. Russell and Lorne Sossin, *Parliamentary Democracy in Crisis* (University of Toronto Press, 2009).

44. Gregory Inwood, Carolyn M. Johns, and Patricia L. O'Reilly, "Formal and Informal Dimensions of Intergovernmental Administrative Relations in Canada," *Canadian Public Administration,* vol. 50, no. 1 (Spring 2007), pp. 21–41.

45. Speech by the Honourable Jim Flaherty, minister of finance, to the Osgoode Hall Law School and the Schulich School of Business LLB/MBA Students' Association Annual General Conference, February 6, 2009.

46. See IMF, "Canada: 2009 Article IV Consultation: Staff Report; Staff Statement; and Public Information Notice on the Executive Board Discussion," May 22, 2009 (www.imf.org/external/pubs/ft/scr/2009/cr09162.pdf).

47. See the alternative federal budget: Canadian Centre for Policy Alternatives, "AFB 2009: Beyond the Crisis" January 2009 (www.policyalternatives.ca/sites/default/files/uploads/publications/National_Office_Pubs/2009/AFB2009_Beyond_the_Crisis.pdf); TD Economics, Special Report, "Priming the Fiscal Pump," April 28, 2009 (www.td.com/document/PDF/economics/special/td-economics-special-db0409-fiscal.pdf).

48. Government of Canada, "Economic Action Plan 2012: Growth and Long-Term Prosperity," p. 314.

49. Tracy Snoddon and Paul A.R. Hobson, "Cost-Sharing and Federal-Provincial Fiscal Relations," in *The 2009 Federal Budget: Challenge, Response, and Retrospect,* edited by Charles M. Beach, Bev Dahlby, and Paul A.R. Hobson (Kingston: John Deutsch Institute, Queen's University, 2010), pp.181–98.

50. Alain G. Gagnon and Richard Simeon, "Canada," in *Diversity and Unity in Federal Countries,* edited by Luis Moreno and César Colino (McGill–Queen's University Press, 2010), pp.109–38.

Contributors

ANDREW G. BIGGS
American Enterprise Institute

CÉSAR COLINO
National Distance Education University (UNED), Madrid

ELOÍSA DEL PINO
Instituto de Políticas y Bienes Públicos (IPP), CSIC, Madrid

HENRIK ENDERLEIN
Hertie School of Governance, Berlin

CORY KOEDEL
University of Missouri–Columbia

CARLOS XABEL LASTRA-ANADÓN
Harvard University

SHAWN NI
University of Missouri–Columbia

AMY NUGENT
Government of Ontario, Canada

JAMES PEARCE
Mowat Centre, University of Toronto, Canada

MICHAEL PODGURSKY
University of Missouri–Columbia

JASON RICHWINE
Public Policy Analyst, Washington, D.C.

JONATHAN RODDEN
Stanford University

DANIEL SHOAG
Harvard University

RICHARD SIMEON
University of Toronto, Canada

CAMILLO VON MÜLLER
University of St. Gallen, Switzerland, and Leuphana University, Germany

DANIEL ZIBLATT
Harvard University

PAUL E. PETERSON is the Henry Lee Shattuck Professor of Government and director of the Program on Education Policy and Governance at Harvard University and a senior fellow at the Hoover Institution. DANIEL NADLER is a visiting scholar at the Federal Reserve and a Ph.D. candidate at Harvard University.

Index

Note: page numbers followed by *t* and *f* refer to tables and figures respectively; those followed by n refer to notes, with note number.

Accounting standards, of academic and professional economists: general acceptance of, 69–70; value of public sector pension plan liabilities under, 62, 63–64, 67, 68–69, 71, 71*t*, 75, 80; value of teacher pensions under, 71–75, 74*t*, 75*t*

Accounting standards, of GASB: criticisms of, 69–70, 76; revisions to, 70; value of public sector pension plan liabilities under, 64, 67, 68–69, 80, 97

Actuarial funding ratio, 99

Actuarially required contribution (ARC), 99, 106–07

Alaska, balanced budget of, 24–25

Alberta (Canada): debt-to-GDP ratio, 215; default of *1930*s, 215; demographics, 203–04; impact of crisis of *2008* on, 213; oil and gas wealth in, 202, 204, 210

Alden v. *Maine* (*1999*), 20

Almos Tassonyi, 215

American exceptionalism, history of, 15–16

American Federation of Teachers (AFT), growth of, 23

Andalucía: and centrally controlled reform, resistance to, 194; GDP decline in, 186; separatism in, 184; strong regional identity in, 186, 187*f*

Annual Survey of Public Employees Retirement Systems (U.S. Census Bureau), 95–96

Argentina: and central control, necessity of, 57; dysfunctional federalism in, 41; failure of fiscal discipline in, 44–46

Arkansas, default during Great Depression, 26

Asset market investments, to meet unfunded liabilities: no return from, ability to pay despite, 99; parallels to default crisis of *1840*s, 95, 107; profits from, 95–97, 96*f*; profits from versus liabilities, 97–98, 97*f*; return on, and pension risk, 99, 106; as risky, 95

Asymmetrical unitary model, in European Union, 124, 129

Aubry, Jean-Pierre, 98

Autonomous communities (ACs), in Spain: blame shifting by, 174; bond market disciplining of, 161, 166, 168–69, 172, 173; budget oversight by EU, benefits of, 196–97; budgets, 164; budget stability and debt goals, failure to comply with, 173, 174; bypassing of by central government in crisis management, 171, 173; capacities of, 163–64; central government loans to, 172; central government political dependence on, 190–92; and competitive federalism, benefits of, 196–97; creation of, 180; debt, growth of, 168, 190; fiscal responsibility before crisis of *2008,* 168; full independence of, as proposal, 194–95; history of, 161–62; incentives to overspend, 165–67, 173; limited autonomy of, 181; prime ministers, influence of, 164; regional government and civil services, 164; and regional identities, (re)creation of, 180; regional political class in, 163–64; relative independence of, and degree of equality, 185, 189; responsibilities of, 181, 182*t*; separatist sentiment in, 174, 179, 186, 189; Spanish move toward centralization and, 159–61, 171, 173–74; Spanish wealth redistribution policies and, 179, 184–89; spending and debt, central government efforts to regulate, 166–67, 172, 174, 184, 190–92, 193; taxation and spending in, 164–66, 167, 171, 174, 180, 181–83, 183*f*, 196

Bailout guarantees. *See entries under* Federal bailout; Federal no-bailout policies
Balanced budget restrictions, of EU states: adoption of as compulsory, 127–28, 131n11
Balanced budget restrictions, of U.S. states: origin of, 47, 95; pension liabilities' exclusion from, 95; success of, 47; voluntary adoption of, 124, 127–28, 131n11
Ballou, Dale, 79n36
Banking system involvement in debt crisis, and federal no-bailout policy, credibility of, 46
Bankruptcies, by state governments: consequences of, 7–8; debate on, 8–9; as looming crisis, 7; as strategy to address state debt, 32

Bankruptcies, municipal: public sector pension plan liabilities and, 80; in U.S., 5–7
Basque Country: as charter regime, 163, 166, 183; debt levels of, 168; fiscal autonomy of, 181, 183, 186; low income inequality in, 189; salary costs of, 170; separatism in, 184, 186, 189; and Spanish competitive federalism, structure of, 195–96; and Spanish redistributive policies, 196; strong regional identity in, 186
Bavarian Association of Savings Banks, 145
Bavarian Court of Audit, 145
Bayerische Landesbank, 144, 145
Benefit calculation formulas for defined benefit pension plans, 83; school administrators as greatest beneficiaries of in education DB plans, 86–90, 87*f*, 88*f*, 93n15; benefit factor changes, impact on liabilities of, 84, 101; enhancements of *1990s–2000*s, 83, 84, 84*t*; private sector changes in, 81
Bergstrom, Fred, 8
Bertelsmann Foundation, 127
Beshears, John, 102
Binkley, Robert, 117
Bird, Richard, 215
Bismark, Otto von, 116, 117, 119
Bloomberg, 6
Blue Bonds, 126
Bond defaults by state and local government, and state sovereign immunity, 21
Bondholders, city bankruptcies and, 6–7
Bond insurance industry, impact on default risk, 61n12
Bond market: bankruptcy of U.S. cities and, 5–7; Canadian provinces and, 214–15; German *Länder* bonds, economic crisis of *2008* and, 26–27, 27*f*, 147–49, 149*f*, 152; joint state/federal Deutschland bonds, 137, 150–51, 152, 158n79; risk premiums for U.S. states, 25–26, 25*f*, 26–31, 27*f*; views on credibility of U.S. no-bailout policy, 54, 55. *See also entries under* Market-based fiscal discipline

Bond yield, in calculation of total pension liabilities, 70, 71, 71*t*, 72, 73*t*, 74, 75*t*

Brady Handgun Violence Prevention Act, and state sovereignty, 21

Brandeis, Louis, 15

Brazil: and central control, necessity of, 57; dysfunctional federalism in, 41; failure of fiscal discipline in, 44–46

British North America Act of *1867,* 208

Bryce, Lord James, 17, 18

Budget deficits, state governments, 8

Buffett, Warren, 7, 33

Build America Bonds, 52

Bull market of *1990s–2000s,* and public sector pension plan enhancements, 81

Bundesrat, and gradual erosion of *Länder* power, 138–39

Bureau of Economic Analysis, 100, 102

Bureau of Labor Statistics, 63, 65–66, 78n32

Bush, George H. W., and federal grants to state and local government, 50

Bush, George W., and federal grants to state and local government, 50

Bush, Jeb, 9

CAFRs (comprehensive annual financial reports) of retirement systems, 98

California: bonds, risk premiums of, 25*f,* 26; budget deficits, 25; credit default swap market and, 54–55, 54*f;* earnings from pension fund investments, 96, 96*f*

Canada: as model for debt reduction, 13; as multinational society, 203, 218; National Policy, 204; spending cuts of *1990s,* 202; unemployment, economic crisis of *2008* and, 213; welfare state, building of, 206, 208

Canada, and economic crisis of *2008:* debt and spending levels in, 214; impact of, 211–14; initial response, 216; stimulus package, 216–18; success in weathering, reasons for, 218–19

Canada Revenue Agency, 209

Canadian central government: and equalization payments, burden of, 210; and implicit bailout guarantee of province debt, 16, 48, 214–15; spending power, and influence over provincial policy, 208–09; Stabilization Agreement and, 215; surpluses, as cushion against crisis of *2008,* 213–14; transfers to provinces, as issue, 209–10

Canadian constitution of *1867,* 206

Canadian energy policy, battle over, 202

Canadian federal system: and Canadian provinces as fiscal actors, 208–11; collaborative federalism, critiques of, 207; collaborative federalism period, 206–07; cooperation in fiscal field, 209; decentralization, high level of, 201, 203, 206, 208, 209; and economic crisis of *2008,* impact of, 201–02; Equalization Program of, 202, 205, 210; as executive federalism, 205, 219; federal government transfers, as issue, 209–10; Great Depression and, 206; history of, 202, 208; influence of, crisis of *2008* and, 209; institutional capacity and strength, 219; institutional structure of, 205–08; intergovernmental transfers in, 201; neoliberal consensus in, 209, 211, 219; as older, experienced federation, 219; open federalism, transition to, 207–08; success of, 201–02; tax administration in, 209; tax powers, decentralization of, 208, 209

Canadian Federation of Independent Business (CFIB), 215–16

Canadian parliamentary system: as executive-centered, 205–06; party discipline in, 205

Canadian provinces: autonomy of, in collaborative federalism system, 206–07; balancing needs of, as challenge, 202, 204–05; cost of borrowing for, 214–15; debt, variation in, 215; defaults of *1930s,* 215; and Economic Action Plan

stimulus package, 217–18; economic
and demographic variety in, 202, 203–
04, 210; and economic crisis of *2008,*
impact of, 213; as fiscal actors, 208–11;
fiscal autonomy of, 201; Great Depression and, 202; implicit federal bailout
guarantee for, 16, 48, 214–15; public
sector pensions costs and, 215–16; surpluses, as cushion against crisis of *2008,*
213–14. *See also* Quebec

Canadian public sector pensions: cost
reduction efforts, 216; unfunded liabilities, 215–16

Catalonia: debt of, 168, 190; GDP decline
in, 186; market disciplining of, 168;
pension funds in, 169; salary costs
in, 170; separatism in, 159, 179, 184,
189, 194–95, 199n21, 200n35; strong
regional identity in, 180, 186

Cavour, Camillo Benso, Count of, 116–17,
117–18, 119, 120

CD Howe Institute, 215–16

Census Bureau, U.S., 95–96, 100

Center for Retirement Research (Boston
College), 63, 98

Central control of state finances: advocates
of, 57; and implied responsibility for
debt, 45; lack of in U.S., 47; limits on, in
federal system, 44, 45; as method of fiscal discipline, 43–44; as necessity, after
collapse of credible federal no-bailout
stance, 57; problems inherent in, 57–58;
U.S. state defaults and, 91; in U.S., problems inherent in, 57–58

Central Falls, Rhode Island, bankruptcy
of, 6–7

Centralization, in EU, 118–19, 129; and
accountability, as issue, 130; likelihood
of, 113–14; necessity of, in economists'
view, 115, 130; possible configura-
tions of, 114; potential unintentional
excesses in, 114; proposals for, 113;
unintentional movement toward, 114,
123–29; and U.S. Hamiltonian moment

as model, 115. *See also* European Union,
potential decentralized federalism in

Centralization, in German federalism,
move toward, 137, 138, 150–51,
151–53

Centralization, in Spain: resistance to
among ACs, 159, 160; as result of
economic crisis of *2008,* 159–61, 171,
173–74, 193, 194

Centralization, unintentional excesses in,
114; federal ideology and, 117–18, 120;
state capacity of subunits and, 119–22,
122–23, 124–29, 125*t,* 130

Centre for the Study of Living Standards
(CSLS), 211

CFIB. *See* Canadian Federation of Independent Business

Chafee, Lincoln, 7

Chaney, Barbara A., 98, 102

Charter schools, and pension plans, 92n6

Chisholm v. *Georgia* (*1793*), 20–21

Chrétien, Jean, 207

Cities, U.S., bankruptcies, 5–7

Civil rights laws, and state sovereign
immunity, 21

Civil War, U.S., and centralization of
government, 57

Clark, Robert L., 65

Collective bargaining in public sector. *See*
Public sector unions

Colorado, earnings from pension fund
investments, 96, 96*f*

Comparative Retirement Studies
(Wisconsin state legislature), 98

Competitive federalism, U.S., 17–20;
potential impact of state defaults on,
31–33; and redistribution programs,
avoidance of, 18–20; stabilizing factors,
whittling away of, 32; and state and
local governments as laboratories, 18;
state and local responsiveness to public
needs, 17–18

Comprehensive annual financial reports
(CAFRs) of retirement systems, 98

Congressional Budget Office, and valuation of pension liabilities, 69

Congressional Financial Crisis Inquiry Commission, 7

Conservative Party (Canada), 207

Conservatives, on U.S. federal system, problems in, 40

Constitution, Canadian (*1867*), 206

Constitution, Spanish (*1978*): federal structure under, 180; spending and borrowing limits in, 172

Constitution, U.S.: Eleventh Amendment, 20; Fourteenth Amendment, 21; and state sovereign immunity, 20–21

Constitution Act of *1982* (Canada), 210

Constitutional Court, German, on bailout guarantees for *Länder,* 141

Constitutional Court, Spanish, and Spanish federal system, 162, 163, 166

Convergència i Unió (CiU), 191

Copley, Paul A., 98, 102

Corporate bond yield, in calculation of total pension liabilities, 70, 71, 71*t,* 74, 75*t*

Council of Finance and Fiscal Policy Ministers (Spain), 166, 173

Council of the Federation (Canada), 207

Craig, Lee A., 65

Credit default swaps, and credibility of U.S. no-bailout policy, 54–55, 54*f*

Credit markets, as tool for disciplining state governments. *See* Market-based fiscal discipline

Creditors: bond insurance industry as, and default risk, 61n12; identity of, and credibility of federal no-bailout policy, 42, 46, 47; identity of, for U.S. state debt, 53

Credit ratings of states: downgrades, political costs of, 48; importance of to state governments, 47

CSLS. *See* Centre for the Study of Living Standards

Current pension wealth (CPW), and cost of pension enhancements, 85–86

Current Population Survey, 105

Debt of developed nations: increases in, 3–4; pension and health care costs and, 4; possibility of reducing, 4, 13

Decentralized federalism: in Canadian system, 201, 203, 206, 208, 209; in Spain, before crisis of *2008,* 162, 180, 181

Decentralized federalism, potential for in EU, 114, 123–29; and central control, asymmetrical, 124, 129; conditions necessary for success of, 130; defining characteristics of, 113; historical parallels, 114, 115–22; national loyalties and, 114; renewed interest in, 113; as solution to issue of accountability of the political center, 130; and state capacity of subunits, 124–29, 125*t. See also* Centralization, in EU

Default crisis of *1840*s (U.S.), 26; balanced budget restrictions adopted following, 95; causes of, 94–95; parallels with current unfunded pension liabilities, 95, 107; success of federal no-bailout policy in, 31, 46–47

Default crisis of *1870–80*s (U.S.), 26

Deferred compensation: appeal of for governments, 24, 55, 90, 104; valuation of, 66–67

Defined benefit (DB) pension plans: academic administrators' support for, 82; appeal of for governments, 90; benefits provided under, 65; benefits *vs.* defined contribution plans, 65–66, 72–74; decline of in private sector, 63, 80–81; efforts by public sector employees to protect, 70; employee contributions to, 65; fair market valuation of, and pressure for reform, 75; public sector pension plans as, 80, 95; Social Security and, 65; teacher pension plans as, 62–63, 65, 75, 76, 90

Defined benefit (DB) pension plans, benefit calculation formulas for, 83; school administrators as greatest beneficiaries of in education DB plans,

86–90, 87*f,* 88*f,* 93n15; benefit factor changes, impact on liabilities of, 84, 101; enhancements of *1990*s–*2000*s, 83, 84, 84*t;* private sector changes in, 81

Defined contribution (DC) retirement plans: benefits versus those of defined benefit plans, 65–66, 72–74; and market risk, 65; pressure to convert defined benefits plans to, 75

Deis, Bob, 6

Delaware, pension plan enhancements of *1990*s to early *2000*s, 92n4

Delors Report (*1989*), 126

Delpla, Jacques, 126

Democratic Party: and collective bargaining rights for public sector employees, 22–23; share of state legislature, and state default risk, 29–31, 30*t,* 38n91

Detroit, Michigan, bankruptcy of, 7

Deutsche Bank, 144

Deutschland bonds, 137, 150–51, 152, 158n79

Draghi, Mario, 57

Economic Action Plan (Canada), 217

Economic and Fiscal Statement (Canada, *2008*), 216

Economic crisis of *2008:* and EU centralization, 126–27; impact on federal systems, 201

Economic crisis of *2008,* Canada and: debt and spending levels in, 214; impact of, 211–14; initial response, 216; resurgence of federal influence in, 209; stimulus package, 216–18; success in weathering, reasons for, 218–19

Economic crisis of *2008,* Germany and: bond market impact of, 26–27, 27*f,* 147–49, 149*f,* 152; and debt, 134, 135, 136*t,* 142–47; fiscal and legal consequences, 149–51; and *Länder,* impact on, 134, 135, 136*t,* 143–47; and *Landesbanken,* losses by, 144–45; as test of German federal system, 151–52

Economic crisis of *2008,* Spain and: AC spending and, 171, 193; centralizing effect of central government measures, 159–61, 171, 173–74, 193; counter-cyclical stimulus packages, 171; debt, increase in, 168, 190, 192–93, 192*f;* Eurozone design as contributing factor, 167–68; government responses, 170–73; and government spending, 192–93, 192*f;* inherent problems in Spanish federal system and, 160; reform, discussion of, 159; regional spending, efforts to limit, 172–73; severity of impact, 159, 167; Spain's responsible behavior prior to, 167–68; spending cutbacks, 168; systemic factors contributing to, 169–70; two phases of, 167, 171–73; and unsustainability of current federal system, 193; and wealth redistribution policies, 179

Economic growth, rate of, and pension risk, 100, 102–03, 107

Economics, as discipline, and rebirth of political economy, 4

Education costs, teachers unions and, 24

EFSF. *See* European Financial Stability Facility

Eleventh Amendment, and state sovereign immunity, 20

Employee Retirement Income Security Act (ERISA), public sector pensions and, 91

EMU. *See* European Monetary Union

Energy crises of *1970*s–*80*s: and Canadian energy policy, 202; and Canadian federal system, 206

Erie Canal, financing of, 94

ESGP. *See* European Stability and Growth Pact

EU. *See* European Union

Europe, dysfunctional federalism in, 40–41

European Central Bank, purchase of indebted states' bonds, 57

European Commission, warnings to indebted EU nations, 127

European Financial Stability Facility (EFSF), 127

European Fiscal Compact, 172

European government, national debt, increases in, 3–4

European Monetary Union (EMU): and central control, as problematic, 57–58; and central control, necessity of, 57; crises in, and move toward centralization, 125–29; dysfunctional federalism in, 41, 45; failure of fiscal discipline in, 45–46

European Semester, 127

European Stability and Growth Pact (ESGP), 126–27

European Union (EU): intervention in national budgets, impact on federalism, 123–29; public sector workers, increase in, 170; rescue of weak states, unintentional centralization through, 114; and Spanish ACs, debt regulation by, 166; Stability and Growth Pact, 45; success of as trade zone, 113; weakness of central structure, 113. *See also* Centralization, in EU

European Union, potential decentralized federalism in: central control, unintentional movement toward, 114, 123–29; and central control, asymmetrical, 124, 129; conditions necessary for success of, 130; defining characteristics of, 113; historical parallels, 114, 115–22; national loyalties and, 114; renewed interest in, 113; as solution to issue of accountability of the political center, 130; and state capacity of subunits, 124–29, 125*t*

European Union law, failure to comply with, 132n32

Euro Plus Pact, 127

Eurozone Growth and Stability Pact, 193

Expected pension wealth (EPW), and cost of pension enhancements, 86

Farrell, James, 106

Federal bailout, in U.S.: federal funding transfers during downturns as de facto form of, 51–52, 52*f;* impact on federal system, 31–33; likely congressional response to, 53; possibility of, 7–8; states' credible argument for, 50–51. *See also* Federal no-bailout policy, U.S.

Federal bailout guarantee: for Canadian provinces, 16, 48, 214–15; central control of state finances as necessity after collapse of, 57; for German *Länder,* 16, 135, 141–42; and moral hazard problem, 43, 44–46; in some federal systems, 16; state and municipal lobbying for, 32

Federal bailout guarantee, in Spain, 161; and AC incentives, 166–67, 173; dubious financial backing for, 161; explicit guarantee, issuing of, 193; institution of competitive federalism and, 196

Federal grants, U.S., to state and local government: increase in, 48–50, 49*f;* legislative representation as predictor of, 55

Federal ideology, and fiscal centralization, unintentional excesses in, 117–18, 120

Federal no-bailout policies, non-credible, and moral hazard, 44–46

Federal no-bailout policy, U.S.: and federal system, 124; history of, 26; political pressure to abandon, 32–33; success of, in *1840*s, 46–47

Federal no-bailout policy, U.S., credibility of: and implicit guarantees, perception of, 41–43; and market-based fiscal discipline, 41–43, 46–48; modern undermining of, 48–52; and orderly default process, announcement of, 58–59; in *21*st century, 53–56

Federal systems: characteristics of, 16; conditions necessary for success of, 130; and credit risk, 4–5; economic crisis of *2008* and, 201; failures of market-based fiscal discipline in, 44–46; number of globally, 16; potential impact of state defaults on, 31–33; as solution to issue of accountability of the political center, 130; and state debt, federal guarantee of, 16. *See also* Canadian federal system; Decentralized federalism; German federal system; Spanish federal system

Federal system, U.S.: and collective bargaining rights for state and local government employees, 17; as competitive federalism, 17–20; conservative view on problems in, 40; effectiveness of, 17; European and Latin American admiration for, 40–41; exceptional features of, 16; historical origin of, 16–17; limitations imposed on states in, 16–17; modern intertwining of state and federal functions, 48–52, 58; perceived dysfunctionality of, 40–41; progressive view on problems in, 40; and redistribution programs, state and local avoidance of, 18–20; stabilizing factors, whittling away of, 32; state and local defaults, impact of, 107–8; state and local responsiveness to public needs, 17–18; and state budgets, federal refusal to intervene in, 123–24; threat to, from unsustainable level of public sector benefits, 91. *See also* Competitive federalism, U.S.

First Ministers' Conference, 207

First Ministers' Meetings (FMMs) (Canada), 207, 216–17

Fiscal capacity of states, as measure of pension risk, 99–100

Fiscal Compact of EU, and Spanish government authority, 160–61

Fiscal discipline, strategies for, 43–44. *See also* Central control of state finances; Market-based fiscal discipline, in U.S.

Fiscal Stability and Financial Sustainability Act (*2012*), 172

Flaherty, Jim, 217

Florida Retirement System (FRS), 72–74, 73*f*, 73*t*

FMMs. *See* First Ministers' Meetings

FMS Wertmanagement, 143

Fourteenth Amendment, and state sovereign immunity, 21

France, debt in, 127

Franco, Francisco, 180

Friedman, Milton, 3

Fund for Autonomous Community Liquidity, 193

Fund for Financing Payment to Suppliers (Spain), 172

Fund to Guarantee Public Services, 165

Galicia: GDP decline in, 186; separatism in, 184; strong regional identity in, 186, 187*f*

Game theory, market-based fiscal discipline and, 41–43

GASB. *See* Governmental Accounting Standards Board

Gelinas, Nicole, 9

Genscher, Hans-Dieter, 126

German banking system: *Landesbanken* losses in crisis of *2008,* 144; structure of, 144

German Basic Law (*1949*), 138

German bonds: economic crisis of *2008* and, 26–27, 27*f*, 147–49, 149*f*, 152; joint state/federal Deutschland bonds, 137, 150–51, 152, 158n79

German *Bund*: control over *Länder* spending, 139–40; debt brake requirements and, 150; de facto bailout guarantee for *Länder,* 16, 135, 141–42; and joint state/federal Deutschland bonds, 137, 150–51, 152, 158n79; role in federal system, 137

German Constitutional Court, on bailout guarantees for *Länder,* 141

German debt: economic crisis of *2008* and, 136*t,* 142–44; low interest rates, blurring of debt impact by, 143

German federal system: calls for restructuring of, 136–37; centralization, movement toward, 137, 138, 150–51, 151–53;

equalization requirements in, 135, 139, 140–41; key features of, 134–35; legislative powers, distribution of, 138–40; levels of, 137; origins of, 137–38; restructuring, possible direction of, 137

German *Länder:* budgetary crises, in *2012,* 134; budgetary discipline, federal equalization requirements and, 140–41; city states as, 135; cost reduction efforts, 150; de facto bailout guarantee for, 16, 135, 141–42; demographic and infrastructure variety in, 135; economic and fiscal variety in, 135, 136*t;* gradual erosion of powers of, 138–39; and joint state/federal Deutschland bonds, 137, 150–51, 152, 158n79; limited expenditure and taxation autonomy of, 135, 139–40, 151; role in federal system, 137

German *Länder,* and crisis of *2008:* bond market impact, 26–27, 27*f,* 147–49, 149*f,* 152; debt and, 134, 135, 136*t,* 143–47; fiscal and legal consequences, 149–51; impact of, 135, 136*t;* as test of federal system, 151–52

German *Länder* debt: debt brake requirements and, 149–50; debt-to-GDP ratios, variation in, 140; economic crisis of *2008* and, 134, 135, 136*t,* 143–47; *landesbank* liabilities and, 144–45; off-balance sheet items in, 144–47; and unfunded pension claims, 145–47, 147*t*

German reunification: debt level and, 142–43; and EU, support of, 126; and federal system, testing of, 138

German Stability Council, debt restrictions of, 134

Germany: debt brake, 149–50; dysfunctional federalism in, 41; government net assets, decline of, 142, 143

Germany, state formation in: and federal system, structure of, 137–38; parallels to potential EU federalism, 114, 116–17; state capacity and, 120, 120*t,* 123; and success of federalism, 116, 118, 120, 123

Gerring, John, 122

Gingrich, Newt, 9

Governmental Accounting Standards Board (GASB): accounting standards, underestimate of pension liabilities by, 64, 67, 68–69, 97; criticisms of, 69–70, 76; rule revisions by, 70

Great Depression: and Canadian federal system, 206, 208; and Canadian provinces, 202; and federal grants to state and local government, increase in, 48; municipal bankruptcies in, 5; state defaults during, 26

Greece: bailout of, as bailout of European banks, 46; bailout of, mandatory conditions surrounding, 128; credit default swap market and, 54–55, 54*f;* debt, early efforts to address, 127; and moral hazard of bailout guarantees, 45; unions, power of, 133n47

Growth and Stability Pact of *2011,* 199n29

Hall, Peter, 126

Hamilton, Alexander, 26, 31, 57, 123

Harper, Stephen, 207–8

Haverstick, Kelly, 98

Hayek, Friedrich, 3

Health care costs: and debt of developed nations, 4; politicians' failure to address, 4; for public sector employees, as unfunded liability, 24

Hong, Sounman, 28–31, 30*t*

HSH Nordbank, 145

Hypo Real Estate, 143

Illinois: budget deficits, 8; credit default swap market and, 54–55, 54*f*

IMF. *See* International Monetary Fund

Infrastructure Stimulus Fund, 217

Instituto Nacional de la Seguridad Social (INSS), 169

International Monetary Fund (IMF): on debt of developed nations, 3–4; safety net for Greece, 127; on stimulus packages for crisis of *2008,* 216–17

Interventions in subnational states: in European Union, 123–29; and Italian federalism, failure of, 119, 121–22. *See also entries under* Centralization

Ireland: bailout of, as bailout of European banks, 46; credit default swap market and, 54–55, 54*f*; debt, early efforts to address, 127; and moral hazard problem of federal guarantee of state debt, 45

IRS pension regulations, public sector pensions and, 91

Italy, dysfunctional federalism in, 41

Italy, state formation in: and failure of federalism, 116–17, 117–18, 118–19, 119–22, 122–23; limited state capacity of subunits and, 119–22, 120*t*, 122–23; parallels to potential EU federalism, 114, 116–17, 123–25, 124

Izquierda Unida, 190–91

Jackson, Andrew, 9

Johnson, Richard, 102

Juncker, Jean-Claude, 128

Kennedy, Anthony, 20, 21

Kennedy, John F., 22–23

Keynes, John, 3

Kohl, Helmut, 126

Kohn, Donald, 69

Landesbank Baden-Württemberg (LBBW), 144

Landesbanken (LB), losses in economic crisis of *2008*, 144–45

Latin America, dysfunctional federalism in, 40–41

Law *7/2007* (Spain), 170

Law of Budget Stability and Financial Stability (Spain), 193

LBBW. See Landesbank Baden-Württemberg

Legal guarantees for public sector pensions, and pension risk, 103, 104*t*

Lenze, David G., 69

Liabilities, total actuarial, *vs.* state population, as measure of pension risk, 99

Lisbon Treaty, alteration of, 127

Loans, by U.S. federal government, as strategy to address state debt, 32

Local government, in Spain: responsibilities of, 182*t*; spending increases, 183*f*

Local governments, U.S.: employees, teachers as percentage of, 62; employee wages, pressure to remain competitive in, 18; as employer, importance of, 18, 19*f*; as laboratories, in competitive federalism, 18; responsiveness to public needs, in competitive federalism, 17–18; spending by, as percentage of all government spending, 18, 19*f*

Local governments, U.S., federal grants, to: increase in, 48–50, 49*f*; legislative representation as predictor of, 55

Maastricht criterion: German debt and, 142, 143, 150; Spain and, 168, 190

Maastricht Treaty (*1992*), 126

Macdonald, John A., 204, 206

McHenry, Patrick, 32

Manhattan Institute, 9

Market-based fiscal discipline: critics of, 57; failure, causes of, 44–46; Spanish autonomous communities (ACs) and, 161, 166, 168–69, 172, 173; as theoretical option, 44

Market-based fiscal discipline, in U.S.: as best hope, 58; credibility of federal no-bailout claim and, 41–43, 46–48; current success of, 56; future of, 53–56; modern intertwining of state and federal functions and, 48–52, 58; and punishment of most-troubled states, 55; strengthening of, as goal, 41, 58; success of, through *20*th century, 47–48; as unusual arrangement, 41; viability of, 41

Martin, Paul, 207

Mas i Gavarró, Artur, 179

Matching provisions, and state fiscal discipline, 50, 58

Meany, George, 22

Medicaid: cost to states, economic downturns and, 51; and federal grants to state and local government, increase in, 50

Merkel, Angela, 129

Milliman and Co., 72

Mississippi, *19*th century default of, 26

Missouri teacher pension plan. *See* Public School Retirement System (PSRS) (Missouri)

Missouri teachers organizations, political power of, 82

Mitchell, Olivia S., 98, 106

Modigliani-Miller theorem, 67, 77n18

Montana, balanced budget of, 24–25

Moody's Investor Services: and German *Länder* credit rating, 144, 156n53; and valuation of pension liabilities, 69, 80

Municipal bankruptcies: public sector pension plan liabilities and, 80; in U.S., 5–7

Municipal bond yield, in calculation of total pension liabilities, 71, 71*t*, 72, 74, 75*t*

Munnell, Alicia, 98, 104*t*

Nadler, Daniel, 28–31, 30*t*

National Compensation Survey (NCS), 74, 74*t*, 78n33

National Education Association (NEA), and collective bargaining rights, 22

National Energy Program (Canada), 202

National Income and Product Accounts, 63, 69

National Institute on Money in State Politics, 105

National loyalties, and federalism, possibility of, 114, 118–19

National Policy (Canada), 204

Navarra: as charter regime, 163, 166, 183; fiscal authority of, 181, 183; low income inequality in, 189; and Spanish competitive federalism, structure of,

195–96; and Spanish redistributive policies, 196

NCS. *See* National Compensation Survey

New Deal: and centralization of government, 57; and intertwining of state and federal functions, 48

New Hampshire, public sector unions, efforts to reign in, 105

New Jersey, budget deficits, 8, 25

New York: budget deficits, 25; earnings from pension fund investments, 96, 96*f*

New York Times, 8

New York v. United States (1992), 21

Nonsalary benefits for public sector workers, as unfunded liability, 24. *See also* Unfunded pension liabilities

Nordic countries, as model for debt reduction, 13

North Carolina, retirement system contributions, rise in, 63

North Dakota, balanced budget of, 24–25

Novy-Marx, Robert, 75, 80, 97

Obama administration: and federal grants to state and local government, 50; moves toward federal guarantee of state debt, 32

Oeter, Stefan, 117

Ohio: earnings from pension fund investments, 96, 96*f*; public sector unions, efforts to reign in, 105

Ontario: debt-to-GDP ratio, 215; demographics, 203–04; and economic crisis of *2008*, impact of, 213; economy of, 204, 210–11; and federal transfer payments, 209–10, 210–11; and interregional tensions, 202

Oregon, earnings from pension fund investments, 96, 96*f*

Organic Law of Autonomous Community Finances, 189

Parti Liberal (Canada), 203, 207

Parti Québécois (Canada), 203

Peak-value-pension wealth (PVPW), and cost of pension enhancements, 85–86

Pension envy, 63

Pension plans. *See entries under* Public sector pension plans

Pension risk: factors affecting, 99–107; measures of, 99

Pew Center on the States, 100, 101, 108n7

Political climate, and pension risk, 99, 104–05, 107

Political economy: current relevance of, 3–4, 4–5; as founding social science, 3

Political will: cost of inaction, 5; and credibility of federal no-bailout claim, 42; and health care costs, failure to address, 4; and pension costs, failure to address, 4; and unchecked debt growth, 3, 4–5

Portugal, bailout of, as bailout of European banks, 46

Poterba, James, 29

Powell, Jerome H., 5

Printz v. *United States* (*1997*), 21

Private sector bailouts, and credibility of federal no-bailout policy, 52

Progressives, on U.S. federal system, problems in, 40

Public Plans Database (Boston College), 65, 71, 76, 98, 106

Public School Retirement System (PSRS) (Missouri): administration of, 82; school administrators as greatest beneficiaries of, 86–90, 87*f*, 88*f*; administrators' stake in program, as structural flaw, 81, 91; backloading of benefits in, 83–84; characteristics of, 81; eligibility conditions in, 83–84; employee contributions, increases in, 90–91; and rent capture incentives, as structural flaw, 81, 86–90, 91; and Social Security eligibility, 82; unfunded liabilities, hiding of through accounting tricks, 90–91

Public School Retirement System (PSRS) (Missouri) enhancements of *1990*s–*2000*s, 84, 84*t*; school administrators as greatest beneficiaries of,

86–90, 87*f*, 88*f*; school administrators' support for, 82; costs to younger teachers of, 81, 86, 90; fiscal consequences of, 85–86; and quality of education, 86, 89; and rent seeking by school administrators, 86–90; retroactive application of, 81, 86; unfunded liabilities generated by, 86

Public sector employee compensation: cuts in, by Spanish central government, 172, 173; municipal bankruptcies and, 6–7; versus private sector compensation, 64; public calls for reductions in, 63; state and local government pressure to remain competitive in, 18. *See also* Teacher compensation

Public sector health care plans, as unfunded liability, 24

Public sector pension plans, Canadian, unfunded liabilities of, 215–16

Public sector pension plans, Spanish: and fiscal crisis, 169–70; reform of, 172

Public sector pension plans, U.S.: administrator's financial stake in, as structural flaw, 81, 91; consequences of default by, 107–8; defense of, accounting standards and, 70; defense of, and state sovereign immunity, 21; as defined benefit plans, 80, 95; effect of municipal bankruptcies on, 6–7; efforts to reform, 56; generosity of, and pension risk, 99, 101–02, 107; reform, fair market valuation of liabilities and, 75; and rent capture incentives, as structural flaw, 81, 86–90, 91; and state balanced budget restrictions, 95; structural flaws in, as ongoing problem, 91; studies on funding of, 98. *See also* Pension risk; Teacher pension plans

Public sector pension plans, U.S., enhancements of *1990*s–*2000*s, 84, 84*t*; administrators' stake in program, as structural flaw, 81, 91; costs to younger teachers of, 81; and rent capture incentives as structural flaw, 81, 86–90, 91; retroactive application of, 81, 85, 92n4. *See* *also* Public School Retirement System (PSRS) (Missouri) enhancements of 1990s–2000s

Public sector pension plans, U.S., liabilities of: and aggressive investment practices of pension systems, 63; calculating amount of, 65–66; calculating amount of, method of financing and, 66–67; correct discount rate for calculating, 70, 71*t;* draining of funds from other uses, 63; fair market valuation, calls for, 62, 71, 80; under fair market valuation, 62, 63–64, 67, 68–69, 71, 71*t;* under GASB accounting practices, 64, 67, 68–69, 97; under GASB accounting practices, criticisms of, 69–70; and state debt default, likelihood of, 32; true valuation of, and pressure for reform, 75. *See also entries under* Unfunded pension liabilities

Public sector size, and pension risk, 99, 100–01

Public sector unions: concessions demanded of, 56; critique of, 23–24; and education costs, 24; in Europe, containment of costs despite, 133n47; in Greece, power of, 133n47; history of, 22–23; introduction of, 22–23; legislation to curtail power of, 105; and municipal debt crises, 7; and nonsalary benefits, rising cost of, 24; ongoing demands for unsustainable level of benefits, 91; and pension risk, 105–06; political power of, 23–24; and pressure for federal bailout of states, 33; in Spain, and finance crisis, 169, 170; and state bond risk premiums, 28–31, 28*f,* 30*t;* U.S., enforcement of agreements with, and state sovereign immunity, 21

Put options, in valuation of contingent pension liabilities, 68

Quebec: debt-to-GDP ratio, 215; and decentralization, support for, 203, 206, 208, 209; and French culture, determination to maintain, 203; and interregional tensions, 202; Quiet Revolution in, 203; secessionist movement in, 203

Quimby, Laura, 104*t*

Rauh, Joshua, 75, 80, 97

Ravitch, Richard, 70

Reagan administration, and federal grants to state and local government, 50

Redistribution programs, state and local avoidance of, in competitive federalism, 18–20

Redistribution programs in Canada: Canadian commitment to, 205; difficulty of maintaining, 205; origin of, 202; sustainability of, as issue, 210–11

Redistribution programs in Germany, 135, 139, 140–41

Redistribution programs in Spain, 165, 167, 183; AC charter regimes and, 179–80; AC opposition to, 179; ACs' views on, factors affecting, 184–89; and competitive federalism, introduction of, 196; before crisis of *2008,* 190–92; difficulty of changing, 185; economic crisis of *2008* and, 179; impact of, masked by borrowing, 190, 199n21; as less redistribution than other EU countries, 185, 188–89, 188*t;* types of social expenditures, 198n11

Reform: of pension plans, movement toward, 56, 75; Spanish debate on, 159; of teacher pension plans, union opposition to, 82. *See also* State governments, U.S., fiscal reform

Regional Liquidity Fund (Spain), 172

Regional loyalties, and federalism, possibility of, 118

Reinsdorf, Marshall B., 69

Retirement systems, state and local, amount of assets managed by, 95

Revolutionary War debt of U.S. states, federal assumption of, 26

Ricardo, David, 3

Rodden, Jonathan, 31

Roosevelt, Franklin D., 22
Rosengren, Eric, 4–5
Roubini, Nouriel, 52
Rueben, Kim, 29

Scalia, Antonin, 20
Schäuble, Wolfgang, 128
School administrators: financial stake in pension plans, as structural flaw, 81, 91; as greatest beneficiaries of pension plans, 86–90, 87f, 88f; support for defined benefits plans, 82; support for pension enhancements of *1990s–2000s*, 89
Second Bank of the United States, 94
Shoag, Daniel, 106
Single European Act (*1985*), 125–26
"Six-Pack measures," 127
Skeel, David A., Jr., 8–9
Smith, Adam, 3
Smith, Denis Mack, 118
Smith, Robert S., 98, 106
Social security, in Spain, and fiscal crisis, 169–70
Social Security, in U.S.: benefit calculation formulas for, 83; eligibility of public school teachers for, 81; public sector defined benefit (DB) pension plans and, 65
Southern European countries, and moral hazard of bailout guarantee, 45
Spain: centralization, proposed return to, 194; centralization under Franco, 180; constitutional spending and borrowing limits, introduction of, 172; dysfunctional federalism in, 41; EU excessive deficit procedure against, 171; pension system in, and fiscal crisis, 169–70; public sector workers, increase in, 170; regional parties, rise of, 190–91, 191f; social security entitlements, and fiscal crisis, 169–70; social services spending in, 188–89; taxation, downward pressure on with rise in regional identities, 185, 189, 198n14

Spain and economic crisis of *2008:* AC spending and, 171, 193; centralizing effect of central government measures, 159–61, 171, 173–74, 193; counter-cyclical stimulus packages, 171; debt, increase in, 168, 190, 192–93, 192f; Eurozone design as contributing factor, 167–68; government responses, 170–73; and government spending, 192–93, 192f; inherent problems in Spanish federal system and, 160; reform, discussion of, 159; regional spending, efforts to limit, 172–73; severity of impact, 159, 167; Spain's responsible behavior prior to, 167–68; spending cutbacks, 168; systemic factors contributing to, 169–70; two phases of, 167, 171–73; and unsustainability of current federal system, 193; and wealth redistribution policies, 179
Spanish central government: austerity measures, 172, 174; authority of, EU Fiscal Compact rules and, 160–61; budget stability and debt goals, failure to meet, 174; bypassing of ACs, in local stimulus spending, 171; dependence on AC parties for political support, 190–92; framework legislative power of, 163; increased regulation by, 161; loans to ACs, 172; powers reserved for, 162–63; regional spending, efforts to limit, 172–73, 190–92; responsibilities of, 181, 182t; spending increases, 181, 183f; strategy toward AC crisis, as middle way, 161
Spanish central government bailout guarantee, 161; and AC incentives, 166–67, 173; dubious financial capacity for, 161; explicit guarantee, issuing of, 193; institution of competitive federalism and, 196
Spanish Civil War, and Spanish government, 180
Spanish constitution of *1978:* federal structure under, 180; spending and borrowing limits in, 172

Spanish debt: early efforts to address, 127; growth of, before crisis of *2008*, 190; growth of, in economic crisis of *2008*, 168, 190, 192–93, 192*f*; masking of redistribution impact by, 190, 199n21; regional, efforts to regulate, 166–67, 172, 174, 184

Spanish federal system, 161–67, 180–84; AC governments, capacities of, 163–64; and AC incentives to overspend, 165–67; asymmetric powers in, 163; and competitive federalism, potential benefits of introducing, 179–80, 195–96, 195–97; conflict inherent in, 163; current unsustainability of, 193; decentralization trend, before crisis of *2008*, 162, 180, 181; and economic crisis of *2008*, effect of, 174; fatal flaw in, 180; fiscal equalization in, 165, 167; and fiscal indiscipline, literature on, 160; history of, 161–62, 180; inherent problems in, 160; and national solidarity, means of ensuring, 196; opposition to, 162; political dynamic, before crisis of *2008*, 162; proposed alternatives to, 194–95; regional debt, efforts to regulate, 166–67; separatism in, causes of, 184–85; separatist sentiment in, 174, 179, 186, 189; shared responsibility and finances in, 162–63; taxation and spending in, 164–66, 167, 181–83, 183*f*, 192–93, 192*f*; unique features of, 162; unusual origins of, 181

Spanish local government: responsibilities of, 182*t*; spending increases, 183*f*

Spanish nationalist movements, 162

Spanish public sector unions, and fiscal crisis, 169, 170

Spanish regional banks, consolidation of after crisis of *2008*, 171

Spanish regional identities: (re)creation of by AC governments, 180; increase in, and political unrest, 186, 189; rise in, and downward pressure on taxation, 185, 189, 198n14; strength of, as independent of economic status, 185, 186, 187*f*; wealth redistribution policies and, 184–89

Spanish wealth redistribution policies, 183; AC charter regimes and, 179–80; AC opposition to, 179; ACs' views on, factors affecting, 184–89; and competitive federalism, introduction of, 196; before crisis of *2008*, 190–92; difficulty of changing, 185; economic crisis of *2008* and, 179; impact of, masked by borrowing, 190, 199n21; as less redistribution than other EU countries, 185, 188–89, 188*t*; types of social expenditures, 198n11

Splinter, David, 98, 102

Stability and Growth Pact (EU, *1997*), 45, 166

Stabilization Agreement (Canada), 215

Standard and Poor's (S&P), on German *Länder* bailout guarantee, 141–42

State bonds, U.S., risk premiums, 25–26, 25*f*, 26–31, 27*f*

State Budget Crisis Taskforce, 70

State budget deficits, U.S., 8, 24–25; during economic downturns, federal efforts to cover, 51–52; as understated, 25

State budgets, U.S., smoothing of across business cycle, 47, 51, 56, 58

State capacity of subunits, and centralization, 119–22, 122–23, 124–29, 125*t*, 130

State-chartered banks, U.S., and default crisis of *1840s*, 94

State debt, federal guarantees of. *See* Federal bailout guarantee

State debt, U.S.: fiscal discipline after crisis of *1840s*, 46–47; state sovereign immunity and, 20–21; as understated, 55

State debt, U.S., defaults on: after Civil War, 47; and federal regulations, imposition of, 91; orderly procedure for, benefits of announcing, 58–59; risk to federalism in, 31–33, 107–8; strategies for avoiding, 32–33; as strategy to address state debt, 32. *See also entries under* Default crisis

State debt, U.S., risk of default on: current high level of, 7, 22; factors in, 29; share of Democratic Party representation in legislature and, 29–31, 30*t*, 39n91; level of public sector unionization and, 28–31, 28*f*, 30*t*, 33; and state bond risk premiums, 25–26, 25*f*, 26–31, 27*f*

State economic growth, and pension risk, 99

State governments, U.S.: comparative autonomy of, 53; employees, teachers as percentage of employees of, 62; employee wages, pressure to remain competitive in, 18; as employer, importance of, 18, 19*f*; fiscal capacity, and pension risk, 99; as laboratories, in competitive federalism, 18; responsiveness to public needs, in competitive federalism, 17–18; spending, as percentage of all government spending, 18, 19*f*; spending, variation by region, 100

State governments, U.S., bankruptcy of: consequences of, 7–8; debate on, 8–9; as looming crisis, 7; as strategy to address state debt, 32

State governments, U.S., federal grants to: increase in, 48–50, 49*f*; legislative representation as predictor of, 55

State governments, U.S., fiscal reform: centralized control, problems inherent in, 57–58; difficult path to, 56; efforts toward, 56, 59–60; market-based fiscal discipline as best approach to, 58–59; state efforts toward, 56, 60; strategies for, 57–60. *See also* Central control of state finances; Market-based fiscal discipline, in U.S.

States, Canadian. *See* Canadian provinces

States, German. *See* German *Länder*

States, Spanish. *See* Autonomous communities (ACs), in Spain

States, wealthy, subsidizing of poorer states by, 55–56

State sovereign immunity, U.S.: critics of, 57; state debt and, 20–21; Supreme Court jurisprudence on, 20–21

Stimulus packages of Obama administration, as move toward federal guarantee of state debt, 32

Stock, James H., 102

Stockton, California, bankruptcy of, 6, 80

Stone, Mary S., 98, 102

Subnational governments: debt of, and political will, 3, 4–5; spending by, difficulty of controlling, 201

Subnational governments, interventions in: in European Union, 123–29; and Italian federalism, failure of, 119, 121–22. *See also entries under* Centralization

Supreme Court, U.S., on state sovereign immunity, 20–21

Switzerland, and state debt, federal lack of obligation for, 16, 48

Taxation: in Canada, 208, 209; in Germany, 135, 139–40, 151; in Spain, 164–66, 167, 181–83, 183*f*, 185, 189, 192–93, 192*f*, 198n14; taxpayer mobility, and market-based fiscal discipline, 44

TD Economics, 211

Teacher compensation: current levels of as unsustainable, 62; as percentage of state and local payroll, 63; *vs.* private sector compensation, 62, 64, 72–74, 76; public calls for reductions in, 63; reduction of, as cost reduction strategy, 72, 76

Teacher pension plans: benefits provided by, 65; cost to employee of, 65; as defined benefit plans, 62–63, 65, 75, 76, 90; eligibility conditions in, 83; fair market value, calculation of, 71–75, 74*t*, 75*t*; reform, teachers unions' opposition to, 82; as typically statewide, 81; value of, versus private sector pensions, 71–75, 74*t*, 75*t*. *See also* Public School Retirement System (PSRS) (Missouri)

Teachers: hiring of, poor practices in, 76, 79n36; as percentage of state and local government employees, 62

Teachers unions: and cost of education, 24; history of, 22–23; and nonsalary benefits, rising cost of, 24; opposition to pension reform, 82; political power of, 23–24

Texas, budget deficits, 25

Tocqueville, Alexis de, 15

Treasury bond yield, in calculation of total pension liabilities, 70, 71, 71*t*, 72, 73*t*, 74, 75*t*

Treaty on Stability, Coordination, and Governance (*2012*), 127

Troika inspectors, 128

UAAL. *See* Unfunded actuarial accrued liability

Umbach, Maiken, 118

Unfunded actuarial accrued liability (UAAL), 99; ratio to state GDP, as measure of pension risk, 99

Unfunded mandates, and state fiscal discipline, 58

Unfunded pension liabilities: in Canada, 215–16; and debt of developed nations, 4; fair market valuation of, and increased pressure for reform, 75; and German *Länder* debt, 145–47, 147*t*; hiding of budget problems through, 55; nonsalary benefits for public sector workers as, 8, 24; parallels with default crisis of *1840*s, 95, 107; politicians' failure to address, 4; pressure on states to deal with, 55; of Public School Retirement System (PSRS) (Missouri), hiding of through accounting tricks, 90–91; in public sector pension plans, unfunded amount of, 8, 24, 62, 63, 68, 71, 77n11, 80; as significant problem, 41; state budget deficits and, 25; and state defaults, likelihood

of, 32; state fiscal reform efforts and, 56; in U.S., 8, 24, 62, 63, 68, 71, 77n11, 80

Unfunded pension liabilities, asset market investments to meet: no return from, ability to pay despite, 99; parallels to default crisis of *1840*s, 95, 107; profits from, 95–97, 96*f*; profits from versus liabilities, 97–98, 97*f*; return on, and pension risk, 99, 106; as risky, 95

Unions. *See* Public sector unions

United States: Hamiltonian moment, as model for fiscal centralization of EU, 115; municipal bankruptcies in, 5–7; national debt, increases in, 3–4, 8; national debt, liabilities not included in, 8. *See also* Federal no-bailout policy, U.S.; Federal system, U.S.; Local governments, U.S.; Market-based fiscal discipline, in U.S.; *entries under* State; *other specific topics*

University of Freiberg, 145

U.S. Term Limits, Inc. v. *Thornton* (*1995*), 20

Valencia, Spanish bailout of, 166

Vallejo, California, bankruptcy of, 80

Van Rompuy, Herman, 126, 129

Volcker, Paul, 70

Von Weizsäcker, Jakob, 126

Wall Street Journal, 7

Washington, George, 3

West LB, 144, 145

Wisconsin: earnings from pension fund investments, 96, 96*f*; public sector unions, efforts to rein in, 105

Wisconsin Comparative Retirement Study, 101

World War II, and federal system, structure of, 138

Yogo, Motohiro, 102